2025–2026
Remote Pilot
TEST PREP

Pass your test the first time

AVIATION SUPPLIES & ACADEMICS, INC.
NEWCASTLE, WASHINGTON

Remote Pilot Test Prep
2025–2026 Edition

Aviation Supplies & Academics, Inc.
7005 132nd Place SE
Newcastle, Washington 98059
asa@asa2fly.com | 425.235.1500 | asa2fly.com

© 2024 Aviation Supplies & Academics, Inc.

Visit **asa2fly.com/TPUAS** for additional information and resources related to this book.

Sample Federal Aviation Administration (FAA) questions herein contain information as of: August 2024. Stay informed of changes since the book was printed: **asa2fly.com/testupdate**

None of the material in this publication supersedes any documents, procedures or regulations issued by the Federal Aviation Administration.

Aviation Supplies & Academics, Inc. (ASA), assumes no responsibility for any errors or omissions. Neither is any liability assumed for damages resulting from the use of the information contained herein.

Cover photo: akophotography/Envato Elements

ASA-TP-UAS-25
ISBN 978-1-64425-436-3

Additional format available:
eBook PDF ISBN 978-1-64425-437-0

Printed in the United States of America

2026   2025   5 4 3 2

About the Contributors

Jackie Spanitz
General Manager
Aviation Supplies & Academics, Inc.

As ASA General Manager, Jackie Spanitz oversees maintenance and development of more than 1,000 titles and pilot supplies in the ASA product line. Ms. Spanitz has worked with airman training and testing for more than 25 years, including participation in the Airman Certification Standards (ACS) development committees. Jackie holds a Bachelor of Science in Aviation Technology from Western Michigan University, a Master of Science from Embry-Riddle Aeronautical University, and Instructor and Commercial Pilot certificates. She is the author of *Guide to the Flight Review*, and the technical editor for ASA's Test Prep and FAR/AIM series.

David Ison, Ph.D.
Aviation Planner—Emerging Aviation Technologies & Land Use Compatibility, Washington State Department of Transportation Aviation Division

Dr. David Ison has flown as a flight instructor and as an ATP for regional and major airlines, flying both domestic and international routes. Dr. Ison holds a Bachelor of Science in Aviation Management from Auburn University, a Master of Science in Aeronautical Science—Operations Specialization, and a Ph.D. in Educational Studies/Higher Education Leadership with a Specialization in Aviation Education from Embry-Riddle Aeronautical University. He is the co-author of two books, *Small Unmanned Aircraft Systems Guide: Exploring Designs, Operations, Regulations, and Economics* and *The Complete Remote Pilot*; and the author of *Aircraft Dispatcher Oral Exam Guide* and *Navigating Weather: A Pilot's Guide to Airborne and Datalink Weather Radar*.

Aviation Supplies & Academics, Inc. (ASA) is an industry leader in the development and sale of aviation supplies and publications for pilots, flight instructors, aviation mechanics, aircraft dispatchers, air traffic controllers, and drone operators. ASA has provided trusted training materials to millions of aviators resulting in successful airman certification for over 80 years. Visit **asa2fly.com** to learn more.

Stay informed with ASA online resources.

Website	Updates	Blog	Author Talks	Follow, like, share.
asa2fly.com	asa2fly.com /testupdate	learntoflyblog.com	asapresents.net	instagram.com/asa2fly facebook.com/asa2fly youtube.com/asa2fly linkedin.com/company/asa2fly

Contents

Instructions
Updates and Practice Tests v
Introduction vi
Description of the Tests vii
    Knowledge Test Registration vii
    Acceptable Forms of Authorization viii
    Acceptable Materials viii
    Testing Procedures for Applicants Requesting Special Accommodations ix
    Test Reports ix
    Retesting Procedures ix
    Cheating or Other Unauthorized Conduct x
    Test-Taking Tips x
Remote Pilot Certificate Eligibility Requirements xi
Knowledge Exam References xii
Acronyms xiii
ASA Test Prep Layout xiv

Chapter 1 Regulations
Introduction 1–3
Remote Pilot Certification 1–6
Remote Pilot Privileges 1–8
Supporting Crew Roles 1–9
Falsification, Reproduction, or Alteration 1–11
Accident Reporting 1–11
FAA Inspections 1–13
sUAS Registration 1–14
Remote Identification (Remote ID) 1–15
Preflight Action and Inspection 1–17
Carriage of Hazardous Material 1–18
Operation at Night 1–18
Visual Line of Sight (VLOS) 1–20
Operating Limitations 1–21
Right-of-Way Rules 1–22
Operation Over Human Beings 1–24
Operation from Moving Vehicles or Aircraft 1–26
Privacy and Other Considerations 1–27
Alcohol and Drugs 1–28
Change of Address 1–31
Waivers 1–31

Chapter 2 National Airspace System
Introduction 2–3
    NOTAMs 2–3
    Other Airspace Resources 2–4
Airspace Classification 2–7
Topography 2–15
Airport Operations 2–20
Airport Markings and Signs 2–22
Collision Avoidance 2–27
    Inflight Hazards 2–27

Chapter 3 Weather
Introduction 3–3
Wind 3–4
Air Masses and Fronts 3–5
Atmospheric Stability 3–7
Visibility and Clouds 3–8
Thunderstorms 3–10
Icing 3–13
Fog 3–14
Density Altitude 3–16
Weather Briefing 3–17
Weather Reports, Forecasts and Charts 3–17
    Surface Aviation Weather Observations 3–18
    Aviation Weather Reports 3–19
    Aviation Forecasts 3–21
    Convective Significant Meteorological Information (WST) 3–22

Chapter 4 Preflight Considerations
Introduction 4–3
Determining Speed and Altitude 4–4
Loading 4–6
    Computing Weight and Balance 4–7
Load Factor 4–8
Stalls 4–10
Performance 4–12
Physiology 4–14
Maintenance and Inspection Procedures 4–18

Chapter 5 **Operations**

Introduction 5–3
Communication Procedures 5–5
   sUAS Frequencies 5–9
Emergency Procedures 5–13
   Lost Link 5–13
   Flight Termination 5–14
   Flyaways 5–14
   Loss of GPS 5–14
   Battery Fires 5–15
Aeronautical Decision Making 5–17

Cross References

A: Question Number and Page Number A–1
B: Airman Knowledge Test Report
     Codes and Question Numbers B–1

FAA Figures

Airman Knowledge Testing Supplement for Sport Pilot, Recreational Pilot, Remote Pilot, and Private Pilot (FAA-CT-8080-2H)

Updates and Practice Tests

Free Test Updates for the One-Year Life Cycle of Test Prep Books

The FAA modifies tests as needed throughout the year. ASA keeps abreast of changes to the tests and posts free Test Updates on the ASA website. Before taking your test, be certain you have the most current information by visiting the ASA Test Updates webpage: **asa2fly.com/testupdate**. Additionally, sign up for free email notifications, which are sent when new Test Updates are available.

We Invite Your Feedback

After you take your FAA exam, let us know how you did. Were you prepared? Did ASA's products meet your needs and exceed your expectations? We want to continue to improve these products to ensure applicants are prepared and become safe aviators. Send your feedback to: **cfi@asa2fly.com**.

prepware.com

Online practice to prepare for written exams.

As the experts in FAA Knowledge Exam preparation, we want you to have the confidence needed before heading to the testing center, and help eliminate the hassle and expense of retaking exams.

See inside front cover for **FREE** account!

Realistic Test Simulation
Test maps and time allowed mirror the official FAA exams

Performance Graphs
Review explanations for missed questions and track your performance

Gain Confidence
Go into your exam fully prepared after practicing simulated tests

Succeed
Pass your exam and review your airman knowledge test report to prepare for your checkride

Remote Pilot | Sport Pilot | Private Pilot | Instrument Rating | Commercial Pilot | Flight Instructor | Ground Instructor
Fundamentals of Instructing | Flight Engineer | Airline Transport Pilot | Aviation Mechanic General | Airframe | Powerplant

Practice tests are also available as an app! **asa2fly.com/apps**

Introduction

Welcome to the Aviation Supplies & Academics, Inc., (ASA) Test Prep Series. This series has been helping pilots prepare for the FAA Knowledge Tests for more than 60 years with great success. We are confident that with proper use of this book you will score very well on your Remote Pilot certificate test.

Begin your studies with a classroom or home-study ground school course, which will involve reading a comprehensive textbook. Visit the Reader Resources for this Test Prep (**asa2fly.com/TPUAS**) and become familiar with the FAA guidance materials available for this certification exam. Then use this Test Prep to prepare for your exam: read the question, select your choice for the correct answer, and then read the explanation. Use the references that conclude each explanation to identify additional resources for further study of a subject. Upon completion of your studies, take practice tests at **prepware.com** (see inside the front cover for your activation code).

The questions in this book have been arranged into chapters based on subject matter to promote better understanding, aid recall, and provide a more efficient study guide.

Prior to taking an FAA Airman Knowledge Test, all applicants must establish an FAA Tracking Number (FTN) by creating a profile in the Integrated Airman Certification and Rating Application (IACRA) system at **iacra.faa.gov**. Then visit **faa.psiexams.com** to register for your exam and take FAA-created practice tests to become familiar with the computer testing platform.

It is important to answer every question assigned on your FAA Knowledge Test. If in their ongoing review, the FAA decides a question has no correct answer, is no longer applicable, or is otherwise defective, your answer will be marked correct no matter which one you chose. However, you will not be given the automatic credit if you have not marked an answer. Unlike some other exams you may have taken, there is no penalty for guessing in this instance.

The FAA exams are "closed tests" which means the exact database of questions is not available to the public. The question and answer choices in this book are based on our extensive history and experience with the FAA testing and airman certification process. You might see similarly worded questions on your official FAA exam, or answer stems might be rearranged from the order you see in this book. Therefore, be sure to fully understand the intent of each question and corresponding answer while studying, rather than memorizing the letter associated with the correct response. You may be asked a question that has unfamiliar wording; studying and understanding the information in this book and the associated references will give you the tools to answer question variations with confidence.

If your study leads you to question an answer choice, we recommend you seek the assistance of a local instructor. We welcome your questions, recommendations, and concerns—send them to:

Aviation Supplies & Academics, Inc.
7005 132nd Place SE
Newcastle, WA 98059-3153
Phone: 425.235.1500
Email: cfi@asa2fly.com
Website: asa2fly.com

The FAA appreciates testing experience feedback. You can contact them at:

Federal Aviation Administration, AFS-810
Training & Certification Group, Testing Standards Section
PO Box 25082
Oklahoma City, OK 73125
Email: TestingStandardsComments@faa.gov

Description of the Tests

The FAA Knowledge Exam is an objective, multiple choice test. Each question can be answered by one of the three choices. Each test question is independent of the others—a correct response to one question does not depend on the correct response to another. You must score at least 70 percent to pass the test. Applicants who do not meet the requirements in 14 CFR §107.61 (d)(1), must pass the knowledge test before preparing an application for a Remote Pilot Certificate with a Small UAS Rating.

The table below lists the number of questions for each topic and the allotted time for the test. Study all the questions in the book to prepare for your test. Reference the Remote Pilot Airman Certification Standards (FAA-S-ACS-10) for additional information on expected knowledge within each topic.

Remote Pilot Unmanned Aircraft General – Small (UAG)

Test Code	Test Name	Number of Questions	Minimum Age	Allotted Time (hrs)
UAG	Unmanned Aircraft General —Small	60	14	2.0
UAS Topics		**Percentage of Items on Test**		
I. Regulations		15–25%		
II. Airspace & Requirements		15–25%		
III. Weather		11–16%		
IV. Loading and Performance		7–11%		
V. Operations		35–45%		

Knowledge Test Registration

The FAA testing provider authorizes hundreds of test center locations that offer a full range of airman knowledge tests. For information on authorized testing centers and to register for the knowledge test, visit **faa.psiexams.com**.

When you contact a knowledge testing center, be prepared to select a test date and make payment. You may register for test(s) several weeks in advance online or by phone, and you may cancel in accordance with the testing center's cancellation policy.

Regardless of your registration method, you will need an FAA Tracking Number (FTN) prior to registering for the FAA Airman Knowledge Test. This FTN will follow you throughout your aviation career. You will obtain your FTN as part of the test registration process, by creating a profile in the Integrated Airman Certificate and Rating Application (IACRA) system at **iacra.faa.gov/IACRA**. This FTN will be printed on your Airman Knowledge Test Report (AKTR).

The test registration process includes collection of this information: name, FTN, physical address, date of birth, email address, photo identification, phone number, test authorization (credentials of the individual such as an instructor endorsement), and previous number of test attempts.

For more information, contact:
PSI Services LLC
844-704-1487 or examschedule@psionline.com
faa.psiexams.com

Acceptable Forms of Authorization

You must be at least 14 years of age to take the FAA Knowledge Exam. When you take your FAA Knowledge Test, you will be required to show proper identification which contains your photograph, signature, date of birth, and current government-issued address (if your permanent mailing address is a post office box number).

The UAG test does not require an instructor endorsement or other form of written authorization.

For retesting, see Retesting Procedures.

Acceptable Materials

The applicant may use the following aids, reference materials, and test materials during the test, as long as the material does not include actual test questions or answers.

Acceptable Materials	Unacceptable Materials	Notes
Supplement book provided by proctor.	Written materials that are handwritten, printed, or electronic.	Testing centers may provide calculators and/or deny the use of personal calculators.
All models of aviation-oriented calculators or small electronic calculators that perform only arithmetic functions.	Electronic calculators incorporating permanent or continuous type memory circuits without erasure capability.	Test proctor may prohibit the use of your calculator if he or she is unable to determine the calculator's erasure capability.
Calculators with simple programmable memories, which allow addition to, subtraction from, or retrieval of one number from the memory; or simple functions, such as square root and percentages.	Magnetic cards, magnetic tapes, modules, computer chips, or any other device upon which pre-written programs or information related to the test can be stored and retrieved.	Printouts of data must be surrendered at the completion of the test if the calculator incorporates this design feature.
Scales, straight-edges, protractors, plotters, navigation computers, blank log sheets, holding pattern entry aids, and electronic or mechanical calculators that are directly related to the test.	Dictionaries.	Before, and upon completion of the test, while in the presence of the test proctor, actuate the ON/OFF switch or RESET button, and perform any other function that ensures erasure of any data stored in memory circuits.
Manufacturer's permanently inscribed instructions on the front and back of such aids, such as formulas, conversions, regulations, signals, weather data, holding pattern diagrams, frequencies, weight and balance formulas, and ATC procedures.	Any booklet or manual containing instructions related to use of test aids.	Test proctor makes the final determination regarding aids, reference materials, and test materials.

Testing Procedures for Applicants Requesting Special Accommodations

If you are an applicant with a learning or reading disability, you may request approval from the local FAA office to take an airman knowledge test, using the special accommodations procedures outlined in the most current version of FAA Order 8080.6 Conduct of Airman Knowledge Tests.

Prior to approval of any option, the FAA Aviation Safety Inspector must advise you of the regulatory certification requirement of being able to read, write, speak, and understand the English language.

Test Reports

Your test will be graded immediately upon completion and your score will display on the computer screen. You will receive your Airman Knowledge Test Report (AKTR), which will state your score.

Visit **faa.psiexams.com** to request a duplicate or replacement AKTR due to loss or destruction.

Airman Knowledge Test Reports are valid for 24 calendar months preceding the month you complete the practical test. If the AKTR expires before completion of the practical test, you must retake the knowledge test.

The AKTR lists the Airman Certification Standard (ACS) code for questions answered incorrectly. The total number of ASCs shown on the AKTR is not necessarily an indication of the total number of questions answered incorrectly. Study these knowledge areas to improve your understanding of the subject matter. See Cross-Reference B in the back of this book for a listing of ASCs and their associated questions.

An ACS code consists of four elements. This code is deciphered as follows:

UA.I.B.K10

UA—Applicable ACS (Unmanned Aircraft Systems)
I—Area of Operation (Regulations)
B—Task (Operating Rules)
K10—Task element (Knowledge 10: Visual line of sight aircraft operations)

Retesting Procedures

Applicants retesting *after failure* are required to submit the applicable AKTR indicating failure, along with an endorsement (on the test report) from an authorized instructor, who gave the applicant the additional training, certifying the applicant is competent to pass the test. The original failed AKTR and retest endorsement presented as authorization shall be retained by the proctor and attached to the applicable sign-in/out log. The latest test taken will reflect the official score.

Applicants retesting *in an attempt to achieve a higher passing score* may retake the same test for a better grade after 30 days. The latest test taken will reflect the official score. Applicants are required to submit the original applicable AKTR indicating previous passing score to the testing center prior to testing. Testing center personnel must collect and destroy this report prior to issuing the new test report.

Cheating or Other Unauthorized Conduct

Computer testing centers must follow strict security procedures to avoid test compromise. These procedures are established by the FAA and are covered in FAA Order 8080.6 Conduct of Airman Knowledge Tests. The FAA has directed testing centers to terminate a test at any time a test proctor suspects a cheating incident has occurred. An FAA investigation will then be conducted. If the investigation determines that cheating or unauthorized conduct has occurred, then any airman certificate or rating that you hold may be revoked, and you will be prohibited for one year from applying for or taking any test for a certificate or rating under 14 CFR Part 61, Part 107, or Part 65.

Test-Taking Tips

Prior to launching the actual test, the test proctor's testing software will provide you with an opportunity to practice navigating through the test. This practice (or tutorial) session may include a "sample" question(s). These sample questions have no relation to the content of the test, but are meant to familiarize you with the look and feel of the system screens, including selecting an answer, marking a question for later review, time remaining for the test, and other features of the testing software.

Follow these time-proven tips, which will help you develop a skillful, smooth approach to test-taking:

- Be careful to fully understand the intent of each question and corresponding answer while studying, rather than memorize the A, B, C answer choice—answer stems may appear in a different order than you studied and have some wording differences.

- Remember to bring a photo I.D., the testing fee if you didn't pay at the time of registration, calculator, flight computer (ASA's E6-B or CX-3 Flight Computer), plotter, magnifying glass, and a sharp pointer, such as a safety pin.

- Your first action when you sit down should be to write any formulas and information you can remember from your study on the scratch paper they will provide. Remember, some of the formulas may be on your E6-B.

- Read each question carefully before looking at the possible answers. You should clearly understand the problem before attempting to solve it.

- After formulating an answer, determine which answer choice corresponds the closest with your answer. The answer chosen should completely resolve the problem.

- From the answer choices given, it may appear that there is more than one possible answer. However, there is only one answer that is correct and complete. The other answers are either incomplete, erroneous, or represent popular misconceptions.

- Answer each question in accordance with the latest regulations and guidance publications.

- If a certain question is difficult for you, tag it for REVIEW and proceed to the other questions. After you answer the less difficult questions, return to those which you tagged and answer them. Be sure to untag these questions once you have answered them. The review marking procedure will be explained to you prior to starting the test. Although the computer should alert you to unanswered questions, make sure every question has an answer recorded. This will allow you to use the available time to your maximum advantage.

- Perform each math calculation twice to confirm your answer. If adding or subtracting a column of numbers, reverse your direction the second time to reduce the possibility of error.

- When solving a calculation problem, select the answer nearest to your solution.

- Remember that information is provided in the Legends and Figures contained within the Airman Knowledge Testing Supplement (FAA-CT-8080 document) you'll be using during the test.
- Remember to answer every question, even the ones with no completely correct answer, to ensure the FAA gives you credit for a bad question.
- Take your time and be thorough but relaxed. Take a minute off every half-hour or so to relax your brain and body. Stay hydrated.

Remote Pilot Certificate Eligibility Requirements

When applying for a Remote Pilot Certificate with a Small UAS Rating, in addition to the eligibility requirements of 14 CFR §107.61, you must meet one of the following:

- Applicant must provide an AKTR, which shows that you have passed the UAG aeronautical knowledge test as described in §107.73.
- If you hold a pilot certificate issued under Part 61 and meet the recency requirements specified in §61.56, you must provide a certificate of completion of a Part 107 initial training course. A qualifying initial training course is available at **faasafety.gov**. You must also show, via logbook entry or other method acceptable to the Administrator, that you meet the flight review requirements of §61.56.

The application must be submitted to a Flight Standards District Office (FSDO), a designated pilot examiner (DPE), an airman certification representative for a pilot school, a certified flight instructor (CFI), or other person authorized by the Administrator to process the application.

English Language Proficiency

In accordance with the requirements of §107.61(b) and the FAA Aviation English Language Proficiency standard, throughout the application and testing process, you must demonstrate the ability to read, write, speak, and understand the English language.

Knowledge Exam References

The FAA references the following documents to write the FAA Knowledge Exam questions. You should be familiar with all of these as part of your ground school studies, which you should complete before starting test preparation.

FAA-H-8083-2 *Risk Management Handbook*
FAA-H-8083-3 *Airplane Flying Handbook*
FAA-G-8082-22 *Remote Pilot sUAS Study Guide*
FAA-H-8083-25 *Pilot's Handbook of Aeronautical Knowledge*
FAA-H-8083-28 *Aviation Weather Handbook*

AC 91-57 *Model Aircraft Operating Standards*
AC 107-2 *Small Unmanned Aircraft Systems (sUAS)*
AC 150-5200-32 *Reporting Wildlife Aircraft Strikes*

SAFO 09013 *Fighting Fires Caused By Lithium Type Batteries in Portable Electronic Devices*
SAFO 10015 *Flying in the Wire Environment*
SAFO 10017 *Risks in Transporting Lithium Batteries in Cargo by Aircraft*
SAFO 15010 *Carriage of Spare Lithium Batteries in Carry-on and Checked Baggage*

Chart Supplements U.S.

Aeronautical Information Manual (AIM)
14 CFR Parts 1, 48, 61, 68, 89, 91, 107
49 CFR Part 1544

Visit **asa2fly.com** for these and many more titles and pilot supplies for your aviation endeavors.
Visit **asa2fly.com/TPUAS** for reader resources useful to both remote pilots and manned pilots operating in the presence of unmanned aircraft systems.

Acronyms

For reference, acronyms appearing in this book are defined below.

AC	Advisory Circular	LOA	Letter of Agreement
ACS	Airman Certification Standard	LOC	loss of control
ADDS	Aviation Digital Data Services (NOAA)	METAR	aviation routine weather report
ADM	aeronautical decision making	MOA	Military Operation Area
AGL	above ground level	MOC	means of compliance
AIM	Aeronautical Information Manual	MSL	mean sea level
AIRMET	airman's meteorological information	MTR	Military Training Route
AIS	Abbreviated Injury Scale	NAS	National Airspace System
AKTR	Airman Knowledge Test Report	NAVAID	navigational aid
ASOS	Automated Surface Observing System	NFDC	National Flight Data Center
ATC	air traffic control	NM	nautical mile
ATCT	air traffic control tower	NMACS	FAA Near Midair Collision System
ATIS	Automatic Terminal Information Service	NOTAM	Notice to Air Missions
AWC	Aviation Weather Center	NTIA	National Telecommunications and Information Administration (Department of Commerce)
AWOS	Automated Weather Observing System		
CFI	certified flight instructor	NTSB	National Transportation Safety Board
CG	center of gravity	OAT	outside air temperature
CoW	Certificate of Waiver	OTC	over-the-counter
CRM	crew resource management	PIC	pilot-in-command
CS	control station	POH	pilot's operating handbook
CTAF	Common Traffic Advisory Frequency	ROC	Regional Operations Center (FAA)
DOC	Declaration of Compliance	RVR	runway visual range
DPE	designated pilot examiner	SAA	Special Activity Airspace
FB	winds and temperatures aloft forecast	SIDA	Security Identification Display Area
FCC	Federal Communications Commission	SIGMET	significant meteorological information
FL	flight level	SM	statute mile
FLIP	Flight Information Publication (Department of Defense)	SMS	safety management system
		sUA	small unmanned aircraft
FRIA	FAA-recognized identification area	sUAS	small unmanned aircraft system
FSDO	Flight Standards District Office	TAC	Terminal Area Chart
FSS	Flight Service Station	TAF	terminal aerodrome forecast
FTP	flight termination point	TFR	temporary flight restriction
GPS	Global Positioning System	TSA	Transportation Security Administration
IACRA	Integrated Airman Certificate and/or Rating Application	UA	unmanned aircraft
ICAO	International Civil Aviation Organization	UTC	Coordinated Universal Time
IFR	instrument flight rules	VFR	visual flight rules
ILS	instrument landing system	VLOS	visual line-of-sight
IR	IFR Military Training Route	VO	visual observer
LAA	Local Airport Advisory	VR	VFR Military Training Route

ASA Test Prep Layout

Sample FAA questions have been sorted into chapters according to subject matter. Within each chapter, similar questions are grouped together following introductory chapter text. Figures referenced in the chapter text are numbered with the appropriate chapter number, e.g., "Figure 1-1" is Chapter 1's first chapter text figure.

Some sample FAA questions refer to Figures or Legends immediately following the question number, e.g., "1201. (Refer to Figure 14.)." These are FAA Figures and Legends from the Airman Knowledge Testing Supplement (FAA-CT-8080-2H) that can be found at the back of this book. This supplement will be provided to you as a separate booklet when you take your FAA test.

Following each sample FAA test question is ASA's explanation in italics. The last line of the explanation contains an ACS code and a reference for further study. Some questions include an explanation for the incorrect answers for added clarity. When you encounter a difficult question, find the ACS code in the table in Cross-Reference B, and then look for material relating to the subject description within the given reference(s). Refer to Cross-Reference B for more information on how to use ACS codes for effective studying.

Answers to each question are found at the bottom of each page.

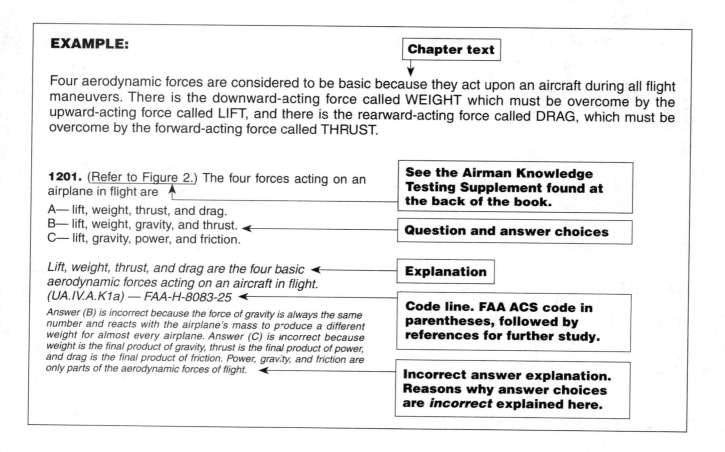

Chapter 1
Regulations

Introduction *1–3*

Remote Pilot Certification *1–6*

Remote Pilot Privileges *1–8*

Supporting Crew Roles *1–9*

Falsification, Reproduction, or Alteration *1–11*

Accident Reporting *1–11*

FAA Inspections *1–13*

sUAS Registration *1–14*

Remote Identification (Remote ID) *1–15*

Preflight Action and Inspection *1–17*

Carriage of Hazardous Material *1–18*

Operation at Night *1–18*

Visual Line of Sight (VLOS) *1–20*

Operating Limitations *1–21*

Right-of-Way Rules *1–22*

Operation Over Human Beings *1–24*

Operation from Moving Vehicles or Aircraft *1–26*

Privacy and Other Considerations *1–27*

Alcohol and Drugs *1–28*

Change of Address *1–31*

Waivers *1–31*

Introduction

The Federal Aviation Administration (FAA) has adopted specific rules to allow the operation of civil **small unmanned aircraft systems (sUAS)** in the **National Airspace System (NAS)** for purposes other than hobby and recreation. The rules are specified in Title 14 of the Code of Federal Regulations (14 CFR) Part 107, "Small Unmanned Aircraft Systems." Part 107 addresses sUAS classification, certification, and operational limitations and applies to the operation of certain civil small unmanned aircraft within the NAS. Except for certain excluded aircraft operations, any aircraft that meets the criteria below is considered a small unmanned aircraft.

Small unmanned aircraft:

- Weigh less than 55 pounds (25 kg), including everything that is onboard or otherwise attached to the aircraft.
- Are operated without the possibility of direct human intervention from within or on the aircraft.

You will see a number of different terms throughout this book used to refer to sUAS. This includes unmanned aircraft, small unmanned aircraft, UA, UAS, and sUAS. Any of these terms may be found on your FAA Knowledge Exam.

An sUAS includes the unmanned aircraft itself and its associated elements that are required for safe operation, such as communication links and components that control the aircraft.

Not all small unmanned aircraft are subject to 14 CFR Part 107. Part 107 does not apply to model aircraft that meet the criteria in 14 CFR §101.41 (for aircraft that meet the conditions in section 336 of Public Law 112-95), e.g. amateur rockets, moored balloons or unmanned free balloons, kites, operations conducted outside the United States, public aircraft operations, and air carrier operations. Hobbyists conducting recreational operations should follow the procedures in Advisory Circular (AC) 91-57, *Model Aircraft Operating Standards*, as well as 14 CFR §§101.41 and 101.43.

An inflight emergency is an unexpected and unforeseen serious occurrence or situation that requires urgent, prompt action. In case of an inflight emergency, the remote pilot-in-command (PIC) is permitted to deviate from any rule of Part 107 to the extent necessary to respond to that emergency. A remote PIC who exercises this emergency power to deviate from the rules of Part 107 is required, upon FAA request, to send a written report to the FAA explaining the deviation. Emergency action should be taken in such a way as to minimize injury or damage to property.

The following defined terms are pertinent to the Remote Pilot with an sUAS rating:

- **Control station (CS)**—An interface used by the remote pilot or the person manipulating the controls to control the flight path of the sUA.
- **Corrective lenses**—Spectacles or contact lenses.
- **Model aircraft**—A UA that is:
  - Capable of sustained flight in the atmosphere;
  - Flown within **visual line-of-sight (VLOS)** of the person operating the aircraft; and
  - Flown for hobby or recreational purposes.
- **Person manipulating the controls**—A person other than the remote PIC who is controlling the flight of an sUAS under the supervision of the remote PIC.
- **Public aircraft**—Means any of the following:
  - An aircraft used only for the U.S. government.
  - An aircraft owned by the U.S. government and operated by any person for purposes related to crew training, equipment development, or demonstration.

Chapter 1 **Regulations**

- An aircraft owned and operated by the government of a state, the District of Columbia, or a territory or possession of the United States or a political subdivision of one of these governments.
- An aircraft exclusively leased for at least 90 continuous days by the government of a state, the District of Columbia, or a territory or possession of the United States or a political subdivision of one of these governments.
- An aircraft owned or operated by the armed forces or chartered to provide transportation or other commercial air service to the armed forces.

- **Remote pilot-in-command (remote PIC or remote pilot)**—A person who holds a remote pilot certificate with an sUAS rating and has the final authority and responsibility for the operation and safety of an sUAS operation conducted under Part 107.
- **Small unmanned aircraft (sUA)**—A UA weighing less than 55 pounds, including everything that is onboard or otherwise attached to the aircraft, and can be flown without the possibility of direct human intervention from within or on the aircraft.
- **Small unmanned aircraft system (sUAS)**—An sUA and its associated elements (including communication links and the components that control the sUA) that are required for the safe and efficient operation of the sUA in the NAS.
- **Unmanned aircraft (UA)**—An aircraft operated without the possibility of direct human intervention from within or on the aircraft.
- **Visual observer (VO)**—A person acting as a flightcrew member who assists the sUA remote PIC and the person manipulating the controls to see and avoid other air traffic or objects aloft or on the ground.

1001. You are operating a 1,280 g (2.8 lb) quadcopter for your own enjoyment. What FAA regulation is this sUAS operation subject to?

A—14 CFR Part 107.
B—14 CFR Part 48.
C—This operation is not subject to FAA regulations.

This operation is recreational in nature. However, Part 48 "Registration and Marking Requirements for sUAS" applies for all operations of an sUAS over .55 pounds, whether for work or your own enjoyment. (UA.I.B.K1) — 14 CFR §107.1

1002. You have accepted football tickets in exchange for using your sUAS to videotape a future construction zone. What FAA regulation is this sUAS operation subject to?

A—14 CFR Part 107.
B—14 CFR Part 101.
C—This operation is not subject to FAA regulations.

This sUAS operation is subject to 14 CFR Part 107 because compensation (money or otherwise) makes the operation commercial in nature. (UA.I.A.K1) — 14 CFR §107.1

1003. You plan to operate a 33 lb sUAS to capture aerial imagery over real estate for use in sales listings. What FAA regulation is this sUAS operation subject to?

A—14 CFR Part 107.
B—14 CFR Part 101.
C—This operation is not subject to FAA regulations.

This sUAS operation is subject to 14 CFR Part 107 because the aerial imagery is for the furtherance of a business, making it commercial in nature. (UA.I.A.K1) — 14 CFR §107.1

1004. According to 14 CFR Part 107, an sUAS is an unmanned aircraft system weighing

A—less than 55 lbs.
B—55 kg or less.
C—55 lbs or less.

Small unmanned aircraft (sUAS) means an unmanned aircraft weighing less than 55 pounds on takeoff, including everything that is on board or otherwise attached to the aircraft. (UA.I.A.K2) — 14 CFR §107.1, AC 107-2

Answers

1001 [B]   1002 [A]   1003 [A]   1004 [A]

Chapter 1 **Regulations**

1005. "Unmanned aircraft" is defined as a device operated

A—during search and rescue operations other than public.
B—without the possibility of direct human intervention from within or on the aircraft.
C—for hobby and recreational use when not certificated.

An unmanned aircraft means an aircraft operated without the possibility of direct human intervention from within or on the aircraft. (UA.I.A.K2) — 14 CFR §§107.1 and 107.3, AC 107-2

1006. Which of the following types of operations are excluded from the requirements in 14 CFR Part 107?

A—Model aircraft for hobby use.
B—Quadcopter capturing aerial imagery for crop monitoring.
C—UAS used for motion picture filming.

14 CFR Part 107 does not apply to model aircraft that meet the criteria in 14 CFR §101.41, amateur rockets, moored balloons or unmanned free balloons, kites, operations conducted outside the United States, public aircraft operations, and air carrier operations. (UA.I.A.K1) — 14 CFR §107.1, AC 107-2

1007. Which of the following operations would be regulated by 14 CFR Part 107?

A—Conducting public operations during a search mission.
B—Flying for enjoyment with family and friends.
C—Operating your sUAS for an imagery company.

Part 107 regulates commercial sUAS operations. (UA.I.A.K1) — 14 CFR §107.1

1008. As a remote pilot with an sUAS rating, under which situation can you deviate from 14 CFR Part 107?

A—When conducting public operations during a search mission.
B—Flying for enjoyment with family and friends.
C—In response to an in-flight emergency.

In case of an inflight emergency, the remote PIC is permitted to deviate from any rule of Part 107 to the extent necessary to respond to that emergency. (UA.I.B.K5) — 14 CFR §107.21

1009. What action, if any, is appropriate if the remote pilot deviates from Part 107 during an emergency?

A—Take no special action since you are pilot-in-command.
B—File a detailed report to the FAA Administrator, upon request.
C—File a report to the FAA Administrator, as soon as possible.

Each remote PIC who deviates from a rule in Part 107 must, upon request of the FAA Administrator, send a written report of that deviation to the Administrator. (UA.I.B.K5) — 14 CFR §107.21

1280. Which of these operations must comply with 14 CFR Part 107?

A—Civil operations.
B—Civil and public operations.
C—Public and military operations.

Part 107 addresses sUAS operations of certain civil small unmanned aircraft within the NAS. (UA.I.A.K1) — 14 CFR Part 107

1010. To avoid a possible collision with a manned airplane, you estimate that your small unmanned aircraft climbed to an altitude greater than 600 feet AGL. To whom must you report the deviation?

A—Upon request of the Federal Aviation Administration.
B—The National Transportation Safety Board.
C—Air Traffic Control.

Each remote PIC who deviates from a rule in Part 107 must, upon request of the FAA Administrator, send a written report of that deviation to the Administrator. (UA.I.B.K5) — 14 CFR §107.21

1011. When an ATC clearance has been obtained, no remote PIC may deviate from that clearance, unless that pilot obtains an amended clearance. The one exception to this regulation is

A—when the clearance states "at pilot's discretion."
B—an emergency.
C—if the clearance contains a restriction.

Except in an emergency, no person may operate an aircraft contrary to an ATC clearance or instruction. (UA.I.B.K5) — 14 CFR §107.21

Answers

| 1005 [B] | 1006 [A] | 1007 [C] | 1008 [C] | 1009 [B] | 1280 [A] |
| 1010 [A] | 1011 [B] | | | | |

1342. 14 CFR Part 107 applies to
A—public sUAS.
B—civil sUAS.
C—all sUAS.

Part 107 only applies to civil sUAS. (UA.I.A.K1) —
14 CFR Part 107

Remote Pilot Certification

When a pilot certificate is issued, it lists the certification level which defines the privileges and limitations of that certificate holder, such as remote pilot, private pilot, flight instructor, or airline transport pilot (ATP). Additionally, the issued pilot certificate will include the category of aircraft in which the certificate holder is qualified. The term "category" means a broad classification of aircraft, such as airplane, rotorcraft, glider, and lighter-than-air. Small unmanned aircraft is a "rating."

An sUAS operation may involve one individual or a team of crewmembers. These sUAS crew roles are a remote PIC, a person manipulating, and a VO.

In the aviation context, the FAA typically refers to "licensing" as "certification." Just like a manned aircraft PIC, the remote PIC of an sUAS is directly responsible for, and is the final authority as to, the operation of that UAS. Additionally, a person manipulating the controls can participate in flight operations under certain conditions.

A person acting as a remote PIC of an sUAS in the NAS under Part 107 must obtain a Remote Pilot Certificate with an sUAS rating issued by the FAA prior to sUAS operation. The remote PIC must have this certificate easily accessible during flight operations.

To apply for a Part 107 Remote Pilot Certificate with an sUAS Rating, you must satisfy the following eligibility requirements:

- Be at least 16 years old;
- Be able to read, speak, write, and understand the English language (FAA may make exceptions for medical reasons);
- Be in a physical and mental condition that would not interfere with the safe operation of sUAS; and
- Fulfill training and testing requirements (defined in 14 CFR Part 107).

Applicants for a Part 107 Remote Pilot Certificate with an sUAS Rating must meet the following requirements in order to gain and retain the knowledge necessary to safely operate UAS in the NAS.

Applicant	Initial Requirements	Recurrent Requirements (every 24 months)
Part 61 Pilot Certificate Holder with a Current Flight Review (per 14 CFR §61.56)	The **faasafety.gov** initial online course, or the FAA UAG Knowledge Exam	The recurrent online course at **faasafety.gov**
Any Other Applicant	The FAA UAG Knowledge Exam	The recurrent online course at **faasafety.gov**

After you satisfy the applicable training or testing requirements, you may apply for a Part 107 Remote Pilot Certificate with an sUAS Rating through an online or paper process. The FAA encourages the use of

Answers
1342 [B]

an online application through the **Integrated Airman Certificate and/or Rating Application (IACRA)**. A paper process is available using FAA Form 8710-13, Remote Pilot Certificate and/or Rating Application, however the paper application requires increased processing time and will delay the issuance of your permanent certificate. The application must be submitted to a **Flight Standards Office (FSDO)**, a designated pilot examiner (DPE), an airman certification representative for a pilot school, a certified flight instructor (CFI), or other person authorized by an FAA Administrator to process the application. A temporary certificate will be issued, valid until receipt of the permanent certificate or for up to 120 calendar days.

After the FAA receives the application, the Transportation Security Administration (TSA) will automatically conduct a background security screening of the applicant prior to issuance of a remote pilot certificate. If the security screening is successful, the FAA will issue a permanent remote pilot certificate. If the security screening is not successful, the applicant will be disqualified and a pilot certificate will not be issued. Individuals who believe that they improperly failed a security threat assessment may appeal the decision to the TSA.

Remote Pilot Certificate holders with an sUAS rating must meet the recurrent training requirements every 24 months. This retraining can be satisfied by completing the online FAA course or taking the FAA Knowledge Exam.

1012. Which of the following individuals may process an application for a Part 107 Remote Pilot Certificate with an sUAS Rating?

A—Commercial balloon pilot.
B—Remote pilot-in-command.
C—Designated Pilot Examiner.

The remote pilot application must be submitted to a FSDO, a DPE, an airman certification representative for a pilot school, a CFI, or other person authorized by the Administrator to process the application. (UA.I.C.K3) — 14 CFR §§107.63 and 61.56

1013. After receiving a Part 107 Remote Pilot Certificate with an sUAS Rating, how often must you satisfy recurrent training requirements?

A—Every 6 months.
B—Every 12 months.
C—Every 24 months.

Remote Pilot Certificate holders with an sUAS Rating must meet the recurrent training requirements every 24 months. This retraining can be satisfied by completing the online FAA course or taking the FAA Knowledge Exam. (UA.I.C.K4) — 14 CFR Part §§107.63 and 107.65, AC 107-2

1014. To satisfy medical requirements, all sUAS crewmembers must

A—hold a valid Third Class Medical Certificate.
B—be free of any physical or mental condition that would interfere with the safe operation of the small unmanned aircraft system.
C—complete a physical with an Aviation Medical Examiner.

No person may manipulate the flight controls of a small unmanned aircraft system or act as a remote PIC, VO, or direct participant in the operation of the sUA if he or she knows or has reason to know that he or she has a physical or mental condition that would interfere with the safe operation of the sUAS. (UA.I.B.K22) — 14 CFR §107.17

1015. Which of the following would medically disqualify a remote pilot?

A—Taking a prescription medication that does not have any noticeable side effects.
B—A migraine headache with the side effect of blurred vision.
C—Occasional muscle soreness following exercise.

No person may manipulate the flight controls of an sUAS or act as a remote PIC, VO, or direct participant in the operation of the sUA if he or she knows or has reason to know that he or she has a physical or mental condition that would interfere with the safe operation of the sUAS. (UA.I.B.K3) — 14 CFR §107.17

Answers

1012 [C]   1013 [C]   1014 [B]   1015 [B]

Chapter 1 **Regulations**

Remote Pilot Privileges

The remote PIC is directly responsible for and is the final authority as to the operation of the sUAS conducted under Part 107. He or she must:

- Be designated before each flight (but can change during the flight).
- Ensure that the operation poses no undue hazard to people, aircraft, or property in the event of a loss of control of the aircraft for any reason.
- Operate the small unmanned aircraft to ensure compliance with all applicable provisions and regulations.

Being able to safely operate the sUAS relies on, among other things, the physical and mental capabilities of the remote PIC, person manipulating the controls, VO, and any other direct participant in the sUAS operation. Though the person manipulating the controls of an sUAS and VO are not required to obtain an airman medical certificate, they may not participate in the operation of an sUAS if they know or have reason to know that they have a physical or mental condition that could interfere with the safe operation of the sUAS.

A person may not operate or act as a remote PIC or VO in the operation of more than one UA at the same time. Additionally, Part 107 allows transfer of control of an sUAS between certificated remote pilots. Two or more certificated remote pilots transferring operational control (i.e., the remote PIC designation) to each other may do so only if they are both capable of maintaining VLOS of the sUA and without loss of control (LOC). For example, one remote pilot may be designated the remote PIC at the beginning of the operation, and then at some point in the operation another remote pilot may take over as remote PIC by positively communicating that he or she is doing so. As the person responsible for the safe operation of the UAS, any remote pilot who will assume remote PIC duties should meet all of the requirements of Part 107, including awareness of factors that could affect the flight.

1016. Who is responsible for ensuring that there are enough crewmembers for a given sUAS operation?
A—Remote pilot-in-command.
B—Person manipulating the controls.
C—Visual observer.

The remote PIC is ultimately responsible for assessing the needs of the operation and preparing sufficient support crewmembers to ensure the safety of the operation. (UA.I.B.K4) — 14 CFR §107.12

1017. Who is ultimately responsible for preventing a hazardous situation before an accident occurs?
A—Remote pilot-in-command.
B—Person manipulating the controls.
C—Visual observer.

The remote PIC is ultimately responsible for identifying hazards and taking appropriate action (or intervening when another person is manipulating the controls) to ensure the safety of the flight. (UA.I.B.K4) — 14 CFR §107.12

1018. Which crewmember must hold a remote pilot certificate with an sUAS rating?
A—Remote pilot-in-command.
B—Person manipulating the controls.
C—Visual observer.

The remote PIC must hold a Part 107 Remote Pilot Certificate with an sUAS Rating before conducting any sUAS operation. (UA.I.B.K4) — 14 CFR §107.12

1019. When using a small unmanned aircraft in a commercial operation, who is responsible for briefing the participants about emergency procedures?
A—The lead visual observer.
B—The FAA inspector-in-charge.
C—The remote pilot-in-command.

Prior to flight, the remote PIC must ensure that all persons directly participating in the small unmanned aircraft operation are informed about the operating conditions, emergency procedures, contingency procedures, roles and responsibilities, and potential hazards. (UA.I.B.K4) — 14 CFR §107.49, AC 107-2

Answers

1016 [A]   1017 [A]   1018 [A]   1019 [C]

1020. The remote PIC may operate how many sUAS at a time?
A—1.
B—5.
C—No more than 2.

A person may not operate or act as a remote PIC or VO in the operation of more than one unmanned aircraft at the same time. (UA.I.B.K12) — 14 CFR §107.35

Supporting Crew Roles

A person who does not hold a Remote Pilot Certificate or a remote pilot that that has not met the recurrent testing/training requirements of Part 107 may operate the flight controls of an sUAS under Part 107, as long as he or she is directly supervised by a remote PIC and the remote PIC has the ability to immediately take direct control of the sUAS. This ability is necessary to ensure that the remote PIC can quickly address any hazardous situation before an accident occurs.

The remote PIC can take over the flight controls by using a number of different methods. For example, the operation could involve a "buddy box" type of system that uses two **control stations (CS)**: one for the person manipulating the flight controls, and one for the remote PIC that allows the remote PIC to override the other CS and immediately take direct control of the sUA. Another method involves the remote PIC standing close enough to the person manipulating the flight controls to be able to physically take over the CS from that person. A third method could employ the use of an automation system whereby the remote PIC could immediately engage that system to put the sUA in a pre-programmed "safe" mode (such as in a hover, in a holding pattern, or "return home").

An **autonomous operation** is when the autopilot onboard the sUA performs certain functions without direct pilot input. For example, the remote pilot can input a flight route into the CS, which then sends it to the autopilot that is installed in the sUA. During autonomous flight, flight control inputs are made by components onboard the aircraft, not from a CS. Thus, the remote PIC could lose the control link to the sUA and the aircraft would still continue to fly the programmed mission and/or return home to land.

When the sUA is flying autonomously, the remote PIC also must have the ability to change routing or altitude, or to command the aircraft to land immediately. The ability to direct the sUA may be through manual manipulation of the flight controls or through commands using automation. The remote PIC must retain the ability to direct the sUA to ensure compliance with the requirements of Part 107. There are different methods a remote PIC may utilize to direct the sUA to ensure compliance with Part 107. For example, the remote PIC may transmit a command for the autonomous aircraft to climb, descend, land now, proceed to a new waypoint, enter an orbit pattern, or return to home. Any of these methods may be used to satisfactorily avoid a hazard or give right-of-way. The use of automation does not allow a person to simultaneously operate more than one sUA.

The role of VOs is to alert the rest of the crew about potential hazards during sUAS operations. The use of VOs is optional. However, the remote PIC may use one or more VOs to supplement situational awareness and VLOS responsibilities while the remote PIC is conducting other mission-critical duties (such as checking displays). The remote PIC must make certain that all VOs:

- Are positioned in a location where they are able to see the sUAS continuously and sufficiently to maintain VLOS.
- Possess a means to effectively communicate the sUAS position and the position of other aircraft to the remote PIC and person manipulating the controls.

Answers
1020 [A]

1021. Which crewmember is required to be under the direct supervision of the remote PIC when operating an sUAS?

A—Remote pilot-in-command.
B—Person manipulating the controls.
C—Visual observer.

A non-certificated person may manipulate the controls of the sUAS only if he or she is under the direct supervision of the remote PIC. (UA.I.B.K4a) — 14 CFR §107.12

1022. A person without a Part 107 Remote Pilot Certificate may operate an sUAS for commercial operations

A—under the direct supervision of a remote PIC.
B—only when visual observers participate in the operation.
C—alone, if operating during daylight hours.

A person who does not hold a Remote Pilot Certificate or a remote pilot that that has not met the recurrent testing/training requirements of Part 107 may operate the sUAS under Part 107, as long as he or she is directly supervised by a remote PIC and the remote PIC has the ability to immediately take direct control of the sUAS. (UA.I.B.K4a) — 14 CFR §107.12

1023. Whose sole task during an sUAS operation is to watch the sUAS and report potential hazards to the rest of the crew?

A—Remote pilot-in-command.
B—Person manipulating the controls.
C—Visual observer.

The VO (when asked by the remote PIC) maintains visual line of sight with the sUAS and reports any potential hazards to the remote PIC and person manipulating the controls. (UA.I.B.K11) — 14 CFR §107.33

1024. Which of the following crewmembers must be used during Part 107 sUAS operations?

A—Remote PIC.
B—Remote PIC and visual observer.
C—Remote PIC, visual observer, and person manipulating the controls.

A remote PIC must be used during Part 107 sUAS operations. A VO is optional. The person manipulating the controls may be the remote PIC, or must be operating under the direct supervision of the remote PIC. (UA.I.B.K4) — 14 CFR §107.19

1025. An autonomous operation requires the following crewmembers.

A—Remote PIC.
B—Remote PIC and visual observer.
C—Remote PIC, visual observer, and person manipulating the controls.

An autonomous operation does not negate the requirement for a remote PIC. An autonomous operation is generally considered an operation in which the remote pilot inputs a flight plan into the control station, which sends it to the autopilot onboard the sUA. (UA.I.B.K4) — AC 107-2

Answers

1021 [B]   1022 [A]   1023 [C]   1024 [A]   1025 [A]

Falsification, Reproduction, or Alteration

The FAA relies on information provided by owners and remote pilots of sUAS when it authorizes operations or when it has to make a compliance determination. Accordingly, the FAA may take appropriate action against an sUAS owner, operator, remote PIC, or anyone else who fraudulently or knowingly provides false records or reports, or otherwise reproduces or alters any records, reports, or other information for fraudulent purposes. Such action could include civil sanctions and the suspension or revocation of a certificate or waiver.

1026. Under Title 14 of the Code of Federal Regulations, what is the maximum penalty for falsification, alteration, or fraudulent reproduction of certificates, logbooks, reports, and records?

A—Ineligibility to receive any certificate or rating for one year.
B—Imprisonment for one year and a $5,000.00 fine.
C—Suspension or revocation of any certificate held.

14 CFR §65.20 states that any person who falsifies or makes a fraudulent entry in a logbook, report, or record is subject to the suspension or revocation of any airman or ground instructor certificate or rating held by that person. (UA.I.A.K3) — 14 CFR §107.5

Accident Reporting

The remote PIC must report any sUAS accident to the FAA, within 10 days of the operation, if any of the following thresholds are met:

- Serious injury to any person or any loss of consciousness.
- Damage to any property, other than the small unmanned aircraft, if the cost is greater than $500 to repair or replace the property (whichever is lower).

For example, a sUA damages property of which the fair market value is $200, and it would cost $600 to repair the damage. Because the fair market value is below $500, this accident is not required to be reported. Similarly, if the aircraft causes $200 worth of damage to property whose fair market value is $600, that accident is also not required to be reported because the repair cost is below $500.

The accident report must be made within 10 calendar days of the operation that created the injury or damage. The report may be submitted to the appropriate **FAA Regional Operations Center (ROC)** or FSDO electronically (**faa.gov/uas**) or by telephone. The report should include the following information:

1. sUAS remote PIC's name and contact information;
2. sUAS remote PIC's FAA airman certificate number;
3. sUAS registration number issued to the aircraft, if required (FAA registration number);
4. Location of the accident;
5. Date of the accident;
6. Time of the accident;
7. Person(s) injured and extent of injury, if any or known;
8. Property damaged and extent of damage, if any or known; and
9. Description of what happened.

A serious injury qualifies as Level 3 or higher on the **Abbreviated Injury Scale (AIS)** of the Association for the Advancement of Automotive Medicine. This scale is an anatomical scoring system that

Answers
1026 [C]

Chapter 1 **Regulations**

is widely used by emergency medical personnel. In the AIS system, injuries are ranked on a scale of 1 to 6; Level 1 is a minor injury, Level 2 is moderate, Level 3 is serious, Level 4 is severe, Level 5 is critical, and Level 6 is a nonsurvivable injury. It would be considered a serious injury if a person requires hospitalization, and the injury is fully reversible including, but not limited to:

- Head trauma.
- Broken bone(s).
- Laceration(s) to the skin that requires suturing.

In addition to this FAA report, and in accordance with the criteria established by the National Transportation Safety Board (NTSB), certain sUAS accidents must also be reported to the NTSB.

1027. You are part of a news crew, operating an sUAS to cover a breaking story. You experience a flyaway during landing. The unmanned aircraft strikes a vehicle, causing approximately $800 worth of damage. When must you report the accident to the FAA?

A—Anytime.
B—Within 10 days.
C—Not to exceed 30 days.

Report any sUAS accident to the FAA within 10 days if it results in serious injury, loss of consciousness, or repairs costing over $500. (UA.I.A.K4) — 14 CFR §107.9

1316. A small UA causes an accident and your crew member loses consciousness. When do you report the accident?

A—No accidents need to be reported.
B—When requested by the UA owner.
C—Within 10 days of the accident.

Report any sUAS accident to the FAA within 10 days if it results in serious injury, loss of consciousness, or repairs costing over $500. (UA.I.A.K4) — 14 CFR §107.9

1028. Within how many days must an sUAS accident be reported to the FAA?

A—90 days.
B—10 days.
C—30 days.

Report any sUAS accident to the FAA within 10 days if it results in serious injury, loss of consciousness, or repairs costing over $500. (UA.I.A.K4) — 14 CFR §107.9

1029. While operating a small unmanned aircraft system (sUAS), you experience a flyaway and several people suffer injuries. Which of the following injuries requires reporting to the FAA?

A—An injury requiring an overnight hospital stay.
B—Scrapes and cuts bandaged on site.
C—Minor bruises.

The remote PIC must report any sUAS accident to the FAA, within 10 days of the operation, if a serious injury to any person or any loss of consciousness occurs. It would be considered a serious injury if a person requires hospitalization. (UA.I.A.K4) — 14 CFR §107.9, AC 107-2

1030. As you are flying your sUAS, valued at $1,000, over a home to photograph it for real estate sales purposes, the sUAS has a failure causing it to fall onto an awning causing some minor damage. The fair market value of the awning is $800 but it can be repaired for $400. What type of report is required?

A—An sUAS accident report to the FAA, within 10 days of the operation.
B—An sUAS incident report to the FAA, within 10 days of the operation.
C—No report is required.

No report is required because the damage can be repaired for less than $500. A report is required only when damage to any property, other than the sUA, is greater than $500 to repair or replace the property (whichever is lower). The cost of the sUAS is not considered when determining if an event is considered to be an accident or incident. (UA.I.A.K4) — 14 CFR §107.9, AC 107-2

Answers

1027 [B]   1316 [C]   1028 [B]   1029 [A]   1030 [C]

Chapter 1 **Regulations**

FAA Inspections

You must make available to the FAA, upon request, the sUAS for inspection or testing. In addition, you must verify before flight that all required documentation is physically or electronically available in the event of an on-site FAA inspection. Such documentation may include:

- Pilot certificate;
- Aircraft registration;
- Any necessary waiver or exemption; or
- Other documentation related to the operation.

1031. When must a current remote pilot certificate be in the pilot's personal possession or readily accessible in the aircraft?

A—When acting as a crew chief during launch and recovery.
B—Only when a payload is carried.
C—Anytime when acting as pilot-in-command or as a required crewmember.

No person may act as PIC, or in any other capacity as a required pilot flight crewmember when operating a sUAS unless he or she has in possession or readily accessible a current pilot certificate. (UA.I.A.K5) — 14 CFR §107.7

1032. Each person who holds a pilot certificate, a U.S. driver's license, or a medical certificate shall present it for inspection upon the request of the Administrator, the National Transportation Safety Board, or any

A—authorized representative of the Administrator of the Department of Transportation.
B—authorized representative of the Department of State.
C—federal, state, or local law enforcement officer.

Remote pilots must present their remote pilot certificate for inspection upon a request from the Administrator; an authorized representative of the National Transportation Safety Board; any federal, state, or local law enforcement officer; or an authorized representative of the Transportation Security Administration. (UA.I.A.K5) — 14 CFR §107.7

1304. If requested, to whom must I present my Remote Pilot Certificate?

A—A person of authority.
B—FAA Inspector.
C—Authorized representative of the Department of State.

A remote PIC, owner, or person manipulating the flight controls of a small unmanned aircraft system must, upon request, make available to the Administrator: (1) the Remote Pilot Certificate with an sUAS Rating; and (2) any other document, record, or report required. (UA.I.A.K5) — 14 CFR §107.7

1324. Upon request by the FAA, the remote pilot-in-command must provide

A—a logbook documenting small UA landing currency.
B—a remote pilot certificate with a small UAS rating.
C—any employer issued photo identification.

A remote PIC, owner, or person manipulating the flight controls of a small unmanned aircraft system must, upon request, make available to the Administrator: (1) the Remote Pilot Certificate with an sUAS Rating; and (2) any other document, record, or report required. (UA.I.A.K5) — 14 CFR §107.7

Answers

1031 [C]   1032 [C]   1304 [B]   1324 [B]

Chapter 1 **Regulations**

sUAS Registration

Most sUAS must be registered with the FAA prior to operating in the NAS. Owners must register the sUAS if it is greater than 0.55 pounds, less than 55 pounds, and operated under the provisions of Part 107. The owner must satisfy the registration requirements described in Part 47, "Aircraft Registration," or Part 48, "Registration and Marking Requirements for Small Unmanned Aircraft." The sUAS must be registered by a person who is at least 13 years of age. Part 48 establishes the online registration option for sUAS that will be operated only within the territorial limits of the United States. A Certificate of Aircraft registration expires 3 years after the date of issue unless it is renewed

An sUAS operation requires a Foreign Aircraft Permit if it involves a civil aircraft that is:

- Registered in a foreign country; or
- Owned, controlled, or operated by someone who is not a U.S. citizen or permanent resident.

If either criteria is met, the remote PIC should obtain a Foreign Aircraft Permit pursuant to 14 CFR §375.41 before conducting any operations.

Before operation, mark the sUAS to identify that it is registered with the FAA. The registration marking must be:

- A unique identifier number. This is typically the FAA-issued registration number or the serial number, if authorized during registration.
- Legible and durable. Sample methods include engraving, permanent marker, or self-adhesive label.
- Visible. The unique identifier must be legibly displayed on an external surface of the sUAS.

An FAA airworthiness certification is not required for sUAS. However, the remote PIC must maintain and inspect the sUAS prior to each flight to ensure that it is in a condition for safe operation. For example, inspect the aircraft for equipment damage or malfunctions.

1033. According to 14 CFR Part 48, when would a small unmanned aircraft owner not be permitted to register it?

A—All persons must register their small unmanned aircraft.
B—If the owner does not have a valid United States driver's license.
C—The owner is less than 13 years of age.

The sUAS must be registered by a person who is at least 13 years of age. (UA.I.B.K1) — 14 CFR §§107.13 and 91.203

1034. According to 14 CFR Part 48, when must a person register a small UA with the Federal Aviation Administration?

A—All civilian small UAs weighing greater than .55 pounds must be registered regardless of its intended use.
B—When the small UA is used for any purpose other than as a model aircraft.
C—Only when the operator will be paid for commercial services.

Owners must register the sUAS if it is greater than 0.55 pounds, less than 55 pounds, and operated under the provisions of Part 107 which regulate commercial sUAS operations. (UA.I.B.K1) — 14 CFR §107.13

Answers

1033 [C]   1034 [A]

Chapter 1 **Regulations**

1035. Under what conditions would a small unmanned aircraft not have to be registered before it is operated in the United States?

A—When the aircraft weighs less than .55 pounds on takeoff, including everything that is on-board or attached to the aircraft.
B—When the aircraft has a takeoff weight that is more than .55 pounds but less than 55 pounds, not including fuel and necessary attachments.
C—All small unmanned aircraft need to be registered regardless of the weight of the aircraft before, during, or after the flight.

Owners must register the sUAS if it is greater than 0.55 lbs, less than 55 pounds and operated under the provisions of Part 107. (UA.I.B.K1) — 14 CFR §107.13

Answer (B) is incorrect because the question is asking when registration is not required. Answer (C) is incorrect because sUAS must be registered if the device is between 0.55 and 55 pounds.

1343. A civil small unmanned aircraft operating under Part 107 is permitted to

A—have dual registration in both the U.S. and a foreign country.
B—operate only if possessing a U.S. registration certificate.
C—operate if possessing either a U.S. registration or a foreign registration certificate.

To operate under Part 107 within the United States, a civil sUAS must have an effective U.S. Certificate of Aircraft Registration issued to its owner, the second copy of the Aircraft Registration Application as described by 14 CFR §47.31(c), a Certificate of Aircraft Registration as provided by Part 48, or a registration certification issued under the laws of a foreign country. (UA.I.B.K1) — 14 CFR Part 107

1356. How long is aircraft registration valid for?

A—2 years.
B—3 years.
C—4 years.

A Certificate of Aircraft registration expires 3 years after the date of issue unless it is renewed. (UA.I.B.K1) — 14 CFR §48.100

Remote Identification (Remote ID)

Remote ID is the ability of a drone in flight to provide identification and location information via radio frequency (e.g., Wi-Fi or Bluetooth) that can be received by other parties. This information includes:

- A unique identifier for the drone;
- The drone's latitude, longitude, geometric altitude, and velocity;
- An indication of the latitude, longitude, and geometric altitude of control station (standard) or takeoff location (broadcast module);
- A time mark; and
- Emergency status (standard remote ID drone only).

This information helps the FAA, law enforcement, and other federal agencies find the control station when a drone appears to be flying in an unsafe manner or where it is not allowed to fly. Remote ID also lays the foundation of the safety and security groundwork needed for more complex drone operations.

Effective September 16, 2023, no person may operate an unmanned aircraft within the airspace of the United States unless the operation meets the requirements of 14 CFR §89.110 (standard remote identification) or §89.115 (alternative remote identification) unless otherwise authorized by the FAA.

Standard remote ID broadcasts identification and location information about the drone and its control station. A standard remote ID drone is one that is produced with built-in remote ID broadcast capability in accordance with the remote ID rule's requirements.

Answers

1035 [A]   1343 [C]   1356 [B]

Chapter 1 **Regulations**

A **remote ID broadcast module** is an alternative remote ID device that broadcasts identification and location information about the drone and its takeoff location in accordance with the remote ID rule's requirements. The broadcast module can be added to a drone to retrofit it with remote ID capability. This module is limited to VLOS operations.

The Certificate of Aircraft Registration of the unmanned aircraft used in the operation must include the serial number of the remote ID broadcast module, or the serial number of the unmanned aircraft must be provided to the FAA in a notice of identification prior to the operation.

Standard and alternative remote ID must broadcast from takeoff to shut down. In the event of a broadcast failure, the person manipulating the flight controls must land the unmanned aircraft as soon as practicable.

If the unmanned aircraft operation is being conducted for aeronautical research or to show compliance with regulations, the Administrator may authorize such operations without remote ID capability. Operations without remote ID may also be conducted in an **FAA-recognized identification area (FRIA)**. FRIAs are often community-based organizations or educational institutions that have received prior FAA permission to allow unmanned aircraft to operate in a specified area without remote ID capability.

1344. Under which operational requirement would the unmanned aircraft be restricted to visual line of sight operations?

A—If operating with ADS-B capabilities.
B—If operating with standard remote identification.
C—If operating with a remote identification broadcast module.

The person manipulating the flight controls of the unmanned aircraft system must be able to see the unmanned aircraft at all times throughout the operation if the operation is being conducted using alternative remote ID, like a remote ID broadcast module. (UA.I.F.K2) — 14 CFR §89.115

1345. What must a person who is manipulating the controls of a small unmanned aircraft do if the standard remote identification fails during flight?

A—Land the aircraft as soon as practicable.
B—Notify the nearest FAA Air Traffic Facility.
C—Activate the aircrafts navigation lights.

The person manipulating the flight controls of the unmanned aircraft system must land the unmanned aircraft as soon as practicable if the standard remote ID unmanned aircraft is no longer broadcasting the message elements of 14 CFR §89.305. (UA.I.F.K1) — 14 CFR §89.110

1346. Where must a small unmanned aircraft's serial number be listed when using either standard remote identification or a broadcast module?

A—The aircraft's Document of Compliance.
B—The manufacturer's Method of Compliance.
C—The Certificate of Aircraft Registration.

The Certificate of Aircraft Registration of the unmanned aircraft used in the operation must include the serial number of the unmanned aircraft, as required by Parts 47 and 48, or the serial number of the unmanned aircraft must be provided to the FAA in a notice of identification pursuant to 14 CFR §89.130 prior to the operation. (UA.I.F.K5) —14 CFR §89.130

1347. Under which operational condition may you be approved to fly without remote identification capability?

A—If the operation is being conducted in an FAA-recognized identification area outside line of sight.
B—If the operation is being conducted for aeronautical research.
C—If the operation is being conducted at altitudes of 400 feet AGL and below.

The Administrator may authorize operations without remote ID where the operation is solely for the purpose of aeronautical research or to show compliance with regulations. (UA.I.F.K3) — 14 CFR §89.120

Answer choice (A) is incorrect because operations without remote ID are allowed within FRIAs but must remain within VLOS. Answer choice (C) is incorrect because remote ID requirements are not restricted to specific altitudes.

Answers

1344 [C]　　　　1345 [A]　　　　1346 [C]　　　　1347 [B]

Chapter 1 **Regulations**

1357. Does an sUAS equipped with ADS-B meet the requirements for remote identification?
A—No.
B—Yes.
C—Always.

Automatic Dependent Surveillance–Broadcast (ADS-B) equipment cannot be used to comply with the remote identification requirements of this part. (UA.I.B.K28) — 14 CFR §89.125

Preflight Action and Inspection

The remote PIC must complete a preflight familiarization, inspection, and other actions, such as crewmember briefings, prior to beginning flight operations. Before beginning any sUAS flight operation:

- Assess the operating environment including local weather conditions, local airspace, flight restrictions, the location of persons and property on the surface, and other ground hazards.
- Inform any supporting crewmembers about the operation and their roles including operating conditions, emergency procedures, contingency procedures, roles and responsibilities of each person involved in the operation, as well as potential hazards.
- Inspect the sUAS to see that it is in a condition for safe operation, ensuring that all control links between the control station and the small unmanned aircraft are working properly, there is sufficient power to continue controlled flight operations to a normal landing, any object attached or carried by the sUAS is secure and does not adversely affect the flight characteristics or controllability of the aircraft, and the unique identifier is readily accessible and visible upon inspection of the sUAS.
- Maintain documents required in the event of an on-site FAA inspection, including the remote PIC's Remote Pilot certificate, aircraft registration (if required), and Certificate of Waiver (CoW) (if applicable).

1036. According to 14 CFR Part 107, the responsibility to inspect the small unmanned aircraft system (sUAS) to ensure it is in safe operating condition rests with the
A—owner of the sUAS.
B—visual observer.
C—remote pilot-in-command.

The remote PIC must complete a preflight familiarization, inspection, and other actions, such as crewmember briefings, prior to beginning flight operations. (UA.I.B.K2) — 14 CFR §107.49

1037. Which preflight action is specifically required of the pilot prior to each flight?
A—Check the aircraft logbooks for appropriate entries.
B—Assess the operating environment including local weather conditions, local airspace and any flight restrictions, the location of persons and property on the surface, and other ground hazards.
C—Visually inspect the pilot certificates of all crew members.

Each remote pilot shall, before each flight, assess the operating environment including local weather conditions, local airspace and any flight restrictions, the location of persons and property on the surface, and other ground hazards.(UA.I.B.K20) — 14 CFR §107.49

Answers

1357 [A]   1036 [C]   1037 [B]

Chapter 1 **Regulations**

Carriage of Hazardous Material

A small unmanned aircraft may not carry hazardous material. Hazardous material means a substance or material that the Secretary of Transportation has determined is capable of posing an unreasonable risk to health, safety, and property when transported in commerce. The term includes hazardous substances, hazardous wastes, marine pollutants, elevated temperature materials, and materials that meet the defining criteria for hazard classes and divisions in 49 CFR Part 173.

Lithium batteries that are installed in an sUAS for power during the operation are not considered a hazardous material under Part 107. However, spare (uninstalled) lithium batteries would meet the definition of hazardous material and may not be carried on the sUAS.

1038. Under what circumstances may lithium batteries be carried during sUAS operations?
A—Lithium batteries are prohibited from sUAS operations.
B—Lithium batteries may be carried in a sealed storage container away from the sUAS fuel source.
C—Lithium batteries may be carried only when installed as the primary power for the operation.

Lithium batteries that are installed in an sUAS for power during the operation are not considered a hazardous material under Part 107. However, spare (uninstalled) lithium batteries would meet the definition of hazardous material and may not be carried on the sUAS. (UA.V.C.K2) — AC 107-2

Operation at Night

For operations conducted during civil twilight and night, the sUAS must be equipped with anti-collision lights that are capable of being visible for at least 3 SM. However, the remote PIC may reduce the intensity of the lighting if it would be in the interest of operational safety to do so. For example, the remote PIC may momentarily reduce the lighting intensity if it impacts his or her night vision.

Civil twilight is defined as the period of time before sunrise and after sunset when the sun is not more than six degrees below the horizon.

14 CFR Part 1 defines **night** as the time between the end of evening civil twilight and the beginning of morning civil twilight, as published in the Federal Air Almanac and converted to local time. The Federal Air Almanac provides tables to determine sunrise and sunset at various latitudes. For example:

- In the contiguous United States, evening civil twilight is the period from sunset until 30 minutes after sunset, and morning civil twilight is the period of 30 minutes prior to sunrise until sunrise.
- In Alaska, the definition of civil twilight differs and is described in the Federal Air Almanac.

Answers
1038 [C]

1039. According to 14 CFR Part 107, what is required to operate a small unmanned aircraft within 30 minutes after official sunset?

A—Use of a transponder.
B—Use of lighted anti-collision lights.
C—Must be operated in a rural area.

When sUAS operations are conducted during civil twilight, the sUAS must be equipped with anti-collision lights that are capable of being visible for at least 3 statute miles. (UA.I.B.K9) — 14 CFR §107.29

1348. You intend to conduct an unmanned aircraft operation 60 minutes past the end of evening civil twilight to inspect a flashing beacon atop a radio tower. To conduct this operation, you will be required to

A—obtain a certificate of waiver from the administrator.
B—have functioning anti-collision lighting which is visible for at least 3 statute miles.
C—contact the nearest air traffic control facility to advise them of your operation.

Night operations require an sUAS to have anti-collision lighting visible for at least 3 SM that has a flash rate sufficient to avoid a collision. The remote PIC may reduce the intensity of, but may not extinguish, the anti-collision lighting if it would be in the interest of safety to do so. (UA.I.B.K25) — 14 CFR §107.29

1349. When may a remote pilot reduce the intensity of an aircraft lights during a night flight?

A—At no time may the lights of an sUAS be reduced in intensity at night.
B—When a manned aircraft is in the vicinity of the sUAS.
C—When it is in the interest of safety to dim the aircrafts lights.

The remote PIC may reduce the intensity of, but may not extinguish, the anti-collision lighting if it would be in the interest of safety to do so. (UA.I.B.K25) — 14 CFR §107.29

1352. What should you do if there are high intensity pulsating lights in the area during a night flight?

A—Determine if they are turned on full strength.
B—Ask them to be turned off.
C—Use first person view (FPV).

The remote PIC should determine if the lights will be turned on and at what strength. While operating as remote PIC, avoid direct eye contact with the lighting to avoid ruining your night vision. (UA.I.B.K25) — FAA-H-8083-25

1353. How should the control station backlighting be set for night flight?

A—As bright as possible.
B—As low as possible to maintain night vision.
C—Set to pulsating mode.

The remote PIC or person manipulating the controls should set the backlighting as low as possible to avoid bright light, which could potentially degrade the eyes' night vision capabilities. (UA.I.B.K25) — FAA-H-8083-25

1361. At which frequency must the anti-collision lights flash during a nighttime operation?

A—The anti-collision lights do not need to flash.
B—The flash rate should be sufficient to avoid a collision.
C—The flash rate must be at least 2 flashes per minute.

Night operations require an sUAS to have anti-collision lighting visible for at least 3 SM that has a flash rate sufficient to avoid a collision. (UA.I.B.K25) — 14 CFR §107.29

Answers

1039 [B]   1348 [B]   1349 [C]   1352 [A]   1353 [B]   1361 [B]

Chapter 1 **Regulations**

Visual Line of Sight (VLOS)

The sUAS must remain within VLOS of flight crewmembers. VLOS means any flight crewmember (i.e., the remote PIC, person manipulating the controls, and VOs if used) is capable of seeing the aircraft with vision unaided by any device other than corrective lenses (spectacles or contact lenses). Vision aids such as binoculars may be used only momentarily to enhance situational awareness. For example, the remote PIC, person manipulating the controls, or VO may use vision aids briefly to avoid flying over persons or to avoid conflicting with other aircraft.

Crewmembers must be able to see the small unmanned aircraft at all times during flight. Therefore, the sUA must be operated closely enough to the CS to ensure visibility requirements are met during small unmanned aircraft operations. The VLOS requirement would not prohibit actions such as scanning the airspace or briefly looking down at the CS. The person maintaining VLOS may have brief moments in which he or she is not looking directly at or cannot see the sUA, but still retains the capability to see the sUA or quickly maneuver it back to VLOS. These moments can be for the safety of the operation (e.g., looking at the controller to see battery life remaining) or for operational necessity.

For operational necessity, the remote PIC or person manipulating the controls may intentionally maneuver the sUA so he or she loses sight of it for brief periods of time. Should the remote PIC or person manipulating the controls lose VLOS of the sUAS, he or she must regain VLOS as soon as practicable. For example, a remote PIC stationed on the ground utilizing a sUA to inspect a rooftop may lose sight of the aircraft for brief periods while inspecting the farthest point of the roof. As another example, a remote PIC conducting a search operation around a fire scene with an sUAS may briefly lose sight of the aircraft while it is temporarily behind a dense column of smoke. Although this is a practical application, remote PICs must avoid interfering with emergency responders when operating in and around a fire scene.

Even though the remote PIC may briefly lose sight of the sUA, he or she always has the see-and-avoid responsibilities.

1041. Power company employees use an sUAS to inspect a long stretch of high voltage powerlines. Due to muddy conditions, their vehicle must stay beside the road and the crew must use binoculars to maintain visual line of sight with the aircraft. Is this sUAS operation in compliance with 14 CFR Part 107?

A—Yes, the operation is compliant with Part 107.
B—There is not enough information to make a determination.
C—No, the operation is not compliant with Part 107.

This scenario is not compliant with Part 107. Vision aids such as binoculars may be used only momentarily to enhance situational awareness. They may not be used for the duration of the operation. (UA.I.B.K10) — 14 CFR §107.31

1042. A crew conducting surveillance anticipates losing visual sight with the sUAS within a small segment of the flight plan. The flight

A—may be conducted using binoculars.
B—must be rerouted to maintain visual line of sight.
C—may be conducted if the visual line of sight can be maintained for 50% of the route.

The sUAS must remain within VLOS of flight crewmembers. The VLOS requirement would not prohibit actions such as scanning the airspace or briefly looking down at the sUAS control station. Should the remote PIC or person manipulating the controls lose VLOS of the sUA, he or she must regain VLOS as soon as possible. (UA.I.B.K10) — 14 CFR §107.31

Answer (A) is incorrect because vision aids such as binoculars may be used only momentarily to enhance situational awareness. Answer (C) is incorrect because crewmembers must be able to see the sUAS at all times during flight.

Answers

1041 [C]   1042 [B]

Chapter 1 **Regulations**

Operating Limitations

The sUAS must be operated in accordance with the following limitations:

- Cannot be flown faster than a ground speed of 87 knots (100 miles per hour).
- Cannot be flown higher than 400 feet above ground level (AGL) unless flown within a 400-foot radius of a structure and not flown higher than 400 feet above the structure's immediate uppermost limit. See Figure 1-1.

Crewmembers must operate within the following limitations:

- Minimum visibility, as observed from the location of the control station, must be no less than 3 statute miles.
- Minimum distance from clouds must be no less than 500 feet below a cloud and 2,000 feet horizontally from the cloud.

Note: These operating limitations are intended, among other things, to support the remote pilot's ability to identify hazardous conditions relating to encroaching aircraft or persons on the ground, and to take the appropriate actions to maintain safety.

Figure 1-1. Flying near a tower

1043. In accordance with 14 CFR Part 107, except when within a 400-foot radius of a structure, at what maximum altitude can you operate sUAS?

A—600 feet AGL.
B—500 feet AGL.
C—400 feet AGL.

The sUAS cannot be flown higher than 400 feet AGL unless flown within a 400-foot radius of a structure and is not flown higher than 400 feet above the structure's immediate uppermost limit. (UA.I.B.K21b) — 14 CFR §107.51

1044. What speed limit applies to sUAS operations?

A—200 knots.
B—80 mph.
C—100 mph.

The sUAS cannot be flown faster than a ground speed of 87 knots (100 mph). (UA.I.B.K21a) — 14 CFR §107.51

1045. Unless otherwise authorized, what is the maximum airspeed at which a person may operate an sUAS below 400 feet?

A—200 knots.
B—80 mph.
C—100 mph.

The sUAS cannot be flown faster than a ground speed of 87 knots (100 mph) and must be operated below 400 feet. (UA.I.B.K21a) — 14 CFR §107.51

1322. According to 14 CFR part 107, what is the maximum ground speed for a small UA?

A—87 knots.
B—87 mph.
C—100 knots.

The sUAS cannot be flown faster than a ground speed of 87 knots (100 mph) and must be operated below 400 feet. (UA.I.B.K21a) — 14 CFR §107.51

Answers

1043 [C]   1044 [C]   1045 [C]   1322 [A]

Remote Pilot Test Prep ASA **1–21**

Chapter 1 Regulations

1046. The basic weather minimums for operating an sUAS up to the 400 feet AGL limit are

A—900-foot ceiling and 3 mile visibility.
B—2,000-foot ceiling and 1 miles visibility.
C—clear of clouds and 2 miles visibility.

Part 107 sUAS operations require minimum visibility of 3 SM and the minimum distance from clouds must be no less than 500 feet below the cloud; and 2,000 feet horizontally from the cloud. To maintain 500 feet below the clouds, you must have a 900-foot ceiling to be able to operate to the maximum 400 feet AGL, or a ceiling that would allow the sUAS to operate at a lower AGL altitude. (UA.I.B.K21d) — 14 CFR §107.51

1270. In accordance with 14 CFR Part 107, at what maximum altitude can you operate an sUAS when inspecting a tower with a top at 1,000 feet AGL at close proximity (within 100 feet)?

A—1,400 feet MSL.
B—1,400 feet AGL.
C—400 feet AGL.

The sUAS cannot be flown higher than 400 feet AGL unless flown within a 400-foot radius of a structure and is not flown higher than 400 feet above the structure's immediate uppermost limit. (UA.I.B.K21b) — 14 CFR §107.51

1323. (Refer to Figure 78.) You have been contracted to inspect towers located approximately 4 NM south of the Sioux Gateway (SUX) airport operating an unmanned aircraft. What is the maximum altitude above ground level (AGL) that you are authorized to operate over the top of the towers?

A—400 feet AGL.
B—402 feet AGL.
C—802 feet AGL.

The sUAS cannot be flown higher than 400 feet AGL unless flown within a 400-foot radius of a structure and no higher than 400 feet above the structure's immediate uppermost limit. One of the tower sets south of the SUX airport shows a tower at 402 feet AGL; you may operate over the top of these towers no higher than 802 feet AGL. (UA.I.B.K21b) — 14 CFR §107.51 and Sectional Chart Legend

Right-of-Way Rules

No person may operate a small unmanned aircraft in a manner that interferes with operations and traffic patterns at any airport, heliport, or seaplane base. The remote PIC also has a responsibility to remain clear of and yield right-of-way to all other aircraft, manned or unmanned, and avoid other potential hazards that may affect the remote PIC's operation of the aircraft. This is traditionally referred to as **see and avoid**.

To satisfy this responsibility, the remote PIC must:

- Know the location and flight path of his or her sUA at all times.
- Be aware of other aircraft, persons, and property in the vicinity of the operating area.
- Be able to maneuver the small unmanned aircraft to:
  – Avoid a collision.
  – Prevent other aircraft from having to take evasive action.
- Avoid operating anywhere where the presence of his or her sUA may interfere with operations at the airport, such as approach corridors, taxiways, runways, or helipads.
- Yield right-of-way to all other aircraft, including aircraft operating on the surface of the airport.

Answers

1046 [A]   1270 [B]   1323 [C]

Chapter 1 **Regulations**

First-person view camera cannot satisfy the see-and-avoid requirement. However, such cameras can be used as long as the see-and-avoid requirement is satisfied in other ways, such as using visual observers.

1047. Which aircraft has right-of-way over the other traffic?

A—An airplane.
B—An sUAS.
C—A quadcopter.

The remote pilot operating an sUAS must yield right-of-way to all manned aircraft, including aircraft operating on the surface of the airport. (UA.I.B.K14) — 14 CFR §107.37

1048. What action should the pilots take if a collision is anticipated?

A—The manned aircraft pilot should give way to the right.
B—The remote pilot should adjust the sUAS course.
C—Both pilots should give way to the right.

The remote PIC must be able to maneuver the sUAS to avoid a collision and prevent other aircraft from having to take evasive action. (UA.I.B.K14) — 14 CFR §107.37

1049. What may be used to assist compliance with sUAS see-and-avoid requirements?

A—Binoculars.
B—First-person view camera.
C—remote pilot diligence.

The remote PIC also has a responsibility to remain clear of and yield right-of-way to all other aircraft, manned or unmanned, and avoid other potential hazards that may affect the remote PIC's operation of the aircraft. (UA.I.B.K14) — 14 CFR §107.37

Answer (A) is incorrect because binoculars may be used only momentarily to enhance situational awareness. Answer (B) is incorrect because the first-person view camera cannot satisfy see-and-avoid requirement.

1320. During a flight of your small unmaned aircraft, you observe a hot air balloon entering the area. You should

A—yield the right-of-way to the hot air balloon.
B—ensure the unmanned aircraft passes below, above, or ahead of the balloon.
C—expect the hot air balloon to climb above your altitude.

The remote pilot operating an sUAS must yield right-of-way to all other manned aircraft, including aircraft operating on the surface of the airport. (UA.I.B.K14) — 14 CFR §107.37

Answers

1047 [A]   1048 [B]   1049 [C]   1320 [A]

Operation Over Human Beings

No person may operate an sUAS over a human being unless:

- That human being is directly participating in the operation of the sUAS;
- That human being is located under a covered structure or inside a stationary vehicle that can provide reasonable protection from a falling sUAS; or
- The operation meets the requirements of at least one of the operational categories specified in Subpart D of Part 107 outlined below:
  - To conduct Category 1 Operations the sUAS must meet the requirements of §107.110.
  - To conduct Category 2 Operations the sUAS must meet the requirements of §107.115.
  - To conduct Category 3 Operations the sUAS must meet the requirements of §107.125.
  - To conduct Category 4 Operations the sUAS must meet the requirements of §107.140.

An sUAS may be eligible for one or more of the above categories as long as the remote PIC cannot inadvertently switch between modes or configurations of the categories.

No person may operate an sUAS over a human being located inside a moving vehicle unless it meets one of the four operational categories for operations over people.

- To conduct Category 1 through 3 operations the sUAS must remain within or over a closed- or restricted-access site, all human beings made aware that an sUAS may fly over them, and the sUAS must not maintain sustained flight over the moving vehicle.
- To conduct Category 4 operations the sUAS must have an airworthiness certificate and be operated in accordance with the operating limitations specified in an approved flight manual.

For all operations conducted under Category 2 and 3 the sUAS must meet a means of compliance (MOC) and be listed on a current Declaration of Compliance (DOC) with the FAA.

The MOC must consist of a test, analysis, and inspection of procedures for the sUAS detailing how the sUAS meets the requirements of §107.120(a) for Category 2 and §107.130(a) for Category 3. The description should include conditions, environments, and methods, as applicable. In addition, this information needs to be submitted along with a compliance explanation of how application of the MOC fulfills the requirements of §107.120(a) and/or §107.130(a).

If the FAA determines the sUAS meets the MOC for Category 2 or 3, the operator will then need to submit a DOC to the Administrator for approval. Once approved, the DOC must be retained along with all supporting information and made available to the Administrator upon request for a period of at least 2 years.

Chapter 1 **Regulations**

1050. Which action is specifically required of the remote pilot prior to each flight?

A—Check the aircraft logbooks to ensure maintenance is current.
B—Make a plan to keep non-participants clear, indoors, or under cover.
C—Identify a non-participant who will be near the sUAS operation to help with see-and-avoid procedures.

You may not operate an sUAS directly over another person unless that person is directly involved in the operation (such as a VO or other crewmember) or within a safe cover, such as inside a stationary vehicle or a protective structure that would protect a person from harm if the sUAS were to crash into that structure, or if the sUAS meets one the specified categories of Part 107 Subpart D. If operating in populated/inhabited areas, make a plan to keep non-participants clear, indoors, or under cover. (UA.I.E.K1) — 14 CFR §107.39

1051. To conduct Category 1 operations, a remote pilot in command must use a small unmanned aircraft that weighs

A—0.55 pounds or less.
B—0.65 pounds or less.
C—0.75 pounds or less.

To conduct Category 1 operations, a remote PIC must use an sUAS that weighs 0.55 pounds or less on takeoff and throughout the duration of each operation under Category 1, including everything that is on board or otherwise attached to the aircraft. (UA.I.E.K3a) — 14 CFR §107.110

1052. Which category of small unmanned aircraft must have an airworthiness certificate issued by the FAA?

A—Category 4.
B—Category 3.
C—Category 2.

To be eligible to operate over human beings under Category 4, the sUAS must: (1) have an airworthiness certificate issued under Part 21; (2) be operated in accordance with the operating limitations specified in the AFM or as otherwise specified by the Administrator (the operating limitations must not prohibit operations over human beings); and (3) have maintenance, preventive maintenance, alterations, or inspections performed. (UA.I.E.K3d) — 14 CFR §107.140

1317. A small unmanned aircraft must be operated in a manner which

A—does not endanger the life or property of another.
B—requires more than one visual observer.
C—never exceeds 200 feet AGL.

No person may continue flight of an sUA when he or she knows or has reason to know that the sUAS is no longer in a condition for safe operation. (UA.I.E.K1) — 14 CFR §107.15

1354. What is required to conduct Category 3 operations over people?

A—Have a label displayed on the sUAS indicating eligibility to conduct category 3 operations.
B—Must be ADS-B equipped.
C—Must have an airworthiness certificate.

To be eligible to operate over human beings under Category 3, the sUAS must meet a means of compliance (MOC) and be listed on a current Declaration of Compliance (DOC) with the FAA and display a label on the sUAS indicating Category 3 eligibility. (UA.I.E.K3c) — 14 CFR §107.125

1355. Who is responsible for making sure the sUAS is marked and listed on the declaration of compliance?

A—The person who submits the declaration of compliance for the sUAS.
B—Owner or operator.
C—Remote PIC.

The person who submits the declaration of compliance (DOC) is responsible for making sure the sUAS is marked and listed on the DOC. (UA.I.E.K12) — 14 CFR §107.160

Answers

1050 [B]   1051 [A]   1052 [A]   1317 [A]   1354 [A]   1355 [A]

Chapter 1 **Regulations**

Operation from Moving Vehicles or Aircraft

Part 107 permits operation of an sUAS from a moving land or water-borne vehicle over a sparsely populated (or unpopulated) area. However, operation from a moving aircraft is prohibited. Additionally, sUA that are transporting another person's property for compensation or hire may not be operated from any moving vehicle.

Operations from moving vehicles are subject to the same restrictions that apply to all other Part 107 sUAS operations. Examples include:

- VLOS—the remote PIC (and the person manipulating the controls, if applicable) operating from a moving vehicle or watercraft is still required to maintain VLOS for the sUAS.
- Communication—the VO and remote PIC must still maintain effective communication.
- No reckless operation—Part 107 also prohibits careless or reckless operation of an sUAS. Operating an sUAS while driving a moving vehicle is considered to be careless or reckless because the driver's attention would be hazardously divided. Therefore, the driver of a land vehicle or the operator of a waterborne vehicle must not serve as the remote PIC, person manipulating the controls, or VO. As another example, failure to consider weather conditions near structures, trees, or rolling terrain when operating in a densely populated area could be determined as careless or reckless operation.

Other laws, such as state and local traffic laws, may also apply to the conduct of a person driving a vehicle. Many states currently prohibit distracted driving and state or local laws may also be amended in the future to impose restrictions on how cars and public roads may be used with regard to an sUAS operation. The FAA emphasizes that people involved in an sUAS operation are responsible for complying with all applicable laws and not just the FAA's regulations.

1053. A professional wildlife photographer operates an sUAS from a moving truck to capture aerial images of migrating birds in remote wetlands. The driver of the truck does not serve any crewmember role in the operation. Is this sUAS operation in compliance with 14 CFR Part 107?

A—Compliant with Part 107.
B—Not compliant with Part 107.
C—Not compliant with state and local traffic laws.

You may operate an sUAS from a moving vehicle if you are in a sparsely populated area and the driver does not serve as the remote PIC, person manipulating the controls, or VO. (UA.I.B.K7) — 14 CFR §107.25

1054. In accordance with 14 CFR Part 107, you may operate an sUAS from a moving vehicle when no property is carried for compensation or hire

A—over suburban areas.
B—over a parade or other social event.
C—over a sparsely populated area.

Operation of an sUAS is permitted from a moving land or waterborne vehicle over a sparsely populated (or unpopulated) area. (UA.I.B.K7) — 14 CFR §107.25

1055. Which of the following operations is compliant with 14 CFR Part 107?

A—Remote PIC is driving a moving vehicle while operating an sUAS in a sparsely populated area.
B—Remote PIC is a passenger on an aircraft in flight while operating an sUAS.
C—Remote PIC is a passenger in a moving boat while operating an sUAS in an unpopulated area.

Operation of an sUAS is permitted from a moving land or waterborne vehicle over a sparsely populated (or unpopulated) area. (UA.I.B.K7) — 14 CFR §107.25

1040. Which categories of operation require an FAA accepted current DOC?

A—Categories 1 and 2.
B—Categories 2 and 3.
C—Categories 1 and 4.

In order for an applicant to declare an sUAS is compliant with the requirements of Part 107 Subpart D for Category 2 or Category 3 operations, an applicant must submit a DOC for acceptance by the FAA in a manner specified by the Administrator. (UA.I.E.K13) — 14 CFR §107.160

Answers

1053 [A]   1054 [C]   1055 [C]   1040 [B]

1274. You are conducting a Category 1 operation over a moving vehicle with a human being inside. Because of such operation, the small unmanned aircraft

A—may not fly directly over the vehicle.
B—may maintain sustained flight over the vehicle for any extended period of time.
C—must not maintain sustained flight over the vehicle.

For an operation under Category 1, Category 2, or Category 3, the sUAS must remain within or over a closed or restricted access site, and all human beings located inside a moving vehicle within the closed or restricted access site must be on notice that an sUAS may fly over them, and the sUAS must not maintain sustained flight over moving vehicles. (UA.I.E.K6) — 14 CFR §107.145

Privacy and Other Considerations

No person may operate an sUAS in a careless or reckless manner that would endanger another person's life or property. Part 107 also prohibits allowing an object to be dropped from an sUAS in a way that causes undue hazard to persons or property. Examples of hazardous operation include, but are not limited to:

- Operations that interfere with manned aircraft operations.
- Operating an sUAS over persons not directly participating in the operation.
- Loading the sUAS beyond its capabilities to the point of losing control.

You may operate an sUAS to transport another person's property (cargo) for compensation or hire provided you comply with the additional requirements described below:

- The total weight of the sUA (including the cargo) must remain below 55 pounds.
- The sUAS operation must be within the boundaries of a state (intrastate).
- No items may be dropped from the small unmanned aircraft in a manner that creates undue hazard to persons or property.
- You may not operate the sUAS from a moving land vehicle or waterborne vessel.
- Carriage of hazardous materials is not permitted.

As with other operations in Part 107, sUAS operations involving the transport of property must be conducted within VLOS of the remote pilot. While the VLOS limitation can be waived for some operations under the rule, it cannot be waived for transportation of property. Additionally, Part 107 does not allow the operation of an sUAS from a moving vehicle or aircraft if the sUA is being used to transport property for compensation or hire. This limitation cannot be waived. Additionally, the remote pilot must know the sUAS location in order to determine the attitude, altitude, and direction; to yield the right-of-way to other aircraft; and to maintain the ability to see and avoid other aircraft.

Other laws, such as state and local privacy laws, may apply to sUAS operations. The remote PIC is responsible for reviewing and complying with such laws prior to operation.

In addition, remote PICs are encouraged to review the Department of Commerce National Telecommunications and Information Administration (NTIA) best practices, which address privacy, transparency, and accountability issues related to private and commercial use of sUAS.

Answers

1274 [C]

Chapter 1 **Regulations**

1056. Personnel at an outdoor concert venue use an sUAS to drop promotional T-shirts and CDs over the audience. Is this sUAS operation in compliance with 14 CFR Part 107?

A—Yes, compliant with Part 107.
B—Not compliant with Part 107.
C—No, unless authorized by the venue.

This scenario is not compliant with Part 107. You may not operate over non-participants without safe cover and you may not drop objects in a manner that creates a hazard. (UA.I.B.K6b) — AC 107-2

1057. Under what conditions may objects be dropped from the sUAS?

A—In an emergency.
B—If precautions are taken to avoid injury or damage to persons or property on the surface.
C—If prior permission is received from the Federal Aviation Administration.

No items may be dropped from the sUA in a manner that creates undue hazard to persons or property. (UA.I.B.K6b) — 14 CFR §107.23

1318. You plan to release golf balls from your small unmanned aircraft at an altitude of 100 feet AGL. You must ensure the objects being dropped will

A—not create an undue hazard to persons or property.
B—land within 10 feet of the expected landing zone.
C—not cause property damage in excess of $300.

No items may be dropped from the sUA in a manner that creates undue hazard to persons or property. (UA.I.B.K6b) — 14 CFR §107.23

1058. You wish to start a local delivery business using an sUAS to drop small packages at the front door of customer. The customer's residence is not always within visual line-of-sight (VLOS) of the remote PIC located at the delivery facility. Under which circumstances would this be authorized?

A—With a waiver from the FAA.
B—By utilizing a vehicle to follow the sUAS while enroute to maintain VLOS.
C—There is currently no way to do this in compliance with AC 107-2.

The FAA has stated that they will not provide waivers for beyond VLOS during the carriage of goods for hire. Also, moving vehicles (land or sea) are not authorized to be used during flights upon which goods are carried for hire. (UA.I.B.K6b) — AC 107-2

Answers (A) and (B) are incorrect because these are specifically prohibited per AC 107-2.

Alcohol and Drugs

Part 107 does not allow operation of an sUAS if the remote PIC, person manipulating the controls, or VO is unable to safely carry out his or her responsibilities. It is the remote PIC's responsibility to ensure all crewmembers are not participating in the operation while impaired. While drugs and alcohol use are known to impair judgment, certain over-the-counter (OTC) medications and medical conditions could also affect the ability to safely operate a sUA. For example, certain antihistamines and decongestants may cause drowsiness. Pilots can learn more about the impact of drugs and alcohol on flight operations in the *Pilot's Handbook of Aeronautical Knowledge* (FAA-H-8083-25).

Part 107 prohibits a person from serving as a remote PIC, person manipulating the controls, VO, or other crewmember if he or she:

- Consumed any alcoholic beverage within the preceding 8 hours;
- Is under the influence of alcohol;
- Has a blood alcohol concentration of .04 percent or greater; and/or
- Is using a drug that affects the person's mental or physical capabilities.

Answers

1056 [B]   1057 [B]   1318 [A]   1058 [C]

Chapter 1 **Regulations**

A refusal to submit to a test to indicate the percentage by weight of alcohol in the blood, when requested by a law enforcement officer, or a refusal to furnish or authorize the release of the test results requested by the Administrator, is grounds for:

- Denial of an application for a Remote Pilot Certificate with an sUAS Rating for a period of up to 1 year after the date of that refusal; or
- Suspension or revocation of a Remote Pilot Certificate with an sUAS Rating.

Certain medical conditions, such as epilepsy, may also create a risk to operations. It is the remote PIC's responsibility to determine that their medical condition is under control and they can safely conduct a UAS operation.

1059. Who holds the responsibility to ensure all crewmembers who are participating in the operation are not impaired by drugs or alcohol?

A—Remote pilot-in-command.
B—The FAA.
C—Site supervisor.

The remote PIC or person manipulating the flight controls of an sUAS must comply with the "do not operate while impaired" regulations. (UA.I.B.K8) — 14 CFR §§107.19 (b), 107.19 (d), and 107.57

1060. A person may not act as a crewmember of a sUAS if alcoholic beverages have been consumed by that person within the preceding

A—8 hours.
B—12 hours.
C—24 hours.

No person may act or attempt to act as a crewmember of an sUAS within 8 hours after the consumption of any alcoholic beverage. Remember "8 hours bottle to throttle." (UA.I.B.K8) — 14 CFR §§107.17 and 91.17

1319. After having dinner and wine, your client asks you to go outside to demonstrate the small unmanned aircraft's capabilities. You must

A—pass a self-administered sobriety test before operating a small unmanned aircraft.
B—not operate a small unmanned aircraft within 8 hours of consuming any alcoholic beverage.
C—ensure that your visual observer has not consumed any alcoholic beverage in the previous 12 hours.

No person may act or attempt to act as a crewmember of an sUAS within 8 hours after the consumption of any alcoholic beverage. Remember "8 hours bottle to throttle." (UA.I.B.K8) — 14 CFR §§107.17 and 91.17

1061. No person may attempt to act as a crewmember of a sUAS with

A—.4 percent by weight or more alcohol in the blood.
B—.004 percent by weight or more alcohol in the blood.
C—.04 percent by weight or more alcohol in the blood.

No person may act, or attempt to act, as a crewmember of a civil aircraft while having .04 percent or more, by weight, alcohol in the blood. (UA.I.B.K8) — 14 CFR §§107.27 and 91.17

1062. Which is true regarding the presence of alcohol within the human body?

A—A small amount of alcohol increases vision acuity.
B—Consuming an equal amount of water will increase the destruction of alcohol and alleviate a hangover.
C—Judgment and decision-making abilities can be adversely affected by even small amounts of alcohol.

As little as one ounce of liquor, one bottle of beer, or four ounces of wine can impair flying skills. (UA.I.B.K8) — AIM ¶8-1-1

Answer (A) is incorrect because all mental and physical activities will be decreased with even small amounts of alcohol in the bloodstream. Answer (B) is incorrect because water does not increase the metabolism of alcohol.

Answers

1059 [A]   1060 [A]   1319 [B]   1061 [C]   1062 [C]

Chapter 1 **Regulations**

1063. A law enforcement officer witnesses careless or reckless behavior while observing sUAS operations and requests the operator submit to a drug or alcohol test. What are the consequences if this request is denied?

A—The operator may be denied an application for a Remote Pilot Certificate for up to 30 days.
B—The operator may have to pay a fine but their Remote Pilot Certificate will not be affected.
C—The operator may have their Remote Pilot Certificate with sUAS Rating suspended or revoked.

A refusal to submit to a test to indicate the percentage by weight of alcohol in the blood, when requested by a law enforcement officer, or a refusal to furnish or authorize the release of the test results requested by the Administrator, is grounds for denial of an application for a Remote Pilot Certificate with an sUAS Rating for a period of up to 1 year after the date of that refusal, or suspension or revocation of a Remote Pilot Certificate with an sUAS Rating. (UA.I.C.K2) — 14 CFR §107.59

Answer (A) is incorrect because the remote pilot applicant could be denied application for up to 1 year after the date of refusal. Answer (B) is incorrect because the operator could risk having their remote pilot certificate suspended or revoked.

1325. The refusal of a remote PIC to submit to a blood alcohol test when requested by a law enforcement officer

A—is grounds for suspension or revocation of their Remote Pilot Certificate.
B—can be delayed for a period up to 8 hours after the request.
C—has no consequences to the Remote Pilot Certificate.

A refusal to submit to a test to indicate the percentage by weight of alcohol in the blood, when requested by a law enforcement officer, or a refusal to furnish or authorize the release of the test results requested by the Administrator, is grounds for denial of an application for a Remote Pilot Certificate with an sUAS Rating for a period of up to 1 year after the date of that refusal; or suspension or revocation of a Remote Pilot Certificate with an sUAS Rating. (UA.I.C.K2) — 14 CFR §107.59

1275. When can someone with a marijuana conviction apply for a Remote Pilot Certificate?

A—Never.
B—18 months.
C—1 year.

A conviction for the violation of any federal or state statute relating to the growing, processing, manufacture, sale, disposition, possession, transportation, or importation of narcotic drugs, marijuana, or depressant or stimulant drugs or substances is grounds for denial of an application for a Remote Pilot Certificate with an sUAS Rating for a period of up to 1 year after the date of that act. (UA.I.C.K1) — 14 CFR §107.57

1306. If you are caught smoking marijuana the FAA will

A—Send you to a drug treatment center.
B—Issue an immediate suspension or revocation of your pilot certificate.
C—Deny all future pilot applications.

A conviction for the violation of any federal or state statute relating to the growing, processing, manufacture, sale, disposition, possession, transportation, or importation of narcotic drugs, marijuana, or depressant or stimulant drugs or substances is grounds for suspension or revocation of a Remote Pilot Certificate with an sUAS Rating. (UA.I.C.K1) — 14 CFR §107.57

1281. What FAA resource can pilots reference to learn more about the impact of drugs and alcohol on flight?

A—The *Pilot's Handbook of Aeronautical Knowledge*.
B—The Pilot Operating Handbook.
C—NOTAMs.

The Pilot's Handbook of Aeronautical Knowledge (FAA-H-8083-25) provides information on the physiological effects of alcohol, prescription drugs, and OTC medications. (UA.I.B.K8) — FAA-H-8083-25

Answers

1063 [C]   1325 [A]   1275 [C]   1306 [B]   1281 [A]

Change of Address

If a remote pilot changes his or her permanent mailing address without notifying the FAA Airman's Certification Branch, in writing, within 30 days, then he or she may not exercise privileges of his or her certificate.

1064. If a certificated pilot changes permanent mailing address and fails to notify the FAA Airmen Certification Branch of the new address, the pilot is entitled to exercise the privileges of the pilot certificate for a period of only
A—30 days after the date of the move.
B—60 days after the date of the move.
C—90 days after the date of the move.

The holder of a Remote Pilot Certificate who has made a change in his or her permanent mailing address may not, after 30 days from the date moved, exercise the privileges of his or her certificate unless he or she has notified in writing the FAA Airman Certification Branch. (UA.I.A.K5) — 14 CFR §107.77

Waivers

If the remote PIC determines that the operation cannot be conducted within the regulatory structure of Part 107, he or she is responsible for applying for a Certificate of Waiver (CoW) and proposing a safe alternative to the operation. This CoW will allow an sUAS operation to deviate from certain provisions of Part 107 as long as the FAA finds that the proposed operation can be safely conducted under the terms of that CoW.

The Administrator may issue a CoW authorizing a deviation from any regulation specified in 14 CFR §107.205 as listed below:

- §107.25—Operation from a moving vehicle or aircraft. However, no waiver of this provision will be issued to allow the carriage of property of another by aircraft for compensation or hire.
- §107.29(a)(2) and (b)—Anti-collision light required for operations at night and during periods of civil twilight.
- §107.31—Visual line of sight aircraft operation. However, no waiver of this provision will be issued to allow the carriage of property of another by aircraft for compensation or hire.
- §107.33—Visual observer.
- §107.35—Operation of multiple small unmanned aircraft systems.
- §107.37(a)—Yielding the right of way.
- §107.39—Operation over people.
- §107.41—Operation in certain airspace.
- §107.51—Operating limitations for small unmanned aircraft.
- §107.145—Operations over moving vehicles.

After submitting your CoW application and supporting documentation via **faadronezone.faa.gov**, the FAA will determine if the proposed operation can be conducted safely. If the application is denied, you will receive notification stating the reasons for denial. If the waiver or authorization is granted, you will receive direct notification with:

- The completed FAA Form 7711-1, Certificate of Waiver or Authorization, dated, signed, and approved by the FAA; and
- Specific special provisions that become regulatory for the waiver holder.

Answers
1064 [A]

1065. The FAA may approve your application for a waiver of provisions in Part 107 only when it has been determined that the proposed operation

A—involves public aircraft or air carrier operations.
B—can be safely conducted under the terms of that certificate of waiver.
C—will be conducted outside of the United States.

If the remote PIC determines that the operation cannot be conducted within the regulatory structure of Part 107, he or she is responsible for applying for a CoW and proposing a safe alternative to the operation. This CoW will allow an sUAS operation to deviate from certain provisions of Part 107 as long as the FAA finds that the proposed operation can be safely conducted under the terms of that Certificate of Waiver. (UA.I.D.K1) — 14 CFR §107.200

Answers (A) and (C) are incorrect because these operations fall outside the regulatory scope of Part 107.

1066. When requesting a waiver, the required documents should be presented to the FAA at least how many days prior to the planned operation?

A—30 days.
B—10 days.
C—90 days.

Although not required by Part 107, the FAA encourages applicants to submit their application at least 90 days prior to the start of the proposed operation. The FAA will strive to complete review and adjudication of waivers within 90 days; however, the time required for the FAA to make a determination regarding waiver requests will vary based on the complexity of the request. (UA.I.D.K1) — AC 107-2

Answers

1065 [B]   1066 [C]

Chapter 2
National Airspace System

Introduction *2–3*

    NOTAMs 2–3

    Other Airspace Resources 2–4

Airspace Classification *2–7*

Topography *2–15*

Airport Operations *2–20*

Airport Markings and Signs *2–22*

Collision Avoidance *2–27*

    Inflight Hazards 2–27

Chapter 2 **National Airspace System**

Introduction

The Remote Pilot Certificate with an sUAS Rating will allow operation of an sUAS in the **National Airspace System (NAS)**. There are two categories of airspace or airspace areas: Regulatory (Class A, B, C, D and E airspace areas, restricted, and prohibited areas) and nonregulatory (Class G airspace, Military Operations Areas, warning areas, Alert Areas, and controlled firing areas). Class A, B, C, D, and E airspace areas are referred to as **controlled airspace** and Class G airspace areas are referred to as **uncontrolled airspace**. You must become familiar with the NAS in order to safely operate with the others sharing this airspace, as well as with the nonparticipants on the ground. The following resources are critical for remote PICs to be able to understand airspace and the NAS, as well as invaluable tools for adequately planning safe operations in compliance with regulations and restrictions.

Refer to the *Chart Supplement U.S.* to determine what kind of airspace, ATC facilities, and traffic you can expect near the airport closest to your operations. The *Chart Supplement U.S.* is a publication for pilots containing key information about all airports, seaplane bases, and heliports open to the public including communications data, navigational facilities, and certain special notices and procedures. This supplement is reissued in its entirety every 56 days. See CT-8080-2, Figure 31 for a sample *Chart Supplement U.S.*

The aeronautical map most commonly used by manned pilots are the Sectional Aeronautical Chart and the Terminal Area Chart (TAC). Both charts include aeronautical information such as airports, airways, special use airspace, and other pertinent data. These charts are of tremendous value to the remote pilot operating an sUAS. The scale of the Sectional Aeronautical Chart is 1:500,000 (1 inch = 6.86 NM). Designed for visual navigation of slow speed aircraft in visual conditions (referred to as VFR), this chart portrays terrain relief and checkpoints such as populated places, roads, railroads, and other distinctive landmarks. These charts are revised every 6 months. See CT-8080-2, Legend 1 to become familiar with the Sectional Chart Legend, and Figure 20 on page A-4 for a sample Sectional excerpt. Information found on the TAC is similar to that found on the Sectional Chart, but at a scale of 1:250,000 (1 inch = 3.43 NM). These charts display a specific city with Class B airspace. They show more significant detail than the Sectional Chart, but have small area coverage.

NOTAMs

Notices to Air Missions (NOTAMs) provide the most current information available and can be found by visiting **faa.gov**, or obtained from the FAA's Flight Service by referencing **1800wxbrief.com**. They provide time-critical information on airports and changes that affect the NAS. It is necessary for the sUAS remote PIC to check for NOTAMs before each flight to determine if there are any applicable airspace restrictions.

NOTAM information is classified into five categories: NOTAM (D) or distant, Flight Data Center (FDC) NOTAMs, pointer NOTAMs, Special Activity Airspace (SAA) NOTAMs, and military NOTAMs. In addition to being available from Flight Service Stations (FSS), NOTAM (D)s are transmitted with hourly weather reports. FDC NOTAMs are issued by the National Flight Data Center (NFDC) and contain regulatory information such as temporary flight restrictions or an amendment to instrument approach procedures. Pointer NOTAMs highlight or point out another NOTAM, such as the issuance of an FDC or NOTAM (D). This type of NOTAM will assist pilots in cross-referencing important information that might not be found under an airport or NAVAID identifier. Military NOTAMs pertain to U.S. Air Force, Army, Navy, and Marine NAVAIDs/airports that are part of the NAS. SAA NOTAMs are issued when Special Activity Airspace will be active outside the published schedule times and when required by the published schedule. Pilots and other users are still responsible to check published schedule times for Special Activity Airspace as well as any NOTAMs for that airspace. NOTAM (D)s and FDC NOTAMs are contained in the Notices to Air Missions publication, which is issued every 28 days. Prior to any flight, all types of pilots must check for any NOTAMs that could affect their intended flight.

Chapter 2 **National Airspace System**

An FDC NOTAM will be issued to designate a temporary flight restriction (TFR). The NOTAM will begin with the phrase "FLIGHT RESTRICTIONS" followed by the location of the temporary restriction, effective time period, area defined in statute miles, and altitudes affected. The NOTAM will also contain the FAA coordination facility and telephone number, the reason for the restriction, and any other information deemed appropriate. TFRs are inclusive of sUAS operations; therefore it is necessary for the remote PIC to check for NOTAMs before each flight to determine if there are any applicable airspace restrictions. Common TFRs that relate to sUAS operations include, but are not limited to:

- Presidential TFRs and NOTAMs (e.g., when the President, or other important public figures are travelling or at a specific location).
- Emergency response TFRs and NOTAMs (e.g., forest fires and other disasters).
- Standing TFRs that go into and out of effect (e.g., stadiums for sporting events).

TFRs may also be found at the FAA website: **tfr.faa.gov**.

Other Airspace Resources

Additional resources on the subject of airspace include ACs and the *AIM*. ACs are issued systematically by the FAA to inform the aviation community of non-regulatory material of interest. In many cases, they are the result of a need to fully explain a particular subject (the pilot's role in collision avoidance, for example). They are issued in a numbered-subject system corresponding to the subject areas of the Federal Aviation Regulations. ACs are available from **faa.gov** and are also occasionally issued in print for a fee. Some ACs include additional information on airspace. The *AIM* is the official guide to basic flight information and ATC procedures, which is issued yearly with ongoing revisions. These resources should be reviewed by remote PICs.

1067. The most comprehensive information on a given airport is provided by

A—the *Chart Supplement U.S.*
B—Notices to Air Missions (NOTAMs).
C—Terminal Area Chart (TAC).

The Chart Supplement U.S. is a publication for pilots containing information about airports, seaplane bases, and heliports open to the public including communications data, navigational facilities, and certain special notices and procedures. (UA.V.B.K6b) — FAA-H-8083-25

Answers (B) and (C) are incorrect because these publications do not have comprehensive and specific airport information.

1068. (Refer to Figure 20, Area 5.) How would a remote PIC "CHECK NOTAMS" as noted in the CAUTION box regarding the unmarked balloon?

A—By utilizing the B4UFLY mobile application.
B—By contacting the FAA district office.
C—By obtaining a briefing via an online source such as 1800WXbrief.com.

NOTAMs provide the most current information available and can be found by visiting faa.gov or obtained from an FSS. A comprehensive weather briefing can be obtained as part of a standard preflight briefing. (UA.II.B.K5) — FAA-H-8083-25

Answers
1067 [A]   1068 [C]

1313. An FDC NOTAM will typically contain information
A—regarding public gatherings of large groups.
B—regarding military operations.
C—regarding available hard surface runways.

NOTAMs provide time-critical aeronautical information either temporary in nature or not sufficiently known in advance to permit publication on aeronautical charts or in other operational publications. (UA.II.B.K5) — FAA-H-8083-25

1070. Flight Data Center (FDC) NOTAMS are issued by the National Flight Data Center and contain regulatory information, such as
A—temporary flight restrictions.
B—markings and signs used at airports.
C—standard communication procedures at uncontrolled airports.

FDC NOTAMs are issued by the National Flight Data Center and contain regulatory information, such as TFRs. (UA.II.B.K5) — FAA-H-8083-25

1071. Time-critical information on airports and changes that affect the national airspace system are provided by
A—Notices to Air Missions (NOTAMs).
B—The *Chart Supplement U.S.*
C—Advisory Circulars (ACs).

Notices to Air Missions (NOTAMs) provide the most current information available. They provide time-critical information on airports and changes that affect the NAS. (UA.II.B.K5) — FAA-H-8083-25

Answer (B) is incorrect because the Chart Supplement U.S. is only revised every 8 weeks. Answer (C) is incorrect because the FAA systematically issues ACs to inform the aviation public of nonregulatory material.

1072. One of the purposes for issuing a temporary flight restriction (TFR) is to
A—announce Parachute Jump Areas.
B—protect public figures.
C—identify Airport Advisory Areas.

TFRs are imposed in order to:
1. *Protect persons and property in the air or on the surface from an existing or imminent flight associated hazard;*
2. *Provide a safe environment for the operation of disaster relief aircraft;*
3. *Prevent an unsafe congestion of sightseeing aircraft above an incident;*
4. *Protect the President, Vice President, or other public figures; and,*
5. *Provide a safe environment for space agency operations.*

Pilots are expected to check appropriate NOTAMs during flight planning when conducting flight in an area where a TFR is in effect. (UA.II.A.K3) — FAA-H-8083-25

Answer (A) is incorrect because this is done through NOTAMs. Answer (C) is incorrect because these are identified through the sectional and Chart Supplement U.S.

1073. Public figures are protected by
A—special use airspace.
B—prohibited areas.
C—temporary flight restrictions.

TFRs are imposed in order to:
1. *Protect persons and property in the air or on the surface from an existing or imminent flight associated hazard;*
2. *Provide a safe environment for the operation of disaster relief aircraft;*
3. *Prevent an unsafe congestion of sightseeing aircraft above an incident;*
4. *Protect the President, Vice President, or other public figures; and,*
5. *Provide a safe environment for space agency operations.*

Pilots are expected to check appropriate NOTAMs during flight planning when conducting flight in an area where a TFR is in effect. (UA.II.A.K3) — FAA-H-8083-25

Answer (A) is incorrect because special use airspace is the broad category to include alert, controlled firing, military operations, prohibited, restricted, and warning areas; none of these are used to protect public figures. Answer (B) is incorrect because prohibited areas are blocks of airspace within which the flight of all aircraft is prohibited.

Answers

1313 [A]   1070 [A]   1071 [A]   1072 [B]   1073 [C]

Chapter 2 **National Airspace System**

1350. Your surveying company is a title sponsor for a race team at the Indianapolis 500. To promote your new aerial surveying department, you decide to video part of the race using a small unmanned aircraft. The FAA has issued a TFR for the race in the area you plan to fly. In this situation

A—you may fly your drone in the TFR since your company is sponsoring a team at the race.
B—the TFR applies to all aircraft; you may not fly in the area without a Certificate of Waiver or Authorization.
C—flying your drone is allowed if you notify all non-participating people of the closed course small unmanned aircraft operation.

A Certificate of Waiver or Authorization is required to operate an sUAS in an area where the FAA has issued a TFR. (UA.II.A.K3) — FAA-H-8083-25

1074. The FAA publication that provides the aviation community with basic flight information and Air Traffic Control procedures for use in the National Airspace System of the United States is the

A—*Aeronautical Information Manual (AIM).*
B—*Chart Supplement U.S.*
C—*Advisory Circular Checklist (AC 00-2).*

The AIM is the official guide to basic flight information and ATC procedures. (UA.II.A.K4) — AIM

Answer (B) is incorrect because the Chart Supplement U.S. contains information on airports and various other pertinent special notices essential to operating in the NAS. Answer (C) is incorrect because AC 00-2 is the Advisory Circular Checklist for the status of all other FAA publications.

1075. (Refer to Figure 31.) Within what airspace is Coeur D'Alene Pappy Boyington Fld located?

A—Class B.
B—Class E.
C—Class D.

The Chart Supplement U.S. includes airport details, including the airspace the airport lies in. Figure 31 shows Coeur D'Alene airport lies within Class E airspace. (UA.II.A.K1d) — Chart Supplement U.S.

1076. (Refer to Figure 52.) What special conditions do remote pilots need to be on the lookout for while operating near Lincoln Airport?

A—Deer near the runway.
B—Birds in the vicinity.
C—Parachute operations.

The Chart Supplement U.S. includes airport details, including remarks unique to that airport. Figure 52 shows an abbreviated remark for Lincoln Airport, "Birds invof aipt." (UA.II.B.K4) — Chart Supplement U.S.

1276. Checking the NOTAMs confirms the Blue Angels are scheduled to perform at the local airport. When can UAS operations resume relative to this NOTAM?

A—Once the Blue Angels have landed.
B—With ATC authorization.
C—Immediately, so long as a 1 NM distance is maintained.

A NOTAM may be issued for reasons including hazards, such as air shows. The NOTAM will include the location and time for the affected region. UAS operations should stay away from these locations during the timeframe defined by the NOTAM. Once the NOTAM is over, UAS operations may resume with ATC authorization. (UA.II.B.K5) — FAA-H-8083-25

Answers

1350 [B]   1074 [A]   1075 [B]   1076 [B]   1276 [B]

Airspace Classification

It is very important that sUAS remote PICs be aware of the type of airspace in which they will be operating their sUA. Referring to the B4UFLY app or a current aeronautical chart (**faacharts.faa.gov**) of the intended operating area will aid a remote PIC's decision making regarding sUAS operations in the NAS.

Though many sUAS operations will occur in uncontrolled airspace, there are some that may need to operate in controlled airspace. Operations in what is called controlled airspace, i.e., Class B, Class C, or Class D airspace, or within the lateral boundaries of the surface area of Class E airspace designated for an airport, are not allowed unless that person has prior authorization from ATC.

The sUAS remote PIC must understand airspace classifications and requirements. The authorization process can be found at **faa.gov/uas**. Although sUAS will not be subject to Part 91, the equipment and communications requirements outlined in Part 91 were designed to provide safety and efficiency in controlled airspace. Accordingly, while sUAS operating under Part 107 are not subject to Part 91, as a practical matter, ATC authorization or clearance may depend on operational parameters similar to those found in Part 91. The FAA has the authority to approve or deny aircraft operations based on traffic density, controller workload, communication issues, or any other type of operations that could potentially impact the safe and expeditious flow of air traffic in that airspace. Those planning sUAS operations in controlled airspace are encouraged to contact the FAA as early as possible.

Many sUAS operations can be conducted in uncontrolled, Class G airspace without further permission or authorization. However, controlled airspace operations require prior authorization from ATC and therefore it is incumbent on the remote PIC to be aware of the type of airspace in which they will be operating their sUAS. As with other flight operations, the remote PIC should refer to current aeronautical charts and other navigation tools to determine position and related airspace.

Controlled airspace, that is, airspace within which some or all aircraft may be subject to air traffic control, consists of those areas designated as Class A, Class B, Class C, Class D, and Class E airspace. Much of the controlled airspace begins at either 700 feet or 1,200 feet above the ground. The lateral limits and floors of Class E airspace of 700 feet are defined by a magenta vignette (shading) on the Sectional Chart; while the lateral limits and floors of 1,200 feet are defined by a blue vignette on the

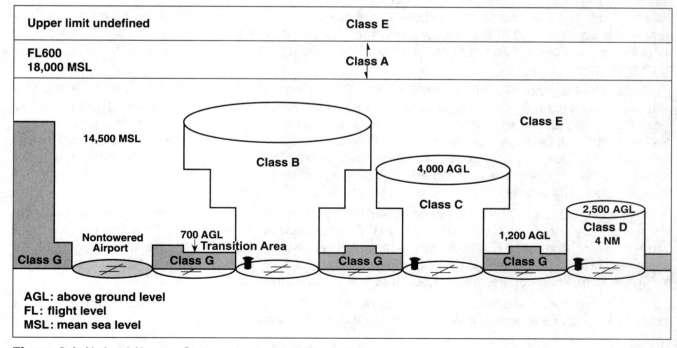

Figure 2-1. National Airspace System: airspace classification

Sectional Chart if it abuts uncontrolled airspace. Floors other than 700 feet or 1,200 feet are indicated by a number indicating the floor. See Figure 2-1.

Class A—Class A airspace extends from 18,000 feet MSL up to and including flight level (FL) 600 (60,000 feet) and is not depicted on VFR sectional charts. No flight under VFR is authorized in Class A airspace.

Class B—Class B airspace consists of controlled airspace extending upward from the surface or higher up to specified altitudes. Class B airspace size, altitudes, and layouts vary greatly from one site to another which are centered around one or more primary airports. Each Class B airspace sector, outlined in blue on the Sectional Chart, is labeled with its delimiting arcs, radials, and altitudes. Within each segment, the floor and ceiling are denoted by one number over a second number or the letters SFC. Class B airspace is also depicted on the Terminal Area Chart; on these each Class B airspace sector is, again, outlined in blue and is labeled with its delimiting arcs, radials, and altitudes. An ATC clearance is required prior to operating within Class B airspace. Some large, very busy airports are designated as Class B Primary airports; these require the pilot hold at least a Private Pilot Certificate and may have additional operating requirements or limitations.

Class C—All Class C airspace shares the same dimensions with minor site variations. Class C is composed of two circles, both centered on the primary airport. The inner surface area has a radius of 5 NM and extends from the surface up to 4,000 feet above the airport. The "outer shelf" area has a radius of 10 NM and extends vertically from 1,200 feet AGL up to 4,000 feet above the primary airport. In addition to the Class C airspace proper, there is an outer area with a radius of 20 NM that has vertical coverage from the lower limits of the radio/radar coverage up to the top of the approach control facility's delegated airspace. Within the outer area, pilots are encouraged to participate but it is not a requirement. Class C airspace service to aircraft proceeding to a satellite airport is terminated at a sufficient distance to allow time to change to the appropriate tower or advisory frequency. On aeronautical charts, Class C airspace is depicted by solid magenta lines. Class C requires two-way radio communications equipment, a transponder, and an encoding altimeter.

Class D—Class D airspace extends upward from the surface to approximately 2,500 feet AGL (the actual height is as needed). Class D airspace may include one or more airports and is normally 4 NM in radius centered around a designated airport. The actual size and shape is depicted on sectional charts by a blue dashed line and numbers showing the top or airspace ceiling. When the ceiling of Class D airspace is less than 1,000 feet and/or the visibility is less than 3 statute miles, additional restrictions exist for manned aircraft and may preclude UAS operations; contact ATC for information during these circumstances.

Class E—Magenta shading on the Sectional Chart identifies Class E airspace starting at 700 feet AGL, and no shading (or blue if next to Class G airspace) identifies Class E airspace starting at 1,200 feet AGL. It may also start at other altitudes. All airspace from 14,500 feet to 17,999 feet and airspace above 60,000 feet is Class E airspace. It also includes the surface area of some airports with an instrument approach but no control tower. An airway is a corridor of Class E airspace extending from 1,200 feet above the surface (or as designated) up to and including 17,999 feet MSL, and 4 NM either side of the centerline. The airway is indicated by a centerline, shown in blue.

Class G—Class G airspace is airspace within which ATC has neither the authority nor responsibility to exercise any control over air traffic. Class G airspace typically extends from the surface to the base of the overlying controlled (Class E) airspace, which is normally 700 or 1,200 feet AGL. In some areas of the western U.S. and Alaska, Class G airspace may extend from the surface to 14,500 feet MSL. An exception to this rule occurs when 14,500 feet MSL is lower than 1,500 feet AGL.

Prohibited Areas are blocks of airspace within which the flight of aircraft is prohibited. Examples include the airspace around the White House and the U.S. Capitol building.

Restricted Areas denote the presence of unusual, often invisible, hazards to aircraft such as artillery firing, aerial gunnery, or guided missiles. Penetration of restricted areas without authorization of the using or controlling agency may be extremely hazardous to the aircraft and its occupants. Per Part 107, entry into restricted airspace is not authorized without permission from the controlling agency.

Warning Areas contain the same hazardous activities as those found in restricted areas, but are located in international airspace. Prohibited, restricted, or warning areas are depicted as shown in CT-8080-2, Legend 1.

Alert Areas may contain a high volume of pilot training activities or an unusual type of aerial activity. Pilots should be particularly alert when flying in these areas. Pilots of participating aircraft as well as pilots transiting the area are equally responsible for collision avoidance.

Military Operations Areas (MOAs) consist of airspace established for the purpose of separating certain military training activities from IFR traffic. Pilots should exercise extreme caution while flying within an active MOA. Prior to entering an active MOA, pilots should contact the controlling agency for traffic advisories.

Military Training Routes (MTRs) have been developed for use by the military for the purpose of conducting low-altitude, high-speed training. Generally, MTRs are established below 10,000 feet MSL for operations at speeds in excess of 250 knots. IFR Military Training Route (IR) operations are conducted in accordance with instrument flight rules, regardless of weather conditions. VFR Military Training Routes (VR) operations are conducted in accordance with visual flight rules. IR and VR at and below 1,500 feet AGL (with no segment above 1,500) will be identified by four digit numbers, e.g., VR1351, IR1007. IR and VR with one or more segments above 1,500 feet AGL (routes can be above or below 1,500 feet AGL) will be identified by three digit numbers, e.g., IR341, VR426. The lateral boundaries of MTRs vary. For more information, pilots should consult the Department of Defense Flight Information Publication (FLIP).

Advisory Circular 91-36, *Visual Flight Rules (VFR) Flight Near Noise-Sensitive Areas*, defines the surface of a National Park area (including parks, forests, primitive areas, wilderness areas, recreational areas, National Seashores, National Monuments, National Lakeshores, and National Wildlife Refuge and Range Areas) as: the highest terrain within 2,000 feet laterally of the route of flight, or the upper-most rim of a canyon or valley. These are marked on sectional charts with a solid blue line on the outside of the area border with blue dots on the inside of the border line. Aircraft are requested to remain at least 2,000 feet above the surface of National Parks, National Monuments, Wilderness and Primitive Areas, and National Wildlife Refuges.

Local Airport Advisory (LAA) is an advisory service provided by Flight Service facilities, which are located on the landing airport, using a discrete ground-to-air frequency or the tower frequency when the tower is closed. LAA services include local airport advisories, automated weather reporting with voice broadcasting, and a continuous Automated Surface Observing System (ASOS)/Automated Weather Observing Station (AWOS) data display, other continuous direct reading instruments, or manual observations available to the specialist.

When ATC authorization is required (at or near an airport with a control tower and/or when operating within controlled airspace), it must be requested and granted before any operation in that airspace. There is currently no established timeline for approval after ATC permission has been requested because the time required for approval will vary based on the resources available at the ATC facility and the complexity and safety issues raised by each specific request. For this reason, remote PICs should contact the appropriate ATC facility as soon as possible prior to any operation in Class B, C and D airspace and within the lateral boundaries of the surface area of Class E airspace designated for an airport. ATC has the authority to approve or deny aircraft operations based on traffic density, controller workload, communication issues, or any other type of operations that could potentially impact the safe and expeditious flow of air traffic in that airspace.

Chapter 2 **National Airspace System**

When ATC authorization is not required (at or near an airport without a control tower and/or when operating within uncontrolled airspace), remote pilots should monitor the Common Traffic Advisory Frequency (CTAF) of any nearby airport(s) to stay aware of manned aircraft communications and operations. The CTAF can be found in the *Chart Supplement U.S.* and on Sectional and Terminal Area Charts (noted by a magenta "C" next to the frequency).

1360. What is required when operating in Class B airspace?

A—Operations in Class B airspace are prohibited.
B—The remote PIC or operator must receive an airspace authorization for operations in Class B airspace.
C—Two-way radio communication and ADS-B capabilities.

No person may operate an aircraft within a Class B airspace area unless the operator receives an ATC clearance from the ATC facility having jurisdiction for that area before operating an aircraft in that area. (UA.II.A.K1a) — AIM ¶3-2-3

1077. (Refer to Figure 25, Area 4.) The floor of Class B airspace overlying Hicks Airport (T67) north-northwest of Fort Worth Meacham Field is

A—at the surface.
B—3,200 feet MSL.
C—4,000 feet MSL.

The thick blue lines on the sectional chart indicate the boundaries of the overlying Class B airspace. Within each segment, the floor and ceiling are denoted by one number over a second number or the letters SFC. The floor of the Class B airspace is 4,000 feet MSL. (UA.II.A.K1a) — AIM ¶3-2-3

1228. (Refer to Figure 25, Area 4.) What is the base of the Class B airspace over Hicks Airport (T67)?

A—3,000 feet AGL.
B—4,000 feet AGL.
C—4,000 feet MSL.

The base of the Class B airspace directly over Hicks airport is 4,000 feet MSL as indicated by the blue 110/40. Class B airspace is always shown on sectional charts in mean sea level (MSL). (UA.II.A.K1a) — FAA-H-8083-25

1326. (Refer to Figure 25, Area 3.) The floor of Class B airspace at Dallas Executive (RBD) is

A—at the surface.
B—3,000 feet MSL.
C—3,100 feet MSL.

The thick blue lines on the sectional chart indicate the boundaries of the overlying Class B airspace. Within each segment, the floor and ceiling are denoted by one number over a second number, or the letters "SFC." The floor of the Dallas Executive (RBD) Class B airspace is 3,000 feet MSL. (UA.II.A.K1a) — AIM ¶3-2-3

1340. (Refer to Figure 23.) You have been hired to inspect a farm 3 miles west of Hilton Head Airport, in what type of airspace will you be operating?

A—Class G.
B—Class E.
C—Class C.

Hilton Head Airport is located in Class C airspace, from the surface up to 4,100 feet MSL (41/SFC) as shown by the solid magenta line encompassing the airport. The surface area Class C airspace extends 5 miles out from the center of the airport. (UA.II.A.K1b) — Sectional Chart Legend

1078. (Refer to Figure 23, Area 3.) What is the floor of the Savannah Class C airspace at the shelf area (outer circle)?

A—1,300 feet AGL.
B—1,300 feet MSL.
C—1,700 feet MSL.

Within the outer magenta circle of Savannah Class C airspace, there is a number 41 directly above the number 13. These numbers depict the floor and ceiling of the Class C airspace; the floor being 1,300 feet MSL and the ceiling being 4,100 feet MSL. (UA.II.A.K1b) — AIM ¶3-2-4

Answers

| 1360 [B] | 1077 [C] | 1228 [C] | 1326 [B] | 1340 [C] | 1078 [B] |

Chapter 2 National Airspace System

1079. According to 14 CFR Part 107, the remote PIC of a small unmanned aircraft planning to operate within Class C airspace

A—is required to receive ATC authorization.
B—is required to file a flight plan.
C—must use a visual observer.

No person may operate an sUA in Class B, Class C, or Class D airspace or within the lateral boundaries of the surface area of Class E airspace designated for an airport unless that person has prior authorization from ATC. (UA.II.B.K2) — 14 CFR §107.41

1080. According to 14 CFR part 107, how may a remote PIC operate an unmanned aircraft in Class C airspace?

A—The remote PIC must have prior authorization from the ATC facility having jurisdiction over that airspace.
B—The remote PIC must contact the ATC facility after launching the unmanned aircraft.
C—The remote PIC must monitor the ATC frequency from launch to recovery.

No person may operate an sUA in Class B, Class C, or Class D airspace or within the lateral boundaries of the surface area of Class E airspace designated for an airport unless that person has prior authorization from ATC. (UA.II.B.K2) — 14 CFR §107.41

1081. The lateral dimensions of Class D airspace are based on

A—the number of airports that lie within the Class D airspace.
B—5 statute miles from the geographical center of the primary airport.
C—the instrument procedures for which the controlled airspace is established.

The dimensions of Class D airspace are as needed for each individual circumstance. The airspace may include extensions necessary for IFR arrival and departure paths. (UA.II.A.K1c) — AIM ¶3-2-5

1082. (Refer to Figure 74, Area 6.) What airspace is Hayward Executive in?

A—Class B.
B—Class C.
C—Class D.

Hayward Executive is located in Class D airspace up to but not including 1,500 feet MSL as depicted by the blue segmented line surrounding it. Note that Class C begins at 1,500 feet MSL in that sector and goes up to the bottom of the overlying Class B (noted by the "T" in the altitude description). (UA.II.A.K1c) — AIM ¶3-2-5

1083. (Refer to Figure 26, Area 5.) The airspace overlying and within 5 miles of Barnes County Airport is

A—Class D airspace from the surface to the floor of the overlying Class E airspace.
B—Class E airspace from the surface to 1,200 feet MSL.
C—Class G airspace from the surface up to but not including 700 feet AGL.

The Barnes County Airport is depicted inside the magenta shading, which is controlled airspace from 700 feet AGL up to but not including 18,000 feet. Therefore, the airspace below 700 feet AGL is Class G. (UA.II.A.K1e) — AIM ¶3-2-1

1084. (Refer to Figure 76.) What ATC permissions are required to operate near Anderson Airport?

A—ATC clearance required.
B—No ATC permission is required.
C—Waiver must be requested.

Refer to CT-8080-2, Legend 1. Anderson Airport is in the bottom right quadrant of the sectional. The lack of shading around the airport indicates it is in Class G airspace. Small UAS operations in Class G airspace may be conducted without ATC permissions. However, remote pilots should exercise vigilance to ensure they cause no interruption to aircraft traffic. (UA.II.B.K2) — Sectional Chart Legend

1085. (Refer to Figure 78.) In what airspace is Onawa (K36) located?

A—Class E.
B—Class G.
C—Class D.

Onawa (K36) is in the bottom right quadrant of the sectional excerpt. It is outside of any shading or lines, which indicates the airport is in Class G airspace up to 1,200 feet AGL. (UA.II.A.K1e) — Sectional Chart Legend

Answers

| 1079 [A] | 1080 [A] | 1081 [C] | 1082 [C] | 1083 [C] | 1084 [B] |
| 1085 [B] | | | | | |

Chapter 2 **National Airspace System**

1327. (Refer to Figure 78, near the center of the chart.) What class of airspace is associated with SIOUX GATEWAY/COL DAY (SUX) Airport?

A—Class B airspace.
B—Class C airspace.
C—Class D airspace.

Sioux Gateway/Col Day Airport (SUX) is located in Class D airspace as depicted by the blue segmented line surrounding it, up to 3,600 feet as indicated by the bracketed [36]. (UA.II.A.K1c) — Sectional Chart Legend

1328. (Refer to Figure 20, Area 1.) The Fentress NALF Airport (NFE) is in what type of airspace?

A—Class C.
B—Class E.
C—Class G.

Fentress NALF Airport (FNE) is in the middle of Areas 1, 2 and 6 on Figure 20. It is located in Class E airspace, depicted by the magenta dashed line surrounding it. (UA.II.A.K1d) — Sectional Chart Legend

1305. The typical outer radius limits of Class C airspace are

A—10 NM.
B—20 NM.
C—30 NM.

The normal radius of the Class C outer area will be 20 NM. This is the area where separation is provided after two-way communication is established. It is only a requirement to contact ATC before entering the 10 NM Class C airspace depicted on the Sectional Chart. (UA.II.A.K1b) — FAA-H-8083-25

1307. (Refer to Figure 25, Area 2.) The airspace directly overlying Addison Airport (ADS) is

A—Class D up to 3,000 feet MSL.
B—Class D up to but not including 3,000 feet MSL.
C—Class E from the surface up to 3,000 feet MSL.

Refer to Legend 1. Class D airspace is depicted with the dashed blue circle, the ceiling defined by the number in brackets [30]. (UA.II.A.K1c) — AIM ¶3-2-5

1295. (Refer to Figure 26, Area 1.) The airspace overlying Tomlinson Airport is

A—Class G up to 18,000.
B—Class E from 1,200 up to but not including 18,000.
C—Class E from 700 up to but not including 18,000.

Refer to Legend 1. Tomlinson Airport is in the top left corner of Figure 26, and lies outside any colored circles. This indicates the airport is within Class E airspace from 1,200 feet AGL up to but not including 18,000 feet MSL. (UA.II.A.K1d) — AIM ¶3-2-5

1282. (Refer to Figure 78.) You have been hired to fly your UA to inspect train tracks from the town of Hinton to the town of Winnebago. Will you be able to conduct this flight without contacting ATC?

A—Yes, because you will remain under 400 feet.
B—No, because you will pass through Echo airspace.
C—No, because you will pass through Delta airspace.

Refer to Legend 1. The town of Hinton is north of Sioux City airport. Winnebago is south of Sioux City airport. This route is through the Class D airspace, depicted with the dashed blue line. You will need to contact ATC before conducting this flight. (UA.II.A.K1c) — Sectional Chart Legend

1321. (Refer to Figure 78.) You have been hired to use your small UAS to inspect the railroad tracks from Blencoe (SE of Sioux City) to Onawa. Will ATC authorization be required?

A—Yes, Onawa is in Class D airspace that is designated for an airport.
B—No, your entire flight is in Class G airspace.
C—Yes, you must contact the Onawa control tower to operate within 5 miles of the airport.

Refer to Legend 1. The entire flight for this route will be in Class G airspace. You do not need ATC authorization to operate in Class G airspace. (UA.II.A.K1e) — Sectional Chart Legend

Answers

1327 [C]   1328 [B]   1305 [B]   1307 [B]   1295 [B]   1282 [C]
1321 [B]

Chapter 2 **National Airspace System**

1338. (Refer to Figure 78.) You are hired to inspect the railroad tracks from the town of Hinton, north of Sioux City, to the town of Winnebago. Will you require ATC authorization?

A—No, the flight will remain clear of controlled airspace.
B—Yes, your route of flight will pass through Class D airspace.
C—Yes, your route of flight will pass through Class E airspace.

The route of flight from Hinton south along the train tracks to Winnebago will pass right through the Class D airspace at Sioux Gateway Airport. (UA.II.A.K1c) — Sectional Chart Legend

Answer (A) is incorrect because you will fly through Class D airspace. Answer (C) is incorrect because the base of the Class E airspace along your route does not begin until 700 feet AGL as shown by the shaded magenta line.

1358. What is required when operating in an MOA?

A—Obtain authorization from the controlling agency prior to operating in the MOA.
B—Exercise extreme caution when military activity is being conducted.
C—Fly only along Military Training Routes (MTRs).

Pilots should exercise extreme caution while flying within an MOA when military activity is being conducted. The activity status (active/inactive) of MOAs may change frequently. Therefore, pilots should contact ATC within 100 miles of the area to obtain accurate real-time information concerning the MOA hours of operation. While no clearance is necessary, prior to entering an active MOA, pilots should contact the controlling agency for traffic advisories. (UA.II.A.K2) — AIM ¶3-4-5

1086. (Refer to Figure 21.) You have been hired by a farmer to use your small unmanned aircraft to inspect his crops. The area that you are to survey is in the Devil's Lake West MOA, east of area 2. How would you find out if the MOA is active?

A—Refer to the legend for special use airspace phone number.
B—This information is available in the Small UAS database.
C—Refer to the Military Operations Directory.

An MOA contains military training activities such as aerobatics, and calls for extreme caution. Any FSS within 100 miles of the area will provide information concerning MOA hours of operation. Prior to entering an active MOA, pilots should contact the controlling agency for traffic advisories, noted in the legend for special use airspace. (UA.II.A.K2) — AIM ¶3-4-5

1087. Responsibility for collision avoidance in an alert area rests with

A—the controlling agency.
B—all pilots.
C—air traffic control.

All activity within an Alert Area shall be conducted in accordance with FAA regulations, without waiver, and pilots of participating aircraft, as well as pilots transiting the area, shall be equally responsible for collision avoidance. (UA.II.A.K2) — AIM ¶3-4-6

1088. (Refer to Figure 22, Area 2.) At Coeur D'Alene, which frequency should be used as a Common Traffic Advisory Frequency (CTAF) to monitor airport traffic?

A—122.05 MHz.
B—135.075 MHz.
C—122.8 MHz.

The CTAF is used for carrying out airport advisory practices and/or position reporting at an uncontrolled airport (which may also occur during hours when a tower is closed). The CTAF may be a UNICOM, MULTICOM, FSS, or tower frequency and is identified in the appropriate aeronautical publications. On charts, CTAF is indicated by a solid dot with the letter "C" inside. When the control tower operates part time and a UNICOM frequency is provided, use the UNICOM frequency. (UA.V.B.K6a) — AIM ¶4-1-9

1341. (Refer to Figure 52.) On what frequency can you expect to monitor air traffic in and around Lincoln Airport?

A—118.5
B—122.95
C—124.0

The communications section of the Chart Supplement U.S. for Lincoln Airport lists 118.5 as the tower frequency and the CTAF when the tower is closed. When operating in the vicinity of an airport, remote pilots are encouraged to monitor the tower frequency or CTAF. (UA.V.B.K6a) — AIM ¶4-1-9

Answers

1338 [B]   1358 [B]   1086 [A]   1087 [B]   1088 [C]   1341 [A]

Chapter 2 National Airspace System

1301. (Refer to Figure 26, Area 3.) What type of flights are being conducted as indicated by IR678?

A—IFR military training route above 1,500 feet AGL.
B—VFR military training route above 1,500 feet AGL.
C—VFR military training route below 1,500 feet AGL.

IR678 identifies an MTR in a south-easterly direction depicted by the solid gray line and directional arrow. The IR represents an IFR route, while the following three-digit number indicates flights along this route are conducted above 1,500 feet AGL. Flights conducted at or below 1,500 feet AGL are identified by a four-digit number. VFR flights are indicated by a VR in place of the IR. (UA.II.A.K3) — FAA-H-8083-25

1089. (Refer to Figure 26, Area 4.) You have been hired to inspect the tower under construction at 46.9N and 98.6W, near Jamestown Regional (JMS). What must you receive prior to flying your unmanned aircraft in this area?

A—Authorization from the military.
B—Authorization from ATC.
C—Authorization from the National Park Service.

The magenta shading around Jamestown airport indicates the floor of the Class E airspace starts 700 feet above the surface. The dashed area means the Class E goes all the way to the surface. No person may operate a small unmanned aircraft in Class B, Class C, or Class D airspace or within the lateral boundaries of the surface area of Class E airspace designated for an airport unless that person has prior authorization from ATC. (UA.II.B.K2) — 14 CFR §107.41, FAA-H-8083-25

1090. (Refer to Figure 59, Area 2.) The chart shows a gray line with "VR1667, VR1617, VR1638, and VR1668." Could this area present a hazard to the operations of a small unmanned aircraft?

A—No, all operations will be above 400 feet.
B—Yes, this is a Military Training Route from 1,500 feet AGL and below.
C—Yes, the defined route provides traffic separation to manned aircraft.

VFR military training routes at and below 1,500 feet AGL (with no segment above 1,500) will be identified by four digit numbers, e.g., VR1351. VR above and below 1,500 feet AGL (segments of these routes may be below 1,500) will be identified by three digit numbers, e.g., VR426. Small UAS must operate below 400 feet. This 4-digit Military Training Route indicates operations below 1,500

feet AGL, which could present a hazard to the sUAS operation. (UA.II.A.K3) — AIM ¶3-5-2

1091. (Refer to Figure 24, Area 5.) You are operating an sUAS in the vicinity of Sulphur Springs Airport (SUR) where there is active air traffic. Who has priority and right-of-way within the traffic pattern area?

A—Priority and right-of-way goes to the aircraft closest to the landing runway.
B—The sUAS.
C—The existing manned aircraft.

No person may operate a small unmanned aircraft in a manner that interferes with operations and traffic patterns at any airport, heliport, or seaplane base. (UA.I.B.K14) — 14 CFR §107.43

1092. (Refer to Figure 71, Area 6.) Sky Way Airport is

A—an airport restricted to use by private and recreational pilots.
B—a restricted military stage field within restricted airspace.
C—a non-public use airport.

The "Pvt" after the airport name indicates Sky Way Airport is a restricted or non-public use airport. (UA.V.B.K6a) — Sectional Chart

Answer (A) is incorrect because the R in the circle indicates the airport is a nonpublic use airport. Answer (B) is incorrect because the blue box near Sky Way Airport indicates an alert area.

1093. (Refer to Figure 71, Area 1.) The floor of the Class E airspace above Georgetown Airport (E36) is at

A—the surface.
B—700 feet AGL.
C—3,823 feet MSL.

Georgetown Airport is outside the magenta shaded area, which indicates the floor of Class E airspace is at 1,200 feet AGL. The airport elevation is given in the airport data as 2,623 feet MSL. Therefore, the Class E airspace above Georgetown Airport is 3,823 feet MSL (2,623 + 1,200). (UA.II.A.K1d) — Sectional Chart

Answer (A) is incorrect because Class E airspace begins at the surface only when surrounded by a magenta segmented circle. Answer (B) is incorrect because Class E airspace begins at 700 feet AGL inside the magenta shaded areas.

Answers

1301 [A] 1089 [B] 1090 [E] 1091 [C] 1092 [C] 1093 [C]

Chapter 2 **National Airspace System**

1094. (Refer to Figure 75.) The airspace surrounding the Gila Bend AF AUX Airport (GXF) (area 6) is classified as Class
A—B.
B—C.
C—D.

The GXF airport is surrounded by a dashed blue line which indicates it is within Class D airspace. (UA.II.A.K1c) — Sectional Chart

1095. Under what condition, if any, may remote pilots fly through a Restricted Area?
A—When flying on airways with an ATC clearance.
B—With the controlling agency's authorization.
C—Regulations do not allow this.

Restricted Areas can be penetrated but only with the permission of the controlling agency. No person may operate an aircraft within a restricted area contrary to the restrictions imposed unless they have the permission of the using or controlling agency. Penetration of restricted areas without authorization from the using or controlling agency may be fatal to the aircraft and its occupants. (UA.II.B.K2) — 14 CFR §107.45, AIM ¶3-4-3

1296. Where can you find information about operating in an MOA along your planned route of flight?
A—Sectional chart.
B—Chart supplement.
C—Aeronautical Information Manual.

Refer to Legend 1. MOAs are depicted on sectional charts with a shaded, hashed magenta line. You can find information about the MOA on the back of the sectional, including times of operation, altitudes affected, and the controlling agency. (UA.II.A.K2) — AIM ¶3-4-5

1309. (Refer to Figure 75, Area 6.) During preflight planning, you plan to operate in R-2305. Where would you find additional information regarding this airspace?
A—In the Special Use Airspace area of the chart.
B—In the Aeronautical Information Manual.
C—In the Charts Supplements U.S.

Refer to Legend 1. Restricted areas are identified on sectional charts with an "R" followed by a number. You can find information about restricted areas on the back of the sectional chart. (UA.II.A.K2) — FAA-H-8083-25

1331. (Refer to Figure 24, Area 6.) What type of airport is Card Airport?
A—Public towered.
B—Public non-towered.
C—Private non-towered.

Card Airport (located south of Figure 24, area 6) is a Private airport, indicated by "PVT" after the airport name and the circled "R." This airport is depicted in magenta, which means it is non-towered. (UA.V.B.K6a) — Sectional Chart Legend

Topography

To identify a point on the surface of the earth, a geographic coordinate, or grid, system was devised. By reference to meridians of longitude and parallels of latitude, any position may be accurately located when using the grid system.

Equidistant from the poles is an imaginary circle called the equator. The lines running east and west, parallel to the equator are called parallels of latitude, and are used to measure angular distance north or south of the equator. From the equator to either pole is 90°, with 0° being at the equator, while 90° north latitude describes the location of the North Pole. See Figure 2-2. Lines called meridians of longitude are drawn from pole

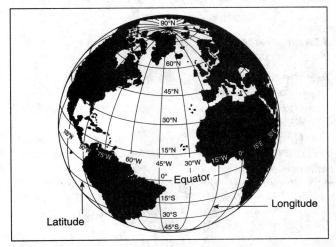

Figure 2-2. Meridians of longitude and parallels of latitude

Answers

1094 [C]   1095 [B]   1296 [A]   1309 [A]   1331 [C]

Chapter 2 **National Airspace System**

to pole at right angles to the equator. The prime meridian, used as the zero degree line, passes through Greenwich, England. From this line, measurements are made in degrees both easterly and westerly up to 180°.

Any specific geographical point can be located by reference to its longitude and latitude. For example, Washington, DC, is approximately 39° north of the equator and 77° west of the prime meridian and would be stated as 39°N 77°W. Note that latitude is stated first.

A Sectional Chart is a pictorial representation of a portion of the Earth's surface upon which lines and symbols in a variety of colors represent features and/or details that can be seen on the Earth's surface. Contour lines, shaded relief, color tints, obstruction symbols, and maximum elevation figures are all used to show topographical information. Explanations and examples may be found in the chart legend. Remote pilots should become familiar with all of the information provided in each Sectional Chart Legend, found in Legend 1 in the CT-8080-2.

In order to describe a location more precisely, each degree (°) is subdivided into 60 minutes (') and each minute further divided into 60 seconds ("), although seconds are not shown. Thus, the location of the airport at Elk City, Oklahoma is described as being at 35°25'55"N 99°23'15"W (35 degrees, 25 minutes, 55 seconds north latitude; 99 degrees, 23 minutes, 15 seconds west longitude). Degrees of west longitude increase moving west from the prime meridian until reaching the international line and degrees of east longitude increase moving east from the prime meridian to the international date line. Degrees of north latitude increase moving north from the equator to the north pole and degrees of south latitude increase moving south from the equator to the south pole.

1096. (Refer to Figure 26.) What does the line of latitude at area 4 measure?

A—The degrees of latitude east and west of the Prime Meridian.
B—The degrees of latitude north and south of the equator.
C—The degrees of latitude east and west of the line that passes through Greenwich, England.

The "47" at area 4 is the line of latitude (also referred to as a parallel) north and south of the equator. (UA.V.B.K6a) — FAA-H-8083-25

1097. (Refer to Figure 69.) What does the line of longitude at area 7 measure?

A—The degrees of longitude north and south of the prime meridian.
B—The degrees of longitude north and south from the equator.
C—The degrees of longitude east and west of the line that passes through Greenwich, England.

The "98" north of area 7 is the line of longitude (also referred to as meridian) east and west of the prime meridian which passes through Greenwich, England. (UA.V.B.K6a) — FAA-H-8083-25

1098. Which statement about longitude and latitude is true?

A—Lines of longitude are parallel to the Equator.
B—Lines of longitude cross the Equator at right angles.
C—The 0° line of latitude passes through Greenwich, England.

Meridians of longitude encircle the earth from pole to pole, and all meridians cross the equator at right angles. (UA.V.B.K6a) — FAA-H-8083-25

Answer (A) is incorrect because lines of latitude are parallel to the equator. Answer (C) is incorrect because the 0° line of longitude passes through Greenwich, England.

1099. (Refer to Figure 21.) What airport is located approximately 47 (degrees) 40 (minutes) N latitude and 101 (degrees) 26 (minutes) W longitude?

A—Mercer County Regional Airport.
B—Semshenko Airport.
C—Garrison Airport.

Graticules on Sectional Charts are the lines dividing each 30 minutes of latitude and each 30 minutes of longitude. Each tick mark represents one minute of latitude or longitude. Latitude increases northward, west longitude increases going westward. The Garrison (Pvt) Airport is located at approximately 47°40"N latitude and 101°26'00"W longitude. (UA.V.B.K6a) — FAA-H-8083-25

Answers

1096 [B]   1097 [C]   1098 [B]   1099 [C]

Chapter 2 **National Airspace System**

1100. (Refer to Figure 20, Area 3.) With ATC authorization, you are operating your small unmanned aircraft approximately 4 SM southeast of Elizabeth City Regional Airport (ECG). What hazard is indicated to be in that area?

A—High density military operations in the vicinity.
B—Unmarked balloon on a cable up to 3,008 feet AGL.
C—Unmarked balloon on a cable up to 3,008 feet MSL.

The sectional chart excerpt includes a blue box note 4 SM southeast of the ECG airport that says "Caution: Unmarked balloon on cable to 3008' MSL. Check NOTAMs." (UA.II.B.K4) — Sectional Chart Legend

1101. (Refer to Figure 20, Area 2.) Why would the small flag at Lake Drummond be important to a remote pilot?

A—This is a VFR check point for manned aircraft, and a higher volume of air traffic should be expected there.
B—This is a GPS check point that can be used by both manned and remote pilots for orientation.
C—This indicates that there will be a large obstruction depicted on the next printing of the chart.

Refer to Legend 1. The flag symbol represents a visual checkpoint used by manned aircraft to identify the position to initiate their contact with Norfolk Approach Control. As a defined checkpoint, a higher volume of air traffic should be expected there. (UA.II.A.K3) — Sectional Chart Legend, FAA-H-8083-25

1102. Which is true concerning the blue and magenta colors used to depict airports on Sectional Aeronautical Charts?

A—Airports with control towers underlying Class A, B, and C airspace are shown in blue, Class D and E airspace are magenta.
B—Airports with control towers underlying Class C, D, and E airspace are shown in magenta.
C—Airports with control towers underlying Class B, C, D, and E airspace are shown in blue.

Refer to Legend 1. Airports having control towers are shown in blue, all others in magenta. (UA.V.B.K6a) — Sectional Chart Legend

Answer (A) is incorrect because Class A airspace is not depicted on a Sectional Chart; Class C airspace is magenta; and Class E airspace is both blue and magenta depending on where the floor of the airspace starts. Answer (B) is incorrect because airports with control towers are shown in blue.

1103. (Refer to Figure 23, Area 3.) What is the height of the lighted obstacle approximately 6 nautical miles southwest of Savannah International?

A—1,500 feet MSL.
B—1,531 feet AGL.
C—1,548 feet MSL.

Refer to Legend 1. The top number, printed in bold, is the height of the obstruction above mean sea level. The second number, printed in parentheses, is the height of the obstruction above ground level. The obstruction is shown as 1,548 feet MSL and 1,534 feet AGL. (UA.V.B.K6a) — Sectional Chart Legend

1104. (Refer to Figure 23, Area 3.) The top of the group obstruction approximately 11 nautical miles from the Savannah VORTAC on the 009° radial is

A—400 feet AGL.
B—454 feet MSL.
C—432 feet MSL.

Refer to Legend 1. On Figure 23, area 3, the group obstruction near the 009° radial has the word "stacks" below 454. The bold number (454) indicates the height of the obstruction above mean sea level. (UA.V.B.K6a) — Sectional Chart Legend

1339. (Refer to Figure 23.) What is the maximum altitude you are permitted to fly when inspecting the high-intensity towers 6 miles southwest of the Savannah/Hilton Head Airport (SAV)?

A—1,945 feet MSL.
B—1,945 feet AGL.
C—1,545 feet MSL.

The high-intensity towers 6 miles southwest of the Savannah/Hilton Head Airport have a maximum elevation of 1,545 feet MSL (1,532 feet AGL). The regulations allow for an sUAS to be operated 400 feet above the structures uppermost limit when within a 400-foot radius of the structure: 1,545 + 400 = 1,945 feet MSL. (UA.V.B.K6a) — Sectional Chart Legend, 14 CFR §107.51

Answer (B) is incorrect because 1,945 feet indicates your maximum altitude in MSL. Answer (C) is incorrect because regulations permit you to operate 400 feet above the structures uppermost limit of 1,545 feet MSL.

Answers

| 1100 [C] | 1101 [A] | 1102 [C] | 1103 [C] | 1104 [B] | 1339 [A] |

Chapter 2 **National Airspace System**

1332. (Refer to Figure 20, Area 4.) A small UA is being launched 2 NM northeast of the town of Hertford. What is the height of the highest obstacle?

A—399 feet MSL.
B—500 feet MSL.
C—500 feet AGL.

Obstacles are depicted as an upside-down V. The top number, printed in bold, is the height of the obstruction above mean sea level. The second number in parentheses is the height of the obstruction above ground level. The highest obstacle 2 NM northeast of Hertford is 500 feet AGL. (UA.V.B.K6a) — Sectional Chart Legend

1333. (Refer to Figure 24, Area 3, and Legend 1.) For information about the parachute operations at Tri-County Airport, refer to

A—notes on the border of the chart.
B—Chart Supplements U.S.
C—the Notices to Air Missions (NOTAM) publication.

Tabulations of parachute jump areas in the U.S. are contained in the Chart Supplements U.S. (UA.V.B.K6b) — Chart Supplements U.S.

1105. (Refer to Figure 24, Area 2.) Operating an sUAS, can you vertically clear the obstacle on the southeast side of Winnsboro Airport?

A—Yes.
B—No.
C—Maybe.

The elevation of the top of the obstacle is shown as 903 feet MSL. Small UAS operations may not exceed 400 feet AGL. Moreover, the sUAS may be operated higher than 400 feet AGL if the sUAS is flown within a 400 foot radius of the structure and does not fly higher than 400 feet above the structure's immediate uppermost limit. (UA.V.B.K6a) — Sectional Chart Legend, 14 CFR §107.51

1362. (Refer to Figure 21.) What is the lowest object altitude near the light blue line denoting V15?

A—300 AGL.
B—1200 AGL.
C—700 AGL.

Obstruction altitudes are identified on sectionals along victor airways with blue numbers (elevation of the top above MSL) and another number in parentheses below (height AGL). The lowest object altitude along V15 is 2264 MSL, 300 AGL. (UA.V.B.K6a) — FAA-H-8083-25

1106. (Refer to Figure 26, Area 1.) You have been asked to inspect the tower just north of Binford. What restrictions should the remote PIC be concerned with prior to operating the sUAS?

A—None, the tower is in Class G airspace up to 1,200 AGL.
B—Class E airspace begins at the ground as indicated by the blue hashed lines surrounding the area.
C—Restricted airspace exists around the tower thus permission is required from the controlling agency.

No person may operate an sUA in prohibited or restricted areas unless that person has permission from the using or controlling agency, as appropriate. (UA.II.A.K2) — Sectional Chart Legend, 14 CFR §107.45

1107. (Refer to Figure 24, Area 1.) How close can the Remote PIC fly their sUAS to the Majors airport (GVT) without having to contact ATC?

A—4 NM
B—4 SM
C—Remote PICs must contact ATC whenever operating within the magenta shading on Sectional Charts.

Contact with ATC must be made when operating within Class D airport, which is indicated by the blue airport and the blue dashed line surrounding it. The radius of Class D in the case is 4 NM, which is the common standard radius, although configuration of Class D is individually tailored for some airports. (UA.II.B.K2) — Sectional Chart Legend, 14 CFR §107.41, AIM ¶3-2-5

Answers

1332 [C]   1333 [B]   1105 [A]   1362 [A]   1106 [C]   1107 [A]

Chapter 2 **National Airspace System**

1108. (Refer to Figure 22, Area 1.) You have been contracted to photograph Lake Pend Oreille from a vantage point just east of Cocolalla. You notice there is a hill which should provide a good place to take panoramic photographs. What is the maximum altitude (MSL) you are authorized to fly over the hill?

A—You cannot operate your sUAS above 400 MSL, and thus cannot operate anywhere in this part of the country.
B—You may operate up to 5,360 feet MSL in Class G airspace.
C—You cannot operate your sUAS without ATC permission because you will be in Class E airspace above 1,200 MSL.

The hill has a height of 4,960 MSL; therefore an sUAS may be flown up to 400 feet AGL, which is 5,360 feet. The floor of airspace such as Class E is in AGL not MSL. (UA.II.A.K1e) — Sectional Chart Legend, 14 CFR §107.51

1109. (Refer to Figure 20, Area 3.) What is the latitude and longitude location of the Elizabeth City CGAS RGL (ECG)?

A—N 36° 16' W 76° 10'
B—W 36° 16' N 76° 10'
C—N 37° 0' W 77° 10'

To measure the latitude and longitude, begin with looking for the hatched black lines with degree numbers on them. Just southeast of ECG there is the 36° latitude line (running east/west) and the 76° longitude line (running north/south). Count the ticks on the latitude line which is approximately 16—these are the number of minutes yielding N 36° 16' (north because the airport is north of the equator). Next, count the ticks west of the longitude line. There are approximately 10, therefore this is W 76° 10' (west because the airport is west of the prime meridian). (UA.V.B.K6a) — Sectional Chart Legend

1110. (Refer to Figure 20, Area 3.) You need to operate your sUAS in close proximity of the Elizabeth City CGAS RGL (ECG) airport. What frequency should be used to contact ATC?

A—122.95
B—124.375
C—120.50

According to the chart, the ATC control tower frequency is 120.50. (UA.V.B.K6a) — Sectional Chart Legend

1229. (Refer to Figure 20, Area 2.) What should you be aware of when operating within the vicinity of Lake Drummond?

A—High intensity of air traffic.
B—Terrain obstruction.
C—Seaplane base.

The purple flag over Lake Drummond is indicating a VFR checkpoint which is used for aircraft to better identify their position to air traffic control or other aircraft in the area. You should expect an increased amount of converging air traffic in and around VFR checkpoints. (UA.II.A.K3) — Sectional Chart Legend

Answers

1108 [B]   1109 [A]   1110 [C]   1229 [A]

Chapter 2 **National Airspace System**

Airport Operations

When operating in the vicinity of an airport, the remote PIC must be aware of all traffic patterns and approach corridors to runways and landing areas. Sources for this airport data include the Sectional Chart and the *Chart Supplement U.S.* The remote PIC must avoid operating anywhere that the presence of the sUAS may interfere with airport operations, such as approach corridors, taxiways, runways, or helipads. Furthermore, the remote PIC must yield right-of-way to all other aircraft, including aircraft operating on the surface of the airport.

Remote PICs are prohibited from operating their sUA in a manner that interferes with operations and traffic patterns at airports, heliports, and seaplane bases. While a sUA must always yield right-of-way to a manned aircraft, a manned aircraft may alter its flightpath, delay its landing, or take off in order to avoid an sUAS that may present a potential conflict or otherwise affect the safe outcome of the flight. For example, an sUA hovering 200 feet above a runway may cause a manned aircraft holding short of the runway to delay takeoff, or a manned aircraft on the downwind leg of the pattern to delay landing. While the sUA in this scenario would not pose an immediate traffic conflict to the aircraft on the downwind leg of the traffic pattern or to the aircraft intending to take off, nor would it violate the right-of-way rules, the sUA would nevertheless have interfered with the operations of the traffic pattern at an airport.

ATC towers are established to promote the safe, orderly, and expeditious flow of air traffic. The tower controller will issue instructions for aircraft to follow the desired flight path while in the airport traffic area whenever necessary by using terminology as shown in Figure 2-3. Manned aircraft use this same terminology to self-announce position and intentions, consistent with recommended traffic advisory procedures.

In order to avoid interfering with operations in a traffic pattern, remote PICs should avoid operating in the traffic pattern or published approach corridors used by manned aircraft. When operational necessity requires the remote PIC to operate at an airport in uncontrolled airspace, the remote PIC should operate the sUA in such a way that the manned aircraft pilot does not need to alter his or her flightpath in the traffic pattern or on a published instrument approach in order to avoid a potential collision. Because remote PICs have an obligation to yield right-of-way to all other aircraft and avoid interfering in traffic pattern operations, the FAA expects that most remote PICs will avoid operating in the vicinity of airports because their aircraft generally do not require airport infrastructure, and the concentration of other aircraft increases in the vicinity of airports.

The FAA has the authority to approve or deny aircraft operations based on traffic density, controller workload, communication issues, or any other type of operations that could potentially impact the safe and expeditious flow of air traffic in that airspace. Those planning sUAS operations in controlled airspace are encouraged to contact the FAA as early as possible.

When ATC authorization is required (at or near an airport with a control tower and/or when operating within controlled airspace), it must be requested and granted before any operation in that airspace. The time required for approval will vary based on the resources available at the ATC facility and the complexity and safety issues raised by each specific request. For this reason, remote PICs should contact the appropriate ATC facility as soon as possible prior to any operation in Class B, C, and D airspace and within the lateral boundaries of the surface area of Class E airspace designated for an airport.

When ATC authorization is not required (at or near an airport without a control tower and/or when operating within uncontrolled airspace), remote pilots should monitor the CTAF to stay aware of

Figure 2-3. Manned aircraft traffic pattern.

Chapter 2 **National Airspace System**

manned aircraft communications and operations. For the sake of safety, it is advisable for remote PICs to announce their sUAS activity on the CTAF to make manned pilots aware of such operations.

For recurring or long-term operations in a given location, prior authorization could include a **Letter of Agreement (LOA)**, established with the controlling ATC facility for that airspace, to establish sUAS operating procedures. This LOA will outline the ability to integrate into the existing air traffic operation and may improve the likelihood of access to the airspace where operations are proposed. This agreement will ensure all parties involved are aware of limitations and conditions and will enable the safe flow of aircraft operations in that airspace. For short-term or short-notice operations proposed in controlled airport airspace, an LOA may not be feasible. Prior authorization is required in all cases.

All areas on-airport that are used for certain cargo and passenger functions, including screening, must be a **Security Identification Display Area (SIDA)**. A SIDA is that portion of an airport within the United States, specified in the security program, in which individuals must display an airport-issued or approved identification and carry out other security measures.

1111. (Refer to Figure 80.) What do the blue shaded lines indicate throughout this sectional excerpt?

A—Military training routes.
B—Airline corridors.
C—Victor airways.

Refer to Legend 1. The routes established between VORs are depicted by blue-tinted bands showing the airway number following the letter "V," and are called "Victor airways." Remote pilots should exercise vigilance in looking for other aircraft when operating near these high density areas. (UA.II.A.K3) — Sectional Chart Legend

1112. The recommended entry position for manned aircraft to enter an airport traffic pattern is

A—45° to the base leg just below traffic pattern altitude.
B—to enter 45° at the midpoint of the downwind leg at traffic pattern altitude.
C—to cross directly over the airport at traffic pattern altitude and join the downwind leg.

The recommended entry position for an airport traffic pattern is 45° to the midpoint of the downwind leg at traffic pattern altitude. (UA.V.B.K4) — AIM ¶4-3-3

1113. When a manned aircraft is approaching to land at an airport in Class G airspace without an operating control tower, the pilot will

A—enter and fly a traffic pattern at 800 feet AGL.
B—make all turns to the left, unless otherwise indicated.
C—fly a left-hand traffic pattern at 800 feet AGL.

When a manned aircraft is approaching to land at an airport in Class G airspace without an operating control tower, each pilot of an airplane will make all turns to the left unless the airport displays approved light signals or visual markings indicating that turns should be made to the right (which will be detailed in the Chart Supplement U.S. (UA.V.B.K4) — 14 CFR §91.126

Answers (A) and (C) are incorrect because the traffic pattern altitude will vary for each airport and aircraft; however, all turns should be to the left unless otherwise indicated.

1114. Entries into traffic patterns by manned aircraft while descending create specific collision hazards and

A—should be avoided.
B—should be used whenever possible.
C—are illegal.

Entries into traffic patterns while descending create specific collision hazards and should be avoided. (UA.V.B.K4) — AIM ¶4-4-15

1115. What is required to enter an airport SIDA?

A—You must pass the TSA screening.
B—You must have an FAA-issued pilot certificate.
C—You must have an airport-issued or approved ID.

On-airport areas that are used for certain cargo functions, including screening, must be a SIDA. A SIDA is that portion of an airport within the United States, specified in the security program, in which individuals must display an airport-issued or approved ID and carry out other security measures. (UA.V.B.K5) — 49 CFR §1544

Answers

1111 [C]   1112 [B]   1113 [B]   1114 [A]   1115 [C]

Airport Markings and Signs

Remote pilots need to be familiar with standard airport markings and signs to exercise vigilant collision avoidance, practice sound see-and-avoid procedures, and not interfere with manned aircraft operations.

Runway numbers and letters are determined from the approach direction. The number is the magnetic heading of the runway rounded to the nearest 10°. For example, a runway facing an azimuth of 183° would result in a runway number of 18; a runway with a magnetic azimuth of 076° would result in a runway numbered 8. If there is more than one runway facing the same direction, the runway will have letters to differentiate between left (L), right (R), or center (C). See Figure 2-4.

The designated beginning of the runway that is available and suitable for the landing of aircraft is called the threshold (Figure 2-5a). A threshold that is not at the beginning of the full-strength runway pavement is a displaced threshold. The paved area behind the displaced threshold is marked by arrows (Figure 2-5b) and is available for taxiing, takeoff, and landing rollout, but is not to be used for landing, usually because of an obstruction in the approach path. See Figure 2-5.

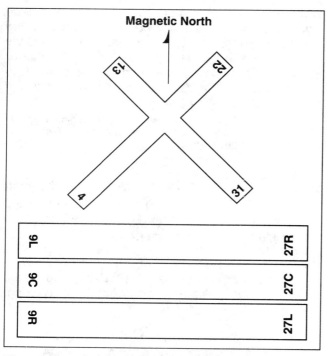

Figure 2-4. Runway numbers and letters

Figure 2-5. Threshold marking

Stopways are found extending beyond some usable runways. These areas are marked by chevrons, and while they appear usable, they are suitable only as overrun areas. See Figure 2-6.

A closed runway which is unusable for various reasons and may be hazardous, even though it may appear usable, will be marked by an "X."

A basic runway may only have centerline markings and runway numbers. Airports supporting instrument operations, higher volumes, and larger aircraft may use additional runway markings. See Figure 2-7.

Figure 2-6. Stopway marking

Chapter 2 **National Airspace System**

Figure 2-7. Selected airport markings and surface lighting

Aircraft use taxiways to transition from parking areas to the runway. Taxiways are identified by a continuous yellow centerline stripe and may include edge markings to define the edge of the taxiway. Where a taxiway approaches a runway, there may be a holding position marker. These consist of four yellow lines (two solid and two dashed). The solid lines are where the aircraft is to hold. Beyond this point, an aircraft is considered to be on the runway.

There are six types of signs that may be found at airports. See Figure 2-8. The more complex the layout of an airport, the more important the signs become to pilots. The six types of signs are:

- Mandatory instruction signs—red background with white inscription. These signs denote an entrance to a runway, critical area, or prohibited area.
- Location signs—black with yellow inscription and a yellow border, no arrows. They are used to identify a taxiway or runway location, to identify the boundary of the runway, or identify an instrument landing system (ILS) critical area.
- Direction signs—yellow background with black inscription. The inscription identifies the designation of the intersecting taxiway(s) leading out of an intersection.
- Destination signs—yellow background with black inscription and arrows. These signs provide information on locating areas, such as runways, terminals, cargo areas, and civil aviation areas.

Chapter 2 **National Airspace System**

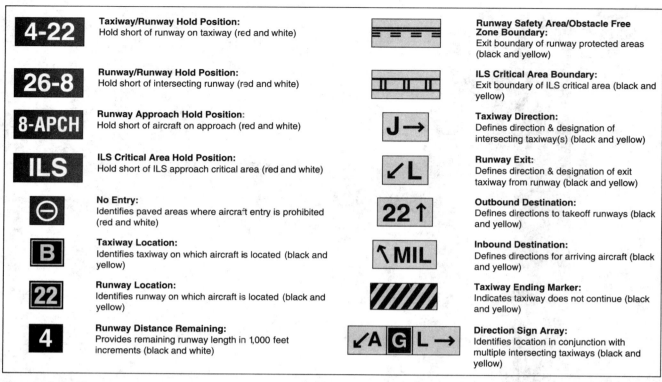

Figure 2-8. Airport signs

- Information signs—yellow background with black inscription. These signs are used to provide the pilot with information on areas that cannot be seen from the control tower, applicable radio frequencies, and noise abatement procedures. The airport operator determines the need, size, and location of these signs.

- Runway distance remaining signs—black background with white numbers. The numbers indicate the distance of the remaining runway in thousands of feet.

1116. The numbers 9 and 27 on a runway indicate that the runway is oriented approximately

A—009° and 027° true.
B—090° and 270° true.
C—090° and 270° magnetic.

The runway number is the whole number nearest one-tenth the magnetic azimuth of the centerline of the runway, measured clockwise from magnetic north. For example: 272° = Runway 27; 087° = Runway 9. (UA.V.B.K3) — AIM ¶2-3-3

1117. (Refer to Figure 26, Area 2.) While monitoring the Cooperstown CTAF you hear an aircraft announce that they are midfield left downwind to RWY 13. Where would the aircraft be relative to the runway?

A—The aircraft is East.
B—The aircraft is South.
C—The aircraft is West.

Cooperstown Airport depicts one runway; Runway 13 means the aircraft will be headed 130 degrees upon landing. "Left downwind" means the aircraft is currently to the left side, heading opposite and midway of the landing runway. This would place the aircraft east of the landing runway. (UA.V.B.K4) — AIM ¶4-1-5

Answers
1116 [C]   1117 [A]

Chapter 2 **National Airspace System**

1118. An aircraft announces that they are on short final for Runway 9. Where will the aircraft be in relation to the airport?
A—North.
B—West.
C—East.

On final approach to Runway 9, the aircraft will be heading from west to east on a 090 heading. Thus the aircraft is west of the airport. (UA.V.B.K4) — AIM ¶4-1-5

1119. You are conducting sUAS operations northeast of a nearby airport. While monitoring the CTAF, an aircraft announces that it is departing Runway 36 utilizing a right traffic pattern. Will the aircraft potentially conflict with your operation?
A—No, the aircraft will be flying on the west side of the airport.
B—No, the aircraft will be flying to the south of the airport.
C—Yes, the aircraft may overfly northeast of the airport.

If taking off of Runway 36, the aircraft will be departing to the north on a 360 heading. With right traffic, it will turn right towards the northeast on the crosswind leg. (UA.V.B.K4) — AIM ¶4-1-5

1120. While operating a sUAS just south of a controlled airport with authorization, ATC notifies you to stay clear of the Runway 6 final approach course. What action should you take to comply with this request?
A—Stay clear of areas to the west and north of your area of operation.
B—Stay clear of areas to the east and north of your area of operation.
C—Stay clear of areas to the west and south of your area of operation.

Runway 6 faces northeast on a 060 heading thus arriving aircraft will be on final approach southwest of the airport. Since you are operating south of the airport, you would want to avoid areas west (which would be closer to the final approach course) and north (closer to the airport and possibly the final approach course for Runway 6). (UA.V.B.K4) — AIM ¶4-1-5

1121. When turning onto a taxiway from another taxiway, what is the purpose of the taxiway directional sign?
A—Indicates direction to take-off runway.
B—Indicates designation and direction of exit taxiway from runway.
C—Indicates designation and direction of taxiway leading out of an intersection.

The taxiway directional sign identifies the designation(s) of the intersecting taxiway(s) leading out of the intersection that a pilot would normally be expected to turn onto or hold short of. (UA.V.B.K3) — AIM ¶2-3-10

Answer (A) is incorrect because this is the purpose of the runway location sign. Answer (B) is incorrect because this is the purpose of the destination sign.

1122. When approaching holding lines from the side with the continuous lines, the pilot
A—may continue taxiing.
B—should not cross the lines without ATC clearance.
C—should continue taxiing until all parts of the aircraft have crossed the lines.

When approaching the holding line from the side with the continuous lines, a pilot should not cross the holding line without ATC clearance at a controlled airport, or without making sure of adequate separation from other aircraft at uncontrolled airports. (UA.V.B.K3) — AIM ¶2-3-5

Answers (A) and (C) are incorrect because no part of the aircraft may cross the hold line without ATC clearance.

1123. What is the purpose of the runway/runway hold position sign?
A—Denotes entrance to runway from a taxiway.
B—Denotes area protected for an aircraft approaching or departing a runway.
C—Denotes intersecting runways.

Mandatory instruction signs are used to denote an entrance to a runway or critical area and areas where an aircraft is prohibited from entering. The runway holding position sign is located at the holding position on taxiways that intersect a runway or on runways that intersect other runways. (UA.V.B.K3) — AIM ¶2-3-8

Answers

1118 [B]   1119 [C]   1120 [A]   1121 [C]   1122 [B]   1123 [C]

Chapter 2 **National Airspace System**

1124. What is the purpose for the runway hold position markings on the taxiway?

A—Holds aircraft short of the runway.
B—Allows an aircraft permission onto the runway.
C—Identifies area where aircraft are prohibited.

Runway holding position markings on taxiways identify the locations on a taxiway where an aircraft is supposed to stop when it does not have clearance to proceed onto the runway. (UA.V.B.K3) — AIM ¶2-3-5

1125. Holding position signs have

A—red inscriptions on white background.
B—white inscriptions on red background.
C—yellow inscriptions on red background.

Hold position signs have white inscriptions on red background. (UA.V.B.K3) — AIM ¶2-3-5

Answers (A) and (C) are incorrect because these color combinations are not used in airport signs.

1126. What is the purpose of the No Entry sign?

A—Identifies a paved area where aircraft are prohibited from entering.
B—Identifies area that does not continue beyond intersection.
C—Identifies the exit boundary for the runway protected area.

The no entry sign prohibits an aircraft from entering an area. Typically, this sign would be located on a taxiway intended to be used in only one direction or at the intersection of vehicle roadways with runways, taxiways or aprons where the roadway may be mistaken as a taxiway or other aircraft movement surface. (UA.V.B.K3) — AIM ¶2-3-8

Answer (B) is incorrect because this is the purpose of a hold position sign. Answer (C) is incorrect because this is the purpose of the runway boundary sign.

1127. The "taxiway ending" marker

A—indicates taxiway does not continue.
B—identifies area where aircraft are prohibited.
C—provides general taxiing direction to named taxiway.

Taxiway ending markers are used to indicate that the taxiway does not continue. (UA.V.B.K3) — AIM ¶2-3-4

1128. Which publication contains an explanation of airport signs and markings?

A—*Aeronautical Information Manual (AIM).*
B—*Advisory Circulars (AC).*
C—*Chart Supplement U.S.*

Both the AIM and the Pilot's Handbook of Aeronautical Knowledge (FAA-H-8083-25) contain explanations of airport signs and markings. (UA.V.B.K3) — AIM Chapter 2, Section 3

Answer (B) is incorrect because ACs provide information on non-regulatory material of interest. Answer (C) is incorrect because the Chart Supplement U.S. provides only comprehensive information on a given airport (such as runway lengths, available services, lighting, etc.).

1129. You have received authorization to operate an sUAS at an airport. When flying the sUAS, the ATC tower instructs you to stay clear of all runways. Which situation would indicate that you are complying with this request?

A—You are on the double dashed yellow line side of markings near the runway.
B—You are over dashed white lines in the center of the pavement.
C—You are on the double solid yellow line side of markings near the runway.

Runway hold markings are indicated by two dashed and two solid yellow lines. You are considered to be on the taxiway on the double solid yellow line side while you are considered to be on the runway if on the double dashed yellow line side. (UA.V.B.K3) — AIM ¶2-3-4

Answer (A) is incorrect because the double dashed yellow line would indicate you are on the taxiway. Answer (B) is incorrect because the dashed white centerline markings would indicate that you are on the runway.

Answers

1124 [A]   1125 [B]   1126 [A]   1127 [A]   1128 [A]   1129 [C]

Chapter 2 **National Airspace System**

Collision Avoidance

A key component to avoiding both manned and unmanned aircraft is active collision avoidance procedures. Scanning the sky for other aircraft is a critical factor in collision avoidance. Remote pilots and visual observers must develop an effective scanning technique that maximizes visual capabilities. Because the eyes focus only on a narrow viewing area, effective scanning is accomplished with a series of short, regularly spaced eye movements. Each movement should not exceed 10°, and each area should be observed for at least one second. Any aircraft that appears to have no relative motion and stays in one scan quadrant is likely to be on a collision course. If a target shows neither lateral nor vertical motion, but increases in size, take evasive action.

Another critical component to collision avoidance is avoiding operations near and under moored balloons and helicopters. The helicopter community performs their critical operations typically at 1,000 feet or less and often in a wire/obstruction rich environment. It is important to note that not all wires are marked.

Inflight Hazards

Although most sUAS cannot be operated in precipitation or other adverse weather conditions, remote PICs should be aware that static electricity buildup (sometimes referred to as P-static) can occur when an aircraft in flight comes in contact with rain, snow, fog, sleet, hail, volcanic ash, dust; any solid or liquid particles. In a very short period of time a substantial negative charge will develop on the skin of the aircraft. If the aircraft is not equipped with static dischargers, or has an ineffective static discharger system, when a sufficient negative voltage level is reached the aircraft may develop a phenomenon called a "corona," a luminous manifestation of the static electricity accumulation. Such buildups may discharge from the extremities of the aircraft, such as the wing tips, horizontal stabilizer, vertical stabilizer, antenna, propeller tips, etc. The visible discharge of static electricity is referred to as "St. Elmo's fire." P-static can also disrupt communications between the sUAS and the control station which may have significant detrimental impact on the ability to control or retrieve the sUAS. Some sUAS may use static dischargers to address this problem.

In recent years, the use of lasers has had more of an impact on all types of flight operations. Of concern to NAS users are those laser events that may affect pilots, e.g., outdoor laser light shows or demonstrations for entertainment and advertisements at special events and theme parks. Generally, the beams from these events appear as bright blue-green in color; however, they may be red, yellow, or white, and some laser systems produce light that is invisible to the human eye. FAA regulations prohibit the disruption of aviation activity by any person on the ground or in the air.

Remote pilots should be aware that illumination from these laser operations are able to create temporary vision impairment miles from the actual location. In addition, these operations can cause permanent eye damage. Remote pilots should therefore use caution when using sUAS in and around known laser activity. Extreme caution should be exercised if an sUAS is fitted with a laser as it could potentially cause hazards to manned aircraft, the public, or even the remote PIC or other crewmembers. Pilots should make themselves aware of where these activities are being conducted and avoid these areas if possible. When these activities become known to the FAA, NOTAMs are issued to inform the aviation community of the events. Pilots should consult NOTAMs or the Special Notices section of the *Chart Supplement U.S.* for information regarding these activities.

Although remote pilots should typically avoid operations in and around power plants, industrial production facilities, or other industrial systems, there may be times when such activity is sanctioned by the owners of these facilities for inspection or imaging. These types of locations often have thermal plumes, which are visible or invisible emissions of large amounts of vertically directed unstable gases. High temperature exhaust plumes may cause significant air disturbances such as turbulence and vertical shear. Other identified potential hazards include, but are not necessarily limited to, reduced visibility,

Chapter 2 National Airspace System

oxygen depletion, engine particulate contamination, exposure to gaseous oxides, and/or icing. Results of encountering a plume may include airframe damage, aircraft upset, and/or engine damage/failure. These conditions could quickly lead to damage and/or loss of control of an sUAS. These hazards are most critical during low altitude flight, especially during maneuvering, takeoff and landing. When able, a pilot should fly upwind of possible thermal plumes. When a plume is visible via smoke or a condensation cloud, remain clear yet at the same time, realize that a plume may have both visible and invisible characteristics. Remote pilots are encouraged to exercise caution when operating in the vicinity of thermal plumes. Refer to the *Chart Supplement U.S.*, where the airport amplifying notes may warn pilots and identify the location of structure(s) emitting thermal plumes.

Most skeletal structures are supported by guy wires, which are very difficult to see in good weather and can be invisible at dusk or during periods of reduced visibility. These wires can extend about 1,500 feet horizontally from a structure; therefore, all skeletal structures should be avoided horizontally by at least 2,000 feet.

Birds and wildlife pose a particular threat to aircraft operations. Although catastrophic events are rare in manned aviation, sUAS are particularly vulnerable to such events. Collision with wildlife will likely cause significant damage and/or loss of control. Remote pilots should report collisions between aircraft and wildlife to assist in the tracking of these incidents and to potentially take action to mitigate future risks of these events. Reports may be sent to the FAA via their Wildlife Strike Report system (**wildlife.faa.gov/strikenew.aspx**). Many airports advise pilots of other wildlife hazards through the *Chart Supplement U.S.* and the NOTAM system.

Collisions between aircraft and animals have been increasing and are not limited to rural airports, as these accidents have also occurred at several major airports. Pilots should exercise extreme caution when warned of the presence of wildlife on and in the vicinity of airports. If you observe birds, deer, or other large animals in close proximity to movement areas, advise the FSS, tower, or airport management. Remote pilots should be aware of bird activity in proximity to their area of operation. It is well documented that some types of birds are agitated by sUAS and may even attack such aircraft. Also, it has been shown that sUAS activity and noise may disturb certain types of wildlife; therefore remote pilots should be cognizant of the potential impact of their operations on the local environment. Many states are considering passing legislation to restrict sUAS operations that may disturb wildlife.

1130. Most midair collision accidents occur during

A—hazy days.
B—clear days.
C—cloudy nights.

The FAA Near Midair Collision System (NMACS) indicates that 81% of the incidents occurred in clear skies and unrestricted visibility conditions. (UA.II.B.K4a) — FAA-H-8083-25

1131. Which technique should a remote pilot use to scan for traffic?

A—Continuously scan the sky from right to left.
B—Concentrate on relative movement detected in the peripheral vision area.
C—Systematically focus on different segments of the sky for short intervals.

Effective scanning is accomplished with a series of short, regularly spaced eye movements that bring successive areas of the sky into the central visual field. Each movement should not exceed 10°, and each area should be observed for at least one second to enable detection. (UA.I.B.K14) — AIM ¶8-1-6

Answers

1130 [B]   1131 [C]

Chapter 2 National Airspace System

1132. Guy wires, which support antenna towers, can extend horizontally; therefore, the towers should be avoided horizontally by at least

A—2,000 feet horizontally.
B—300 feet horizontally.
C—1,000 feet horizontally.

Most skeletal structures are supported by guy wires which are very difficult to see in good weather and can be invisible at dusk or during periods of reduced visibility. These wires can extend about 1,500 feet horizontally from a structure; therefore, all skeletal structures should be avoided horizontally by at least 2,000 feet. (UA.II.B.K4g) — AIM ¶7-6-4

1133. What should remote pilots rely on for wire strike avoidance?

A—Sectional Chart markings.
B—*Chart Supplement U.S.* airport and airspace details.
C—Visual scanning.

The wire-rich environment is typically below 1,000 feet. Not all wires are marked and they can be nearly invisible when viewed from different angles. Remote pilots must exercise vigilance when operating near helicopters, moored balloons and other places where wires are frequently present. (UA.II.B.K4g) — SAFO 10015

1134. What should a remote pilot do if the sUAS they are operating collides with a bird or wildlife?

A—Report the collision to ATC.
B—File an accident report with the NTSB.
C—File a wildlife strike report with the FAA.

Remote pilots should report collisions between aircraft and wildlife to assist in the tracking of these incidents and to potentially mitigate future risks of these events. Reports may be sent to the FAA via their Wildlife Strike Report system (wildlife.faa.gov/strikenew.aspx). (UA.V.B.K7) — AIM ¶7-5-5

1303. What is the most effective way for a remote pilot to scan for traffic?

A—Maintain your focus on the small unmanned aircraft and use your peripheral vision to scan small segments of the sky.
B—A series of short regularly spaced eye movements scanning 10° segments of the sky.
C—Continuously scan the sky from right to left.

Effective scanning is accomplished with a series of short, regularly spaced eye movements that bring successive areas of the sky into the central visual field. Each movement should not exceed 10°, and each area should be observed for at least one second to enable detection. (UA.I.B.K14) — FAA-H-8083-25

1312. A larger UAS is converging head-on; what should you do?

A—The smaller aircraft should adjust course to the right.
B—The larger aircraft should adjust course to the right.
C—Both aircraft should adjust course to the right.

When aircraft are approaching each other head-on, or nearly so, each pilot of each aircraft (regardless of category or size) shall alter course to the right. (UA.I.B.K14) — AC 107-2

Answers

1132 [A]   1133 [C]   1134 [C]   1303 [B]   1312 [C]

Chapter 3
Weather

Introduction *3–3*

Wind *3–4*

Air Masses and Fronts *3–5*

Atmospheric Stability *3–7*

Visibility and Clouds *3–8*

Thunderstorms *3–10*

Icing *3–13*

Fog *3–14*

Density Altitude *3–16*

Weather Briefing *3–17*

Weather Reports, Forecasts and Charts *3–17*

    Surface Aviation Weather Observations *3–18*

    Aviation Weather Reports *3–19*

    Aviation Forecasts *3–21*

    Convective Significant Meteorological Information (WST) *3–22*

Chapter 3 **Weather**

Introduction

As with any flight, the remote PIC should check and consider the weather conditions prior to and during every sUAS flight. Even though sUAS operations are often conducted at very low altitudes, weather factors can greatly influence performance and safety of flight. Specifically, factors that affect sUAS performance and risk management include:

- Atmospheric pressure and stability;
- Wind and currents;
- Uneven surface heating;
- Visibility and cloud clearance; and
- Precipitation.

The major source of all weather is the sun. Every physical process of weather, change, or variation of weather patterns is accompanied by or is a result of unequal heating of the Earth's surface. The heating of the Earth (and therefore the heating of the air surrounding the Earth) is imbalanced around the entire planet. Both north and south of the equator, due to the different angle sunlight hits the Earth, one square foot of sunrays is not concentrated over one square foot of the surface, but over a larger area. This lower concentration of sunrays produces less radiation of heat over a given surface area; therefore, less atmospheric heating takes place in that area. The unequal heating of the Earth's atmosphere creates a large air-cell circulation pattern (wind) because the warmer air has a tendency to rise (associated with low pressure systems) and the colder air has a tendency to settle or descend (associated with high pressure systems) and replace the rising warmer air. This unequal heating, which causes pressure variations, will also cause variations in barometric altimeter settings between weather reporting points.

Different surfaces radiate heat in varying amounts. The resulting uneven heating of the air creates small areas of local circulation called convective currents. Convective currents can cause turbulent air that has the potential to dramatically affect the remote PIC's ability to control unmanned aircraft at lower altitudes. For example:

- Plowed ground, rocks, sand, barren land, pavement, and urban areas give off a large amount of heat and are likely to result in updrafts.
- Water, trees, and other areas of vegetation tend to absorb and retain heat and are likely to result in downdrafts.

1135. Which of the following considerations is most relevant to a remote PIC when evaluating unmanned aircraft performance?

A—Current weather conditions.
B—The number of available ground crew.
C—The type of sUAS operation.

Weather factors can greatly influence sUAS performance and safety of flight. (UA.III.B.K1) — AC 107-2

1136. Every physical process of weather is accompanied by, or is the result of, a

A—movement of air.
B—pressure differential.
C—heat exchange.

Every physical process of weather is accompanied by, or is a result of, unequal heating of the Earth's surface. (UA.III.B.K1c) — FAA-H-8083-28

Answers
1135 [A]   1136 [C]

Chapter 3 **Weather**

1137. What causes variations in altimeter settings between weather reporting points?
A—Unequal heating of the Earth's surface.
B—Variation of terrain elevation.
C—Coriolis force.

All altimeter settings are corrected to sea level. Unequal heating of the Earth's surface causes pressure differences. (UA.III.B.K1c) — FAA-H-8083-28

1138. The development of thermals depends upon
A—a counterclockwise circulation of air.
B—temperature inversions.
C—solar heating.

Thermals are updrafts in convective currents dependent on solar heating. A temperature inversion would result in stable air with very little, if any, convective activity. (UA.III.B.K1c) — FAA-H-8083-28

1139. (Refer to Figure 20.) Over which area should a remote pilot expect to find the highest amount of thermal currents under normal conditions?
A—2.
B—7.
C—5.

Dry areas get hotter than moist areas. Dry fields or dry ground of any nature are better thermal sources than moist areas. This applies to woods or forests, which are poor sources of thermals because of the large amount of moisture given off by foliage. (UA.III.B.K1c) — FAA-H-8083-28

1272. Clouds, fog, or dew will always form when
A—water vapor condenses.
B—water vapor is present.
C—relative humidity reaches 100 percent.

As water vapor condenses or sublimates on condensation nuclei, liquid or ice particles begin to grow. Some condensation nuclei have an affinity for water and can induce condensation or sublimation even when air is almost, but not completely, saturated. (UA.III.B.K1d) — FAA-H-8083-28

Answer (B) is incorrect because the presence of water vapor does not result in clouds, fog, or dew unless condensation occurs. Answer (C) is incorrect because it is possible to have 100% humidity without the occurrence of condensation, which is necessary for clouds, fog, or dew to form.

Wind

Wind and currents can affect sUAS performance and maneuverability during all phases of flight. Be vigilant when operating sUAS at low altitudes, in confined areas, near buildings or other manmade structures, and near natural obstructions (such as mountains, bluffs, or canyons). Consider the following effects of wind on performance:

- Obstructions on the ground affect the flow of wind, may create rapidly changing wind speed and direction, and can be an unseen danger.
- High winds may make it difficult to maintain a geographical position in flight and may consume more battery power or preclude aircraft control and recovery.

Local conditions, geological features, and other anomalies can change the wind direction and speed close to the Earth's surface. For example, when operating close to a building, winds blowing against the building could cause strong updrafts that can result in ballooning or a loss of positive control. On the other hand, winds blowing over the building from the opposite side can cause significant downdrafts that can have a dramatic sinking effect on the unmanned aircraft that may exceed its climb performance.

The intensity of the turbulence associated with ground obstructions depends on the size of the obstacle and the primary velocity of the wind. This same condition is even more noticeable when flying in mountainous regions. While the wind flows smoothly up the windward side of the mountain and the upward currents help to carry an aircraft over the peak of the mountain, the wind on the leeward side

Answers
1137 [A]   1138 [C]   1139 [A]   1272 [A]

does not act in a similar manner. As the air flows down the leeward side of the mountain, the air follows the contour of the terrain and is increasingly turbulent. This tends to push an aircraft into the side of a mountain. The stronger the wind, the greater the downward pressure and turbulence become. Due to the effect terrain has on the wind in valleys or canyons, downdrafts can be severe. Even small hills or odd shaped terrain can have similar effects on local wind conditions. Remote pilots should be aware that terrain/object wind effects may exist for some distance downwind of the actual terrain or object.

1140. While operating around buildings, the remote PIC should be aware of the creation of wind gusts that
A—change rapidly in direction and speed causing turbulence.
B—enhance stability and imagery.
C—increase performance of the aircraft

Local conditions, geological features, and other anomalies can change the wind direction and speed close to the Earth's surface, making it difficult to control and maneuver the sUAS. (UA.III.B.K1b) — FAA-H-8083-25

1141. A strong steady wind exists out of the north. You need to photograph an area to the south of your location. You are located in an open field with no obstructions. Which of the following is not a concern during this operation?
A—Strong wind conditions may consume more battery power at a faster rate than in calm conditions.
B—Turbulent conditions will likely be a significant factor during the operation.
C—Strong wind may exceed the performance of the sUAS making it impossible to recover.

Unmanned aircraft often have limited performance and therefore in high wind conditions, it may consume more power to maintain position or other maneuvers than in calm air. If the wind is strong enough, the sUAS's performance might not be able to adequately counter the wind, making it difficult or impossible to fly back to you for recovery. (UA.III.B.K1b) — FAA-H-8083-25, 14 CFR §107.49

1278. Wind shear can exist
A—at all altitudes.
B—at low altitudes.
C—at high altitudes.

Wind shear is a sudden, drastic change in wind speed and/or direction over a very small area. Wind shear can subject an aircraft to violent updrafts and downdrafts, as well as abrupt changes to the horizontal movement of the aircraft. While wind shear can occur at any altitude, low-level wind shear is especially hazardous due to the proximity of an aircraft to the ground. (UA.III.B.K1b) — FAA-H-8083-28

Air Masses and Fronts

When a body of air comes to rest on, or moves slowly over, an extensive area having fairly uniform properties of temperature and moisture, the air takes on these properties. The area over which the air mass acquires its identifying distribution of temperature and moisture is its source region. As this air mass moves from its source region, it tends to take on the properties of the new underlying surface. The trend toward change is called air mass modification. When an air mass that is different in such properties advances upon a dissimilar air mass, the division line is referred to as a front.

A ridge is an elongated area of high pressure. A trough is an elongated area of low pressure. All fronts lie in troughs. A cold front is the leading edge of an advancing cold air mass. Cold fronts are often accompanied by poor weather ahead of the front, which passes relatively quickly. Once the front has passed, there is a wind shift and, due to the increased wind speeds, turbulence is common for a period of time. More severe cold fronts can also produce thunderstorms, hail, and tornadoes.

A warm front is the leading edge of an advancing warm air mass. Warm fronts move about half as fast as cold fronts and have more widespread impact on weather. They are often preceded by lowered

Answers
1140 [A]   1141 [C]   1278 [A]

Chapter 3 **Weather**

ceilings, increased precipitation, and reduced visibilities. Remote PICs should be aware of ambient and approaching weather systems as they can significantly impact their operations and safety of flight. Frontal waves and cyclones (areas of low pressure) usually form on slower-moving cold fronts or stationary fronts. These types of systems are often accompanied by conditions that may be unfavorable to sUAS operations. Figure 3-1 shows the symbols that would appear on a weather map.

The physical manifestations of a warm or cold front can be different with each front. They vary with the speed of the air mass on the move and the degree of stability of the air mass being overtaken. A stable air mass forced aloft will continue to exhibit stable characteristics, such as stratus clouds, calm air, steady precipitation, and poor visibility, while an unstable air mass forced to ascend will continue to be characterized by cumulus clouds, turbulence, showery precipitation, and good visibility.

Frontal passage will be indicated by the following discontinuities:

1. A temperature change (the most easily recognizable discontinuity);
2. A continuous decrease in pressure followed by an increase as the front passes; and
3. A shift in the wind direction, speed, or both.

Figure 3-1. Weather map symbols

1142. One of the most easily recognized discontinuities across a front is

A—a change in temperature.
B—an increase in cloud coverage.
C—an increase in relative humidity.

Temperature is one of the most easily recognized discontinuities across a front. (UA.III.B.K1d) — FAA-H-8083-28

Answer (B) is incorrect because cloud coverage is not always present across a front. Answer (C) is incorrect because relative humidity is not an easily recognized discontinuity across a front.

1143. One weather phenomenon which will always occur when flying across a front is a change in the

A—wind direction.
B—type of precipitation.
C—stability of the air mass.

Wind direction always changes across a front. (UA.III.B.K1d) — FAA-H-8083-28

Answer (B) is incorrect because precipitation does not always exist with a front. Answer (C) is incorrect because the stability on both sides of the front may be the same.

1144. Which type of weather phenomenon that may concern a remote pilot is common among cold fronts?

A—Long-term periods of reduced visibility.
B—Long periods of steady precipitation.
C—Thunderstorms and heavy rain.

Thunderstorms and heavy rain are common, although not always, associated with cold fronts. (UA.III.B.K1d) — FAA-H-8083-28

Answers (A) and (B) are incorrect because these characteristics would most typically be associated with warm fronts.

1286. What weather provides the best flying conditions?

A—Warm, moist air.
B—Cool, dry air.
C—Turbulence.

The combination of moisture and temperature determine the stability of the air and the resulting weather. Cool, dry air is very stable and resists vertical movement, which leads to good and generally clear weather. (UA.III.B.K1d) — FAA-H-8083-28

Answers

1142 [A] 1143 [A] 1144 [C] 1286 [B]

1277. The zone between different temperature, humidity, and wind is called

A—A front.
B—An air mass.
C—Wind shear.

The zone between two different air masses is a frontal zone or front. Across this zone, temperature, humidity and wind often change rapidly over short distances. (UA.III.B.K1d) — FAA-H-8083-28

Atmospheric Stability

Atmospheric stability is defined as the resistance of the atmosphere to vertical motion. A stable atmosphere resists any upward or downward movement. An unstable atmosphere allows an upward or downward disturbance to grow into a vertical (convective) current.

Determining the stability of the atmosphere requires measuring the difference between the actual existing (ambient) temperature lapse rate of a given parcel of air and the dry adiabatic (3°C per 1,000 feet) lapse rate. Because sUAS operate at low altitudes, it may seem as though lapse rate may not be a factor, but the stability of the local air mass can have significant impact on ambient conditions. Unstable air can often result in weather conditions unfavorable to sUAS operations.

A stable layer of air would be associated with a temperature inversion (a condition in which warm air is situated above cool or cold air). Warming from below, on the other hand, would decrease the stability of an air mass. The conditions shown in Figure 3-2 can be characteristic of stable or unstable air masses.

Unstable Air	Stable Air
Cumuliform clouds	Stratiform clouds and fog
Showery precipitation	Continuous precipitation
Rough air (turbulence)	Smooth air
Good visibility except in blowing obstructions	Fair to poor visibility in haze and smoke

Figure 3-2. Characteristics of stable and unstable air masses

1145. A stable air mass is most likely to have which characteristic?

A—Showery precipitation.
B—Turbulent air.
C—Poor surface visibility.

Characteristics of a stable air mass include stratiform clouds and fog, continuous precipitation, smooth air, and fair to poor visibility in haze and smoke. (UA.III.B.K1c) — FAA-H-8083-25

1146. What are characteristics of a moist, unstable air mass?

A—Turbulence and showery precipitation.
B—Poor visibility and smooth air.
C—Haze and smoke.

Characteristics of a moist, unstable air mass include cumuliform clouds, showery precipitation, rough air (turbulence), and good visibility (except in blowing obstructions). (UA.III.B.K1c) — FAA-H-8083-28

1147. What are characteristics of stable air?

A—Good visibility and steady precipitation.
B—Poor visibility and steady precipitation.
C—Poor visibility and intermittent precipitation.

Characteristics of a stable air mass include stratiform clouds and fog, continuous precipitation, smooth air, and fair to poor visibility in haze and smoke. (UA.III.B.K1c) — FAA-H-8083-25

1148. What measurement can be used to determine the stability of the atmosphere?

A—Atmospheric pressure.
B—Actual lapse rate.
C—Surface temperature.

The difference between the existing lapse rate of a given mass of air and the adiabatic rates of cooling in upward moving air determines if the air is stable or unstable. (UA.III.B.K1c) — FAA-H-8083-28

Answers

1277 [A]   1145 [C]   1146 [A]   1147 [B]   1148 [B]

1149. What would decrease the stability of an air mass?
A—Warming from below.
B—Cooling from below.
C—Decrease in water vapor.

When air near the surface is warm and moist, suspect instability. Surface heating, cooling aloft, converging or upslope winds, or an invading mass of colder air may lead to instability and cumuliform clouds. (UA.III.B.K1c) — FAA-H-8083-28

Answer (B) is incorrect because cooling from the air below would increase the stability of the air. Answer (C) is incorrect because an increase in water vapor will result in a decrease in stability.

1150. Upon your preflight evaluation of weather, the forecasts you reference state there is an unstable air mass approaching your location. Which would not be a concern for your impending operation?
A—Thunderstorms.
B—Stratiform clouds.
C—Turbulent conditions.

Unstable conditions are characterized by cumulus clouds, turbulence, showery precipitation, and good visibility. (UA.III.B.K1c) — FAA-H-8083-28

1285. You have received an outlook briefing from flight service through 1800wxbrief.com. The briefing indicates you can expect a low-level temperature inversion with high relative humidity. What weather conditions would you expect?
A—Smooth air, poor visibility, fog, haze, or low clouds.
B—Light wind shear, poor visibility, haze, and light rain.
C—Turbulent air, poor visibility, fog, low stratus type clouds, and showery precipitation.

When the temperature of the air rises with altitude, a temperature inversion exists. Inversion layers are commonly shallow layers of smooth, stable air close to the ground. The temperature of the air increases with altitude to a certain point, which is the top of the inversion. The air at the top of the layer acts as a lid, keeping weather and pollutants trapped below. If the relative humidity of the air is high, it can contribute to the formation of clouds, fog, haze, or smoke resulting in diminished visibility in the inversion layer. (UA.III.B.K1c) — FAA-H-8083-28

Visibility and Clouds

As in manned aircraft operations, good visibility and safe distance from clouds enhances the remote PIC's ability to see and avoid other aircraft. Similarly, good visibility and cloud clearance may be the only means for other aircraft to see and avoid the unmanned aircraft. Prior to flight, the remote PIC must determine that visibility from the control station is at least 3 SM and that the sUAS is kept at least 500 feet below a cloud and at least 2,000 feet horizontally from a cloud. These standards must be maintained throughout flight operations.

One of the ways to ensure adherence to the minimum visibility and cloud clearance requirements is to obtain local aviation weather reports that include current and forecast weather conditions. If there is more than one local aviation reporting station near the operating area, the remote PIC should choose the closest one that is also the most representative of the terrain surrounding the operating area. If local aviation weather reports are not available, then the remote PIC may not operate the sUA if he or she is unable to determine the required visibility and cloud clearances by other reliable means.

The remote pilot can determine local visibility by verifying that a known point at least 3 SM away is visible. Similarly, an object with a known height can be observed to have clouds above that object, providing information about how much operational altitude is available for use. For example, you know a nearby tower extends to 1,000 feet AGL (referencing a Sectional Chart). The clouds are above the top. Thus you know that even if you climb to the maximum altitude of 400 feet AGL, you have more than the required 500 feet of separation from the clouds. When in doubt, always choose the most conservative and safest option, which sometimes may be to delay the operation. It is imperative that the sUA not be operated above any cloud, and that there are no obstructions to visibility, such as smoke or a cloud, between the sUA and the remote PIC.

Answers

1149 [A]   1150 [B]   1285 [A]

Chapter 3 Weather

1151. What minimum visibility is required for sUAS operations?

A—1 miles.
B—3 miles.
C—4 miles.

Crewmembers must operate sUAS Part 107 operations with a minimum visibility, as observed from the location of the control station, no less than 3 SM. (UA.I.B.K21c) — 14 CFR §107.51

1152. The minimum distance from clouds required for sUAS Part 107 operations is

A—clear of clouds.
B—500 feet below, 2,000 feet horizontally.
C—500 feet above, 1,000 feet horizontally.

Part 107 sUAS operations require the minimum distance of the small unmanned aircraft from clouds must be no less than 500 feet below the cloud and 2,000 feet horizontally from the cloud. (UA.I.B.K21d) — 14 CFR §107.51

1288. (Refer to Figure 69.) You are inspecting the lighted towers approximately 8 NM SW of the Corpus Christi Intl Airport (CRP). What is the lowest cloud cover that will enable you to inspect the top of the tower?

A—1,104 feet MSL.
B—1,604 feet MSL.
C—1,054 feet MSL.

Part 107 requires that the minimum distance of the sUAS from clouds must be no less than 500 feet below the cloud. The towers depicted 8 NM SW of CRP are 1,104 feet MSL. 1,104 + 500 = 1,604 feet MSL. (UA.II.B.K1) — 14 CFR §107.51

1271. The weather report lists the ceiling at 800 feet. What is the highest you can operate your sUAS?

A—200 feet AGL.
B—800 feet AGL.
C—300 feet AGL.

Part 107 requires that the minimum distance of the sUAS from clouds must be no less than 500 feet below the cloud. 800 − 500 = 300 feet AGL. (UA.II.B.K1) — 14 CFR §107.51

1289. (Refer to Figure 23.) What are the VFR minimum visibility requirements over Plantation Airport?

A—1 SM.
B—5 SM.
C—3 SM.

Regardless of the location, crewmembers must conduct sUAS Part 107 operations with a minimum visibility, as observed from the location of the control station, no less than 3 SM. (UA.II.B.K1) — 14 CFR §107.51

1329. (Refer to Figure 23, Area 4.) What is the required flight visibility for a remote pilot operating an unmanned aircraft near the Plantation Airport (JYL)?

A—5 statute miles.
B—1 statute mile.
C—3 statute miles.

Regardless of the location, crewmembers must conduct sUAS Part 107 operations with a minimum visibility, as observed from the location of the control station, no less than 3 SM. (UA.II.B.K1) — 14 CFR §107.51

1310. (Refer to Figure 78.) What is the minimum base of the cloud layer to fly to the top of the towers 4 NM east of Onawa (K36)?

A—792 feet AGL.
B—292 feet AGL.
C—1,335 feet MSL.

Part 107 requires that the minimum distance of the sUAS from clouds must be no less than 500 feet below the cloud. The towers depicted 4 NM east of K36 are 292 feet AGL. 292 + 500 = 792 feet AGL. (UA.II.B.K1) — 14 CFR §107.51

Answers

1151 [B]   1152 [B]   1288 [B]   1271 [C]   1289 [C]   1329 [C]
1310 [A]

Thunderstorms

Thunderstorms present many hazards to flying. Three conditions necessary for the formation of a thunderstorm are:

1. Sufficient water vapor;
2. An unstable lapse rate; and
3. An initial lifting force (upward boost).

The lifting action can be caused by heating from below, frontal lifting, or by mechanical lifting (wind blowing air upslope on a mountain). There are three stages of a thunderstorm: the cumulus, mature, and dissipating stages. See Figure 3-3.

The cumulus stage is characterized by continuous updrafts, and these updrafts create low-pressure areas. Thunderstorms reach their greatest intensity during the mature stage, which is characterized by updrafts and downdrafts inside the cloud. Precipitation inside the cloud aids in the development of these downdrafts, and the start of rain from the base of the cloud signals the beginning of the mature stage. The precipitation that evaporates before it reaches the ground is called virga. Virga is typically associated with very turbulent conditions and should be avoided. The dissipating stage of a thunderstorm is characterized predominantly by downdrafts.

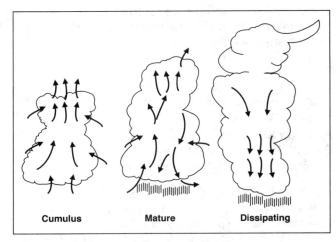

Figure 3-3. Stages of thunderstorms

Lightning is always associated with a thunderstorm. The frequency of lightning is a good indicator of the severity of the storm. Upon observing frequent nearby lightning, remote PICs should recover their crew and sUAS in order to seek cover. One way to determine the distance a storm is from your location is to count the number of seconds it takes between when you see lightning and then hear thunder. Take the result and divide by 5 to give you the distance in statute miles. If there is frequent lightning or multiple storms, this method may not be feasible. Ideally, remote pilots can monitor the weather by electronic means and observe incoming systems with precise detail.

Hail is formed inside thunderstorms by the constant freezing, melting, and refreezing of water as it is carried about by the up- and downdrafts.

Thunderstorms that generally produce the most intense hazard to aircraft are called squall-line thunderstorms. These non-frontal, narrow bands of thunderstorms often develop ahead of a cold front. Embedded thunderstorms are those that are obscured by massive cloud layers and cannot be seen. A pilot should always expect the hazardous and invisible atmospheric phenomena called wind shear turbulence when operating anywhere near a thunderstorm (within 20 NM).

Microbursts are small-scale intense downdrafts which, as they get near the ground, spread outward from the center in all directions. Maximum downdrafts at the center of a microburst may be as strong as 6,000 feet per minute far exceeding the capabilities of sUAS. Also, wind speeds in excess of 45 knots and shears of 90 knots or more may exist which may cause an upset or loss of control of an sUAS. An individual microburst will seldom last longer than 15 minutes from the time it strikes the ground until dissipation. The horizontal winds continue to increase during the first 5 minutes with the maximum intensity winds and last approximately 2–4 minutes.

The most violent thunderstorms draw air into their cloud bases with great vigor. If the incoming air has any initial rotating motion, it often forms an extremely concentrated vortex from the surface well into the cloud. Meteorologists have estimated that wind in such a vortex can exceed 200 knots with pressure inside the vortex quite low. The strong winds gather dust and debris and the low pressure generates a funnel-shaped cloud extending downward from the cumulonimbus base. If the cloud does not reach the surface, it is a funnel cloud; if it touches a land surface, it is a tornado. Tornadoes occur with both isolated and squall line thunderstorms. Remote pilots should avoid operations during or in close proximity to thunderstorm activity, especially those that appear to be severe.

Remote pilots should be aware that some phenomenon (e.g. hail, lightning, windshear, and microbursts) can occur well away from the center of the storm. Extreme caution is advised when operating in conditions that may generate thunderstorms.

1153. What feature is normally associated with the cumulus stage of a thunderstorm?

A—Roll cloud.
B—Continuous updraft.
C—Frequent lightning.

The key feature of the cumulus stage is an updraft. Precipitation beginning to fall from the cloudbase is the signal that a downdraft has developed also and a cell has entered the mature stage. (UA.III.B.K1e) — FAA-H-8083-28

Answer (A) is incorrect because a roll cloud is associated with a mountain wave. Answer (C) is incorrect because frequent lightning may be present in any stage.

1154. Which weather phenomenon signals the beginning of the mature stage of a thunderstorm?

A—The appearance of an anvil top.
B—Precipitation beginning to fall.
C—Maximum growth rate of the clouds.

The key feature of the cumulus stage is an updraft. Precipitation beginning to fall from the cloudbase is the signal that a downdraft has developed also and the cell has entered the mature stage. (UA.III.B.K1e) — FAA-H-8083-28

Answer (A) is incorrect because the appearance of an anvil top is characteristic of the dissipating stage. Answer (C) is incorrect because the maximum growth rate of the clouds is during the mature stage of a thunderstorm, but it does not signal the beginning of that stage.

1155. What conditions are necessary for the formation of thunderstorms?

A—High humidity, lifting force, and unstable conditions.
B—High humidity, high temperature, and cumulus clouds.
C—Lifting force, moist air, and extensive cloud cover.

For a cumulonimbus cloud or thunderstorm to form, the air must have:

1. *Sufficient water vapor;*
2. *An unstable lapse rate; and*
3. *An initial upward boost (lifting) to start the storm process in motion.*

(UA.III.B.K1e) — FAA-H-8083-28

1156. During the life cycle of a thunderstorm, which stage is characterized predominately by downdrafts?

A—Cumulus.
B—Dissipating.
C—Mature.

Downdrafts characterize the dissipating stage of the thunderstorm cell and the storm dies rapidly. (UA.III.B.K1e) — FAA-H-8083-28

Answer (A) is incorrect because updrafts occur during the cumulus stage. Answer (C) is incorrect because both updrafts and downdrafts occur during the mature stage.

1157. Thunderstorms reach their greatest intensity during the

A—mature stage.
B—downdraft stage.
C—cumulus stage.

All thunderstorm hazards reach their greatest intensity during the mature stage. (UA.III.B.K1e) — FAA-H-8083-28

Answers

1153 [B]   1154 [B]   1155 [A]   1156 [B]   1157 [A]

Chapter 3 **Weather**

1158. Thunderstorms which generally produce the most intense hazard to aircraft are

A—squall line thunderstorms.
B—steady-state thunderstorms.
C—warm front thunderstorms.

A squall line is a non-frontal, narrow band of active thunderstorms. The line may be too long to easily detour and too wide and severe to penetrate. It often contains severe steady-state thunderstorms and presents the single, most intense weather hazard to aircraft. (UA.III.B.K1e) — FAA-H-8083-28

1159. A nonfrontal, narrow band of active thunderstorms that often develop ahead of a cold front is known as a

A—prefrontal system.
B—squall line.
C—dry line.

A squall line is a nonfrontal, narrow band of active thunderstorms. The line may be too long to easily detour and too wide and severe to penetrate. It often contains severe steady-state thunderstorms and presents the single, most intense weather hazard to aircraft. (UA.III.B.K1e) — FAA-H-8083-28

1160. If there is thunderstorm activity in the vicinity of an airport at which you plan to land, which hazardous atmospheric phenomenon might be expected during recovery/landing of the sUAS?

A—Precipitation static.
B—Wind-shear turbulence.
C—Steady rain.

Wind shear is an invisible hazard associated with all thunderstorms. Shear turbulence has been encountered 20 miles laterally from a severe storm. (UA.III.B.K1e) — FAA-H-8083-28

Answer (A) is incorrect because precipitation static is not considered a hazardous atmospheric phenomenon. Answer (C) is incorrect because showery precipitation is a characteristic of thunderstorm activity.

1161. Which weather phenomenon is always associated with a thunderstorm?

A—Lightning.
B—Heavy rain.
C—Hail.

A thunderstorm is, in general, a local storm invariably produced by a cumulonimbus cloud, and is always accompanied by lightning and thunder. (UA.III.B.K1e) — FAA-H-8083-28

1162. Which is considered to be the most hazardous condition when flying an sUAS in the vicinity of thunderstorms?

A—Static electricity.
B—Lightning.
C—Wind shear and turbulence.

During the mature stage of a thunderstorm, updrafts and downdrafts in close proximity create strong vertical shears and a very turbulent environment. A lightning strike can puncture the skin of an aircraft, damage communication and navigation equipment, or hit the remote pilot or crew on the ground. (UA.III.B.K1e) — FAA-H-8083-28

1163. What is the expected duration of an individual microburst?

A—Two minutes with maximum winds lasting approximately 1 minute.
B—One microburst may continue for as long as 2 to 4 hours.
C—Seldom longer than 15 minutes from the time the burst strikes the ground until dissipation.

An individual microburst will seldom last longer than 15 minutes from the time it strikes the ground until dissipation. However, there may be multiple microbursts in the area. (UA.III.B.K1e) — AIM ¶7-1-24

Answers

1158 [A] 1159 [B] 1160 [B] 1161 [A] 1162 [B] 1163 [C]

1283. In what stage are thunderstorms the strongest?
A—Mature.
B—Dissipating.
C—Cumulus.

Thunderstorm hazards reach their greatest intensity during the mature stage, which is when precipitation begins. (UA.III.B.K1e) — FAA-H-8083-28

1287. Where are squalls most likely to form?
A—High altitude.
B—Low altitude.
C—At any altitude.

A continuous line of thunderstorms, or squall line, may form along or ahead of the front. Squall lines present a serious hazard to pilots as squall type thunderstorms are intense and move quickly. Squalls can occur at any altitude—they are not unique to high- or low-altitude operations. (UA.III.B.K1e) — FAA-H-8083-28

Icing

Structural icing occurs on an aircraft whenever supercooled condensed droplets of water make contact with any part of the aircraft that is also at a temperature below freezing. An inflight condition necessary for structural icing to form is visible moisture (clouds or raindrops). Icing in precipitation (rain) is of concern to the remote pilot because it can occur outside of clouds. Aircraft structural ice will most likely have the highest accumulation in freezing rain which indicates warmer temperature at a higher altitude. The effects of structural icing on an sUAS are as follows:

- Lift decreases;
- Weight and stalling speed increase for fixed wing, and propellers may stall on rotary wing;
- Thrust decreases; and
- Drag increases.

The presence of ice pellets at the surface is evidence that there is freezing rain at a higher altitude, while wet snow indicates that the temperature at your altitude is above freezing. A situation conducive to any icing would be flying in the vicinity of a front.

Remote pilots should avoid flight in conditions that may produce icing. If it appears that ice is accumulating on the sUAS, it should be recovered immediately to avoid loss of control.

1164. The presence of ice pellets at the surface is evidence that there
A—are thunderstorms in the area.
B—has been cold frontal passage.
C—is a temperature inversion with freezing rain at a higher altitude.

Ice pellets always indicate freezing rain at higher altitude. (UA.III.B.K1g) — FAA-H-8083-28

1165. One in-flight condition necessary for structural icing to form is
A—small temperature/dewpoint spread.
B—stratiform clouds.
C—visible moisture.

Two conditions are necessary for structural icing in flight:

1. *The aircraft must be flying through visible water such as rain or cloud droplets, and*
2. *The temperature at the point where the moisture strikes the aircraft must be 0°C (32°F) or colder.*

(UA.III.B.K1g) — FAA-H-8083-28

Answers

1283 [A]   1287 [C]   1164 [C]   1165 [C]

Chapter 3 **Weather**

1166. In which environment is aircraft structural ice most likely to have the highest accumulation rate?
A—Cumulus clouds with below freezing temperatures.
B—Freezing drizzle.
C—Freezing rain.

A condition favorable for rapid accumulation of clear icing is freezing rain below a frontal surface. (UA.III.B.K1g) — FAA-H-8083-28

Answers (A) and (B) are incorrect because although cumulus clouds with below-freezing temperatures and freezing drizzle are conducive to structural icing, they will not have as high an accumulation rate as freezing rain.

1298. What environment is most conducive to frost formation?
A—Dewpoint of surface is below freezing, dewpoint is above freezing.
B—Surface temperature is below freezing, air temperature is below freezing.
C—Surface temperature is above freezing, air temperature is below freezing.

On cool, clear, calm nights, the temperature of the ground and objects on the surface can cause temperatures of the surrounding air to drop below the dew point. When this occurs, the moisture in the air condenses and deposits itself on the ground, buildings, and other objects like cars and aircraft. This moisture is known as dew and sometimes can be seen on grass and other objects in the morning. If the temperature is below freezing, the moisture is deposited in the form of frost. (UA.III.B.K1g) — FAA-H-8083-28

Fog

Fog is a surface-based cloud (restricting visibility) composed of either water droplets or ice crystals. Fog may form by cooling the air to its dew point or by adding moisture to the air near the ground. A small temperature/dew point spread is essential to the formation of fog. An abundance of condensation nuclei from combustion products makes fog prevalent in industrial areas.

Fog is classified by the way it is formed:

- **Radiation fog** (ground fog) is formed when terrestrial radiation cools the ground, which in turn cools the air in contact with it. When the air is cooled to its dew point (or within a few degrees), fog will form. This fog will form most readily in warm, moist air over low, flatland areas on clear, calm (no wind) nights.

- **Advection fog** (sea fog) is formed when warm, moist air moves (wind is required) over colder ground or water (e.g., an air mass moving inland from the coast in winter).

- **Upslope fog** is formed when moist, stable air is cooled to its dew point as it moves up along sloping terrain (wind is required). Cooling will be at the dry adiabatic lapse rate of approximately 3°C per 1,000 feet.

- **Precipitation-induced (rain or drizzle) fog** is most commonly associated with frontal activity and is formed by relatively warm drizzle or rain falling through cooler air. Evaporation from the precipitation saturates the cool air and fog forms. This fog is especially critical because it occurs in the proximity of precipitation and other possible hazards such as icing, turbulence, and thunderstorms.

- **Steam fog** forms in the winter when cold, dry air passes from land areas over comparatively warm ocean waters. Low-level turbulence can occur and icing can become hazardous in a steam fog.

- Remote pilots should be cautious when conditions are conducive to the formation of fog (e.g., when temperature and dew points are converging), especially at dusk or before dawn. Visibility can rapidly change once fog begins to form. The sUAS should be recovered if visibility approaches the 3 SM minimum.

Answers
1166 [C]   1298 [A]

1167. What situation is most conducive to the formation of radiation fog?

A—Warm, moist air over low, flatland areas on clear, calm nights.
B—Moist, tropical air moving over cold, offshore water.
C—The movement of cold air over much warmer water.

Conditions favorable for radiation fog are clear sky, little or no wind, and small temperature/dew point spread (high relative humidity). Radiation fog is restricted to land because water surfaces cool little from nighttime radiation. (UA.III.B.K1i) — FAA-H-8083-28

Answers (B) and (C) are incorrect because radiation fog will not form over water since water surfaces cool little from nighttime radiation.

1168. In which situation is advection fog most likely to form?

A—A warm, moist air mass on the windward side of mountains.
B—An air mass moving inland from the coast in winter.
C—A light breeze blowing colder air out to sea.

Advection fog forms when moist air moves over colder ground or water. It is most common along coastal areas. This fog frequently forms offshore as a result of cold water, then is carried inland by the wind. (UA.III.B.K1i) — FAA-H-8083-28

Answer (A) is incorrect because a warm, moist air mass on the windward side of mountains will form upslope fog and/or rain. Answer (C) is incorrect because a light breeze blowing colder air out to sea will form steam fog.

1169. An air mass moving inland from the coast in winter is likely to result in

A—rain.
B—fog.
C—frost.

Advection fog forms when moist air moves over colder ground or water. It is most common along coastal areas. This fog frequently forms offshore as a result of cold water, then is carried inland by the wind. (UA.III.B.K1i) — FAA-H-8083-28

1170. What types of fog depend upon wind in order to exist?

A—Radiation fog and ice fog.
B—Steam fog and ground fog.
C—Advection fog and upslope fog.

Advection fog forms when moist air moves over colder ground or water. It is most common along coastal areas, but often develops deep in continental areas. Advection fog deepens as wind speed increases up to about 15 knots. Wind much stronger than 15 knots lifts the fog into a layer of low stratus or stratocumulus. Upslope fog forms as a result of moist, stable air being cooled adiabatically as it moves up sloping terrain. Once upslope wind ceases, the fog dissipates. (UA.III.B.K1i) — FAA-H-8083-28

Answer (A) is incorrect because radiation fog and ice fog do not depend upon wind in order to exist. Answer (B) is incorrect because ground fog does not depend on wind in order to exist.

1171. Low-level turbulence can occur and icing can become hazardous in which type of fog?

A—Rain-induced fog.
B—Upslope fog.
C—Steam fog.

Steam fog forms in the winter when cold, dry air passes from land areas over comparatively warm ocean waters. Low-level turbulence can occur and icing can become hazardous in a steam fog. (UA.III.B.K1i) — FAA-H-8083-28

1172. What is the best way for a remote pilot to determine the likelihood of local fog formation?

A—Monitor the temperature/dew point spread.
B—Monitor the wind conditions to ensure the wind speed is not increasing.
C—Monitor the barometric pressure to ensure that it is not decreasing.

Fog is more likely to form when the temperature and dew point converge. A difference between these two temperatures of 3°C (or 5°F) is indicative of possible fog formation. (UA.III.B.K1i) — FAA-H-8083-28

Answers

1167 [A]   1168 [B]   1169 [B]   1170 [C]   1171 [C]   1172 [A]

Chapter 3 **Weather**

Density Altitude

Manufacturer performance information conveys to the remote pilot what can be expected of an sUAS (rate of climb, takeoff roll, etc.) under ideal conditions. Prediction of performance is based upon the conditions a manufacturer chooses, but is often similar to manned aircraft calculations which use a sea level temperature of +15°C (+59°F) and atmospheric pressure of 29.92 "Hg (1013.2 mb). This combination of temperature and pressure is called a standard day. When the air is at a standard density, temperature and/or pressure deviations from standard will change the air density, or the density altitude, and that change affects sUAS performance. Remote pilots should be aware that conditions which deviate away from the manufacturer-calculated or standard conditions will impact performance.

Relative humidity also affects density altitude, but should have minimal impact on sUAS performance. Overall, sUAS flight performance will decrease as atmospheric pressure decreases, altitude increases (in flight or at higher launch sites), temperature increases, and marginally as humidity increases. A combination of high temperature, high humidity, and high altitude result in a density altitude higher than the pressure altitude which, in turn, results in reduced aircraft performance.

1173. How would high density altitude affect the performance of a small unmanned aircraft?

A—No change in performance.
B—Increased performance.
C—Decreased performance.

A combination of high temperature, high humidity, and high altitude result in a density altitude higher than the pressure altitude which, in turn, results in reduced aircraft performance. (UA.III.B.K1a) — FAA-H-8083-25

1174. If the outside air temperature (OAT) at a given altitude is warmer than standard, the density altitude is

A—equal to pressure altitude.
B—lower than pressure altitude.
C—higher than pressure altitude.

If the temperature is above standard, the density altitude will be higher than pressure altitude. (UA.III.B.K1a) — FAA-H-8083-25

1175. What are the standard temperature and pressure values for sea level?

A—15°C and 29.92 "Hg.
B—59°C and 1013.2 millibars.
C—59°F and 29.92 millibars.

Standard sea level pressure is 29.92 "Hg. Standard sea level temperature is 15°C. (UA.III.B.K1a) — FAA-H-8083-25

1176. Which factor would tend to increase the density altitude at a given airport referenced in the weather briefing?

A—An increase in barometric pressure.
B—An increase in ambient temperature.
C—A decrease in relative humidity.

On a hot day, the air becomes "thinner" or lighter, and its density is equivalent to a higher altitude in the standard atmosphere, thus the term high density altitude. (UA.III.B.K1a) — FAA-H-8083-28

Answer (A) is incorrect because an increase in barometric pressure would decrease density altitude. Answer (C) is incorrect because a decrease in relative humidity would decrease density altitude.

1177. What effect does high density altitude have on the efficiency of a small unmanned aircraft propeller?

A—Propeller efficiency is increased.
B—Propeller efficiency is decreased.
C—Density altitude does not affect propeller efficiency.

The propeller produces thrust in proportion to the mass of air being accelerated through the rotating blades. If the air is less dense, propeller efficiency is decreased. (UA.III.B.K1a) — FAA-H-8083-25

Answers

1173 [C]   1174 [C]   1175 [A]   1176 [B]   1177 [B]

Chapter 3 **Weather**

1290. What effect does humidity have on performance?
A—It has no effect on performance.
B—It increases performance.
C—It decreases performance.

An increase in air temperature or humidity or a decrease in air pressure (which results in a higher density altitude) will significantly decrease both power output and propeller efficiency. If an air mass is humid, there is more water in it; therefore, less oxygen. (UA.III.B.K1a) — FAA-H-8083-28

Weather Briefing

Remote PICs are encouraged to obtain weather information from Flight Service prior to flight by visiting **1800wxbrief.com**. Remote PICs can create a free account in order to use the briefing service. While Flight Service does offer a telephone-based service, it is intended for manned aircraft pilots only.

Remote PICs are also encouraged to visit the **NWS Aviation Weather Center (AWC)** at **aviationweather.gov**. This free, web-based service does not require registration and offers all of the weather products important to a remote PIC, such as **aviation routine weather reports (METAR)** and **terminal aerodrome forecasts (TAF)**. While reviewing the weather for your intended operation, it is also critical that the remote PIC review any temporary flight restrictions (TFR) at **tfr.faa.gov**.

Request a standard briefing to get a complete weather briefing. Request an abbreviated briefing to supplement mass disseminated data or when only one or two items are needed. Request an outlook briefing whenever the proposed departure time is six or more hours from the time of briefing.

Remote pilots need to learn the various abbreviations and symbols of textual weather reports in order to interpret them properly, and should familiarize themselves with available graphical products to be able to understand available weather maps and images.

1178. To get a complete weather overview for the planned flight, the remote pilot-in-command should obtain

A—An outlook briefing.
B—An abbreviated briefing.
C—A standard briefing.

A remote PIC should request a standard briefing any time they are planning a flight and have not received a previous briefing. (UA.III.A.K1) — FAA-H-8083-25

Weather Reports, Forecasts and Charts

Remote pilots can access weather reports, forecasts and charts by visiting **aviationweather.gov** or **1800wxbrief.com**.

The **Automated Surface Observing System (ASOS)** is the primary surface weather observing system of the U.S. Automated weather reporting systems are increasingly being installed at airports. These systems consist of various sensors, a processor, a computer-generated voice subsystem, and a transmitter to broadcast local, minute-by-minute weather data directly to the pilot. The **Automated Weather Observing System (AWOS)** observations will include the prefix "AUTO" to indicate that the data is derived from an automated system.

An international weather reporting code is used for weather reports (METAR) and forecasts (TAFs) worldwide. The reports follow the format shown in Figure 3-4. For aviation purposes, the ceiling is the lowest broken or overcast layer, or vertical visibility into an obscuration.

Answers
1290 [C]   1178 [C]

Chapter 3 **Weather**

Figure 3-4. TAF/METAR weather card

Surface Aviation Weather Observations

Surface aviation weather observations are a compilation of elements of the current weather at individual ground stations across the United States. The network is made up of government and privately contracted facilities that provide continuous up-to-date weather information. Automated weather sources, such as AWOS, ASOS, as well as other automated facilities, also play a major role in the gathering of surface observations.

Surface observations provide local weather conditions and other relevant information for a specific airport. This information includes the type of report, station identifier, date and time, modifier (as required), wind, visibility, runway visual range (RVR), weather phenomena, sky condition, temperature/dew point, altimeter reading, and applicable remarks. The information gathered for the surface observation may be from a person, an automated station, or an automated station that is updated or enhanced by a weather observer. In any form, the surface observation provides valuable information about individual airports around the country. These reports cover a small area and will be beneficial to the remote pilot.

Chapter 3 **Weather**

Aviation Weather Reports

Aviation weather reports are designed to give accurate depictions of current weather conditions. Each report provides current information that is updated at different times. Some typical reports are METARs and PIREPs. To view a weather report, go to **aviationweather.gov**.

Aviation Routine Weather Report (METAR)

A METAR is an observation of current surface weather reported in a standard international format. METARs are issued on a regularly scheduled basis unless significant weather changes have occurred. A special METAR (SPECI) can be issued at any time between routine METAR reports. *Example:*

METAR KGGG 161753Z AUTO 14021G26KT 3/4SM +TSRA BR BKN008 OVC012CB 18/17 A2970 RMK PRESFR

A typical METAR report contains the following information in sequential order:

1. Type of report—there are two types of METAR reports. The first is the routine METAR report that is transmitted on a regular time interval. The second is the aviation selected SPECI. This is a special report that can be given at any time to update the METAR for rapidly changing weather conditions, aircraft mishaps, or other critical information.

2. Station identifier—a four-letter code as established by the International Civil Aviation Organization (ICAO). In the 48 contiguous states, a unique three-letter identifier is preceded by the letter "K." For example, Gregg County Airport in Longview, Texas, is identified by the letters "KGGG," K being the country designation and GGG being the airport identifier. In other regions of the world, including Alaska and Hawaii, the first two letters of the four-letter ICAO identifier indicate the region, country, or state. Alaska identifiers always begin with the letters "PA" and Hawaii identifiers always begin with the letters "PH." Station identifiers can be found by searching various websites such as DUATS and NOAA's Aviation Weather Aviation Digital Data Services (ADDS).

3. Date and time of report—depicted in a six-digit group (161753Z). The first two digits are the date. The last four digits are the time of the METAR/SPECI, which is always given in coordinated universal time (UTC). A "Z" is appended to the end of the time to denote the time is given in Zulu time (UTC) as opposed to local time.

4. Modifier—denotes that the METAR/SPECI came from an automated source or that the report was corrected. If the notation "AUTO" is listed in the METAR/SPECI, the report came from an automated source. It also lists "AO1" (for no precipitation discriminator) or "AO2" (with precipitation discriminator) in the "Remarks" section to indicate the type of precipitation sensors employed at the automated station. When the modifier "COR" is used, it identifies a corrected report sent out to replace an earlier report that contained an error (for example: METAR KGGG 161753Z COR).

5. Wind—reported with five digits (14021KT) unless the speed is greater than 99 knots, in which case the wind is reported with six digits. The first three digits indicate the direction the true wind is blowing from in tens of degrees. If the wind is variable, it is reported as "VRB." The last two digits indicate the speed of the wind in knots unless the wind is greater than 99 knots, in which case it is indicated by three digits. If the winds are gusting, the letter "G" follows the wind speed (G26KT). After the letter "G," the peak gust recorded is provided. If the wind direction varies more than 60° and the wind speed is greater than six knots, a separate group of numbers, separated by a "V," will indicate the extremes of the wind directions.

6. Visibility—the prevailing visibility (¾ SM) is reported in statute miles as denoted by the letters "SM." It is reported in both miles and fractions of miles. At times, runway visual range (RVR) is reported following the prevailing visibility. RVR is the distance a pilot can see down the runway in a moving

Chapter 3 **Weather**

aircraft. When RVR is reported, it is shown with an R, then the runway number followed by a slant, then the visual range in feet. For example, when the RVR is reported as R17L/1400FT, it translates to a visual range of 1,400 feet on runway 17 left.

7. Weather—can be broken down into two different categories: qualifiers and weather phenomenon (+TSRA BR). First, the qualifiers of intensity, proximity, and the descriptor of the weather are given. The intensity may be light (–), moderate ( ), or heavy (+). Proximity only depicts weather phenomena that are in the airport vicinity. The notation "VC" indicates a specific weather phenomenon is in the vicinity of five to ten miles from the airport. Descriptors are used to describe certain types of precipitation and obscurations. Weather phenomena may be reported as being precipitation, obscurations, and other phenomena, such as squalls or funnel clouds. Descriptions of weather phenomena as they begin or end and hailstone size are also listed in the "Remarks" sections of the report. See Figure 3-5.

Qualifier					Weather Phenomena			
Intensity or Proximity 1		**Descriptor 2**		**Precipitation 3**		**Obscuration 4**		**Other 5**
–	Light	MI	Shallow	DZ	Drizzle	BR	Mist	PO	Dust/sand whirls
	Moderate (no qualifier)	BC	Patches	RA	Rain	FG	Fog	SQ	Squalls
+	Heavy	DR	Low drifting	SN	Snow	FU	Smoke	FC	Funnel cloud
VC	in the vicinity	BL	Blowing	SG	Snow grains	DU	Dust	+FC	Tornado or waterspout
		SH	Showers	IC	Ice crystals (diamond dust)	SA	Sand	SS	Sandstorm
		TS	Thunderstorms	PL	Ice pellets	HZ	Haze	DS	Dust storm
		FZ	Freezing	GR	Hail	PY	Spray		
		PR	Partial	GS	Small hail or snow pellets	VA	Volcanic ash		
				UP	Unknown precipitation*				

The weather groups are constructed by considering columns 1–5 in this table in sequence: intensity, followed by descriptor, followed by weather phenomena (e.g., heavy rain shower(s) is coded as +SHRA).
*Automated stations only.

Figure 3-5. Descriptors and weather phenomena used in a typical METAR

8. Sky condition—always reported in the sequence of amount, height, and type or indefinite ceiling/height (vertical visibility) (BKN008 OVC012CB, VV003). The heights of the cloud bases are reported with a three-digit number in hundreds of feet AGL. Clouds above 12,000 feet are not detected or reported by an automated station. The types of clouds, specifically towering cumulus (TCU) or cumulonimbus (CB) clouds, are reported with their height. Contractions are used to describe the amount of cloud coverage and obscuring phenomena. The amount of sky coverage is reported in eighths of the sky from horizon to horizon. See Figure 3-6.

Sky Cover	Contraction
Less than 1/8 (Clear)	SKC, CLR, FEW
1/8–2/8 (Few)	FEW
3/8–4/8 (Scattered)	SCT
5/8–7/8 (Broken)	BKN
8/8 (Overcast)	OVC

Figure 3-6. Reportable contractions for sky condition

9. Temperature and dew point—the air temperature and dew point are always given in degrees Celsius (C) or (18/17). Temperatures below 0°C are preceded by the letter "M" to indicate minus.

10. Altimeter setting—reported as inches of mercury ("Hg) in a four-digit number group (A2970). It is always preceded by the letter "A." Rising or falling pressure may also be denoted in the "Remarks" sections as "PRESRR" or "PRESFR," respectively.

11. Zulu time—a term used in aviation for UTC, which places the entire world on one time standard.

12. Remarks—the remarks section always begins with the letters "RMK." Comments may or may not appear in this section of the METAR. The information contained in this section may include wind data, variable visibility, beginning and ending times of particular phenomenon, pressure information, and various other information deemed necessary. An example of a remark regarding weather phenomenon that does not fit in any other category would be: OCNL LTGICCG. This translates as

occasional lightning in the clouds and from cloud to ground. Automated stations also use the remarks section to indicate the equipment needs maintenance.

Example:

METAR KGGG 161753Z AUTO 14021G26KT 3/4SM +TSRA BR BKN008 OVC012CB 18/17 A2970 RMK PRESFR

Explanation:

Routine METAR for Gregg County Airport for the 16th day of the month at 1753Z automated source. Winds are 140 at 21 knots gusting to 26. Visibility is ¾ statute mile. Thunderstorms with heavy rain and mist. Ceiling is broken at 800 feet, overcast at 1,200 feet with cumulonimbus clouds. Temperature 18 °C and dew point 17 °C. Barometric pressure is 29.70 "Hg and falling rapidly.

Aviation Forecasts

Observed weather condition reports are often used in the creation of forecasts for the same area. A variety of different forecast products are produced and designed to be used in the preflight planning stage. The printed forecasts that pilots need to be familiar with are the TAF, inflight weather advisories such as Significant Meteorological Information (SIGMET) and Airman's Meteorological Information (AIRMET), and the winds and temperatures aloft forecast (FB).

Terminal Aerodrome Forecasts (TAF)

A TAF is a report established for the 5 SM radius around an airport. TAF reports are usually given for larger airports. Each TAF is valid for a 24- or 30-hour time period and is updated four times a day at 0000Z, 0600Z, 1200Z, and 1800Z. The TAF utilizes the same descriptors and abbreviations as used in the METAR report. These weather reports can be beneficial to the remote pilot for flight planning purposes. The TAF includes the following information in sequential order:

1. Type of report—a TAF can be either a routine forecast (TAF) or an amended forecast (TAF AMD).
2. ICAO station identifier—the station identifier is the same as that used in a METAR.
3. Date and time of origin—time and date (081125Z) of TAF origination is given in the sixnumber code with the first two being the date, the last four being the time. Time is always given in UTC as denoted by the Z following the time block.
4. Valid period dates and times—The TAF valid period (0812/0912) follows the date/time of forecast origin group. Scheduled 24 and 30 hour TAFs are issued four times per day, at 0000, 0600, 1200, and 1800Z. The first two digits (08) are the day of the month for the start of the TAF. The next two digits (12) are the starting hour (UTC). 09 is the day of the month for the end of the TAF, and the last two digits (12) are the ending hour (UTC) of the valid period. A forecast period that begins at midnight UTC is annotated as 00. If the end time of a valid period is at midnight UTC, it is annotated as 24. For example, a 00Z TAF issued on the 9th of the month and valid for 24 hours would have a valid period of 0900/0924.
5. Forecast wind—the wind direction and speed forecast are coded in a five-digit number group. An example would be 15011KT. The first three digits indicate the direction of the wind in reference to true north. The last two digits state the wind speed in knots appended with "KT." Like the METAR, winds greater than 99 knots are given in three digits.
6. Forecast visibility—given in statute miles and may be in whole numbers or fractions. If the forecast is greater than six miles, it is coded as "P6SM."
7. Forecast significant weather—weather phenomena are coded in the TAF reports in the same format as the METAR.

Chapter 3 **Weather**

8. Forecast sky condition—given in the same format as the METAR. Only CB clouds are forecast in this portion of the TAF report as opposed to CBs and towering cumulus in the METAR.

9. Forecast change group—for any significant weather change forecast to occur during the TAF time period, the expected conditions and time period are included in this group. This information may be shown as from (FM), and temporary (TEMPO). "FM" is used when a rapid and significant change, usually within an hour, is expected. "TEMPO" is used for temporary fluctuations of weather, expected to last less than 1 hour.

10. PROB30—a given percentage that describes the probability of thunderstorms and precipitation occurring in the coming hours. This forecast is not used for the first 6 hours of the 24-hour forecast.

Example:

TAF KPIR 111130Z 1112/1212 15012KT P6SM BKN090 TEMPO 1112/1114 5SM BR FM1500 16015G25KT P6SM SCT040 BKN250 FM120000 14012KT P6SM BKN080 OVC150 PROB30 1200/1204 3SM TSRA BKN030CB FM120400 1408KT P6SM SCT040 OVC080 TEMPO 1204/1208 3SM TSRA OVC030CB

Explanation:

Routine TAF for Pierre, South Dakota...on the 11th day of the month, at 1130Z...valid for 24 hours from 1200Z on the 11th to 1200Z on the 12th...wind from 150° at 12 knots... visibility greater than 6 SM...broken clouds at 9,000 feet... temporarily, between 1200Z and 1400Z, visibility 5 SM in mist...from 1500Z winds from 160° at 15 knots, gusting to 25 knots visibility greater than 6 SM...clouds scattered at 4,000 feet and broken at 25,000 feet...from 0000Z wind from 140° at 12 knots...visibility greater than 6 SM... clouds broken at 8,000 feet, overcast at 15,000 feet...between 0000Z and 0400Z, there is 30 percent probability of visibility 3 SM...thunderstorm with moderate rain showers...clouds broken at 3,000 feet with cumulonimbus clouds...from 0400Z...winds from 140° at 8 knots...visibility greater than 6 miles... clouds at 4,000 scattered and overcast at 8,000... temporarily between 0400Z and 0800Z...visibility 3 miles... thunderstorms with moderate rain showers...clouds overcast at 3,000 feet with cumulonimbus clouds...end of report (=).

Convective Significant Meteorological Information (WST)

Convective SIGMETs are issued for severe thunderstorms with surface winds greater than 50 knots, hail at the surface greater than or equal to ¾ inch in diameter, or tornadoes. They are also issued to advise pilots of embedded thunderstorms, lines of thunderstorms, or thunderstorms with heavy or greater precipitation that affect 40 percent or more of a 3,000 square mile or greater region. A remote pilot will find these weather alerts helpful for flight planning.

1179. Which statement is true concerning ASOS/AWOS weather reporting systems?

A—Each AWOS station is part of a nationwide network of weather reporting stations.
B—ASOS locations perform weather observing functions necessary to generate METAR reports.
C—Both ASOS and AWOS have the capability of reporting density altitude, as long as it exceeds the airport elevation by more than 1,000 feet.

ASOS is designed to support aviation operations and weather forecast activities. The ASOS will provide continuous minute-by-minute observations and perform the basic observing functions necessary to generate a METAR and other aviation weather information. (UA. III.A.K5) — AIM ¶7-1-10

Answer (A) is incorrect because selected individual systems may be incorporated into nationwide data collection and dissemination networks. Answer (C) is incorrect because only the AWOS has the capability of reporting density altitude.

1180. (Refer to Figure 12.) The wind direction and velocity at KJFK is from:

A—180° true at 4 knots.
B—180° magnetic at 4 knots.
C—040° true at 18 knots

The wind is reported as a five-digit group (six digits if speed is over 99 knots). The first three digits is the direction the wind is blowing from rounded to the nearest tens of degrees relative to true (not magnetic) north, or "VRB" if the direction is variable. The next two digits is the speed in knots, or if over 99 knots, the next three digits. If the wind is gusty, it is reported as a "G" after the speed followed by the highest gust reported. The abbreviation "KT" is appended to denote the use of knots for wind speed. The wind group for KJFK is 18004KT which means the wind is from 180° at 4 knots. (UA. III.A.K2) — FAA-H-8083-28

1181. (Refer to Figure 12.) What are the current conditions for Chicago Midway Airport (KMDW)?

A—Sky 700 feet overcast, visibility 1-1/2 SM, rain.
B—Sky 7,000 feet overcast, visibility 1-1/2 SM, heavy rain.
C—Sky 700 feet overcast, visibility 11, occasionally 2 SM, with rain.

The current conditions at KMDW are 1-1/2 SM visibility (1-1/2 SM) with rain (RA), ceiling overcast at 700 feet (OVC007). (UA.III.A.K2) — FAA-H-8083-28

1182. (Refer to Figure 15.) In the TAF for KMEM, what does "SHRA" stand for?

A—Rain showers.
B—A shift in wind direction is expected.
C—A significant change in precipitation is possible.

"SH" stands for showers, and "RA" stands for rain. (UA. III.A.K3) — FAA-H-8083-28

Answers (B) and (C) are incorrect because a permanent change in existing conditions during the valid period of the TAF is indicated by the change groups FMHH (FroM) and BECMG (BECoMinG) HHhh.

1183. (Refer to Figure 15.) Between 1000Z and 1200Z the visibility at KMEM is forecast to be

A—1/2 statute mile.
B—3 statute miles.
C—6 statute miles.

Between 1000Z and 1200Z, the visibility at KMEM is forecast to be 3 statute miles (BECMG 1012…3SM). (UA.III.A.K3) — FAA-H-8083-28

1184. (Refer to Figure 15.) What is the forecast wind for KMEM from 1600Z until the end of the forecast?

A—No significant wind.
B—Variable in direction at 4 knots.
C—Variable in direction at 6 knots.

From 1600Z until the end of the forecast, wind will be variable in direction at 6 knots (VRB06KT). (UA.III.A.K3) — FAA-H-8083-28

1185. (Refer to Figure 15.) According to the KMEM forecast, what is the earliest time on the 12th (today) at which the visibility may be reduced below the 3 SM minimum for sUAS operations?

A—1720Z
B—2200Z
C—2000Z

Between 2000Z and 2200Z there is a 40% probability (PROB) that the visibility will drop to 1 SM due to a thunderstorm (TS) and moderate rain (RA). (UA.III.A.K3) — FAA-H-8083-28

Answers

1179 [B] 1180 [A] 1181 [A] 1182 [A] 1183 [B] 1184 [C]
1185 [C]

1311. What will a convective SIGMET be issued for?
A—Squall line thunderstorms.
B—Visibility less than 3 miles.
C—Surface winds greater than 40 knots.

Any convective SIGMET implies severe or greater turbulence, severe icing, and low-level wind shear. The forecast may be issued for any of the following—severe thunderstorms due to:

1. *Surface winds greater than or equal to 50 knots, or*
2. *Hail at the surface greater than or equal to 3/4 inch in diameter, or*
3. *Tornadoes, embedded thunderstorms, lines of thunderstorms.*

(UA.III.A.K1) — FAA-H-8083-28

1292. (Refer to Figure 12.) The remarks section for KMDW has "RAB35" listed. This entry means
A—blowing mist has reduced the visibility to 1-1/2 SM.
B—rain began at 1835Z.
C—the barometer has risen .35 "Hg.

The entry RAB35 means that rain began 35 minutes past the hour. (UA.III.A.K2) — FAA-H-8083-28

Answer (A) is incorrect because mist is reported as BR. Answer (C) is incorrect because there is no format for reporting an altimeter change in a METAR.

Answers

1311 [A]   1292 [B]

Chapter 4
Preflight Considerations

Introduction *4–3*

Determining Speed and Altitude *4–4*

Loading *4–6*

    Computing Weight and Balance *4–7*

Load Factor *4–8*

Stalls *4–10*

Performance *4–12*

Physiology *4–14*

Maintenance and Inspection Procedures *4–18*

Chapter 4 Loading and Performance

Introduction

The remote PIC is responsible for ensuring the sUAS is in a condition for safe operation. Part of this involves checking for proper loading, so that the device operates to the expected performance standards.

Prior to each flight, the remote PIC must ensure that any object attached to or carried by the small unmanned aircraft is secure and does not adversely affect the flight characteristics or controllability of the aircraft. For example, some sUA do not have a set holder or slot for the battery; instead, it is simply attached with hook-and-loop or other type of fastener. This allows some leeway on the lateral and longitudinal location of the battery on the sUA. Remote pilots should ensure the battery is installed in the proper location so it does not adversely affect the controllability of the aircraft. The attachments must be secure so the battery does not move during flight. Similar concerns exist and cautions advised if any external attachments are installed. Also be sure to close and lock (if applicable) all panels or doors.

Follow all manufacturer recommendations for evaluating performance to ensure safe and efficient operation. This manufacturer information may include operational performance details for the aircraft such as launch, climb, range, endurance, descent, and landing. It is important to understand the significance of the operational data to be able to make practical use of the aircraft's capabilities and limitations. The manufacturer's information regarding performance data is not standardized; availability and how this information is conveyed can vary greatly between sUAS types. If manufacturer-published performance data is unavailable, the remote pilot should seek out performance data that may have already been determined and published by other users of the same sUAS manufacturer model, and use that data as a starting point.

Check weather conditions prior to and during every sUAS flight and consider the effects of weather on aircraft performance.

Airplane flight control systems consist of primary and secondary systems. The ailerons, elevator (or stabilator) and rudder constitute the primary control system and are required to control an airplane safely during flight. Wing flaps, leading edge devices, spoilers and trim systems constitute the secondary control system and improve the performance characteristics of the airplane or relieve the pilot of excessive control forces. See Figure 4-1.

A helicopter has four flight control inputs: cyclic, collective, antitorque pedals, and throttle. The cyclic can vary the pitch of the rotor blades throughout each revolution of the main rotor system to develop lift (thrust). The result is to tilt the rotor disc in a particular direction, resulting in the helicopter moving in that direction.

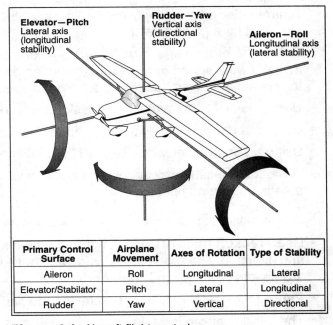

Figure 4-1. Aircraft flight controls

Chapter 4 **Loading and Performance**

1186. Before each flight, the remote PIC must ensure that

A—ATC has granted clearance.
B—the site supervisor has approved the flight.
C—objects carried on the sUAS are secure.

Prior to each flight, the remote PIC must ensure that any object attached to or carried by the small unmanned aircraft is secure and does not adversely affect the flight characteristics or controllability of the aircraft. (UA.I.B.K2) — AC 107-2

1300. What purpose does a rudder perform on an sUAS airplane?

A—The rudder controls yaw.
B—The rudder controls bank.
C—The rudder controls pitch.

The purpose of the rudder is to control yaw. (UA.IV.A.K1b) — FAA-H-8083-25
Answer (B) is incorrect because the ailerons control bank. Answer (C) is incorrect because pitch is controlled by the elevator.

Determining Speed and Altitude

The remote pilot must not exceed these regulatory limitations for operating an sUAS:

- Cannot be flown faster than a ground speed of 87 knots (100 miles per hour).
- Cannot be flown higher than 400 feet AGL unless flown within a 400-foot radius of a structure and is not flown higher than 400 feet above the structure's immediate uppermost limit.

Some of the possible ways to ensure that 87 knots is not exceeded include:

- Installing a GPS device on the sUAS that reports ground speed information to the remote pilot, wherein the remote pilot takes into account the wind direction and speed and calculates the sUAS airspeed for a given direction of flight;
- Timing the ground speed of the sUAS when it is flown between two or more fixed points, taking into account wind speed and direction between each point, then noting the power settings of the sUAS to operate at or less than 87 knots ground speed;
- Using the sUAS manufacturer's design limitations (e.g., installed ground speed limiters);
- Using a radar gun to measure speed of the sUAS;
- Using an anemometer coupled with inertial information from onboard sensors; or
- Using inertial sensors capable of detecting wind speed and velocity as well as sUAS movement to determine ground speed.

These navigation terms are used in aviation as related to ground speed:

- **Dead reckoning** is navigation solely by means of computations based on time, airspeed, distance, and direction. The products derived from these variables, when adjusted by windspeed and velocity, are heading and ground speed.
- **Pilotage** is navigation by reference to landmarks or checkpoints.
- The **wind triangle** is navigation using triangulation. The true heading and the ground speed can be found by drawing a wind triangle of vectors. One side of the triangle is the wind direction and velocity; another side is the true heading and true airspeed, the last side is the track, or true course, and the ground speed. Each side of a wind triangle is the vector sum of the other two sides.

Answers

1186 [C]   1300 [A]

Chapter 4 **Loading and Performance**

Some possible ways for a remote pilot to determine altitude above the ground or structure are as follows:

- Install a calibrated altitude reporting device on the sUAS that reports the sUAS altitude above mean sea level to the remote pilot, wherein the remote pilot subtracts the MSL elevation of the control station from the sUAS-reported MSL altitude to determine the sUAS altitude above the terrain or structure.
- Install a GPS device on the sUAS that also has the capability of reporting MSL altitude to the remote pilot (note that there may be minor errors associated with using this type of altitude reporting).
- With the sUAS on the ground, have the remote pilot and VO pace off 400 feet from the sUAS to get a visual perspective of the sUAS at that distance, wherein the remote pilot and VO maintain that visual perspective or closer while the sUAS is in flight.
- Use the known height of local rising terrain and/or structures as a reference.
- If the control station has a measure of distance between it and the sUA, fly directly overhead until reaching 400 feet and note the visual perspective.

In addition to local resources, the Sectional Chart for that region should be consulted for information on the altitude of the terrain and structures. Towers and other known obstructions are depicted with their altitude noted. It is critical to understand that altitude dimensions of airspace depicted on Sectional Charts are in MSL; remote pilots must be careful to properly convert between AGL and MSL as applicable to their equipment, operation, and regulation restrictions. See Legend 1 in the CT-8080-2.

1187. You are operating an sUAS that does not have GPS or an installed ground speed limiter. How can you determine the speed you are operating?

A—Dead reckoning.
B—Pilotage.
C—Wind triangle.

Without a GPS or manufacturer performance data, you can determine speed by timing the ground speed of the sUAS when it is flown between two or more fixed points, taking into account wind speed and direction between each point, then noting the power settings of the sUAS to operate at or less than 87 knots ground speed. This is a form of dead reckoning. (UA.IV.A.K2) — FAA-H-8083-25, AC 107-2

Answer (B) is incorrect because pilotage will help with navigating the Sectional Chart but cannot be used to determine ground speed. Answer (C) is incorrect because the wind triangle requires that you know true airspeed to determine ground speed; without instrumentation installed on the sUAS you won't have that information.

1188. How can a remote pilot determine the altitude of the terrain and structures where the flight will be conducted?

A—Sectional Chart.
B—Manufacturers data.
C—Road maps.

Refer to Legend 1. In addition to local resources, the sectional chart for that region should be consulted for information on the altitude of the terrain and structures. Towers and other known obstructions are depicted with their altitude noted. (UA.V.B.K6a) — Sectional Chart

1189. You are operating an sUAS that does not have GPS or an installed altimeter. How can you determine the altitude you are operating?

A—Gaining a visual perspective of what 400 feet looks like on the ground before the flight.
B—Operating a second sUAS that has an altimeter to gain a visual perspective of 400 feet from the air.
C—Operating the sUAS in close proximity of a tower known to be 400 feet tall.

To determine altitude, with the sUAS on the ground, the remote pilot and VO should pace off 400 feet from the sUAS to get a visual perspective of the sUAS at that distance, wherein the remote pilot and VO maintain that visual perspective or closer while the sUAS is in flight. (UA.IV.A.K2) — AC 107-2

Answer (B) is incorrect because a person may not operate or act as a remote PIC or VO in the operation of more than one UA at the same time. Answer (C) is incorrect because the remote PIC needs to adhere to wire strike avoidance procedures when operating near towers, which are likely to have guy wires.

Answers

1187 [A]   1188 [A]   1189 [A]

Loading

As with any aircraft, compliance with weight and balance limits is critical to the safety of flight for sUAS. An unmanned aircraft that is loaded out of balance may exhibit unexpected and unsafe flight characteristics. An overweight condition may cause problematic control or performance limitations. Before any flight, verify that the unmanned aircraft is correctly loaded by determining the weight and balance condition.

- Review any available manufacturer weight and balance data and follow all restrictions and limitations.
- If the manufacturer does not provide specific weight and balance data, apply general weight and balance principals to determine limits for a given flight. For example, add weight in a manner that does not adversely affect the aircraft's **center of gravity (CG)** location—a point at which the sUA would balance if it were suspended at that point. Usually this is located near the geographical center of multi-copters but may vary along the centerline of the fuselage of fixed-wing and single-rotor sUA.

Although a maximum gross launch weight may be specified, the aircraft may not always safely take off with this load under all conditions. Or if it does become airborne, the unmanned aircraft may exhibit unexpected and unusually poor flight characteristics. Conditions that affect launch and climb performance, such as high elevations, high air temperatures, and high humidity (high density altitudes) as well as windy conditions may require a reduction in weight before flight is attempted. Other factors to consider prior to launch are runway/launch area length, surface, slope, surface wind, and the presence of obstacles. These factors may require a reduction in weight prior to flight.

Weight changes during flight also have a direct effect on aircraft performance. Fuel burn is the most common weight change that takes place during flight. As fuel is used, the aircraft becomes lighter and performance is improved, but this could have a negative effect on balance. For battery-powered sUAS operations, weight change during flight may occur when expendable items are used on board (e.g., a jettisonable load such as an agricultural spray). Changes of mounted equipment between flights, such as the installation of different cameras, battery packs, or other instruments may also affect the weight and balance and performance of an sUAS.

Adverse balance conditions (i.e., weight distribution) may affect flight characteristics in much the same manner as an excess weight condition. Limits for the location of the CG may be established by the manufacturer and may be covered in the pilot operating handbook (POH) or sUAS flight manual. The CG is not a fixed point marked on the aircraft; its location depends on the distribution of aircraft weight. As variable load items are shifted or expended, there may be a resultant shift in CG location. The remote PIC should determine how the CG will shift and the resultant effects on the aircraft. If the CG is not within the allowable limits after loading or do not remain within the allowable limits for safe flight, it will be necessary to relocate or shed some weight before flight is attempted.

Excessive weight reduces the flight performance in almost every respect. In addition, operating above the maximum weight limitation can compromise the structural integrity of an sUA. The most common performance deficiencies of an overloaded aircraft are:

- Reduced rate of climb;
- Lower maximum altitude;
- Shorter endurance; and
- Reduced maneuverability.

Prior to conducting a mission or extended flight, it is recommended to test-fly the sUA to determine if there are any unexpected performance issues due to loading. This testing should be done away from obstacles and people.

Computing Weight and Balance

The **empty weight** is obtained from manufacturers' documentation. It includes the airframe, power source, all fixed equipment, and unusable fuel. The **useful load** includes the power source (battery or fuel) and payload or mission equipment (such as a camera). The launch weight is the empty weight plus the useful load. The landing weight is the launch weight minus any fuel used or jettisoned load.

The **arm** is the horizontal distance measured in inches from the datum line (a reference point along the longitudinal axis indicated by the manufacturer) to a point on the sUAS. If measured aft, toward the defined rear of the aircraft, the arm is given a positive (+) value; if measured forward, toward the defined front, the arm is given a negative (-) value.

The **moment** is the product of the weight of an object multiplied by its arm and is expressed in pound-inches (lbs-in). The moment is essentially a force being applied at a location along the longitudinal axis, which must be countered by the control capabilities of the aircraft. If moment(s) exceed the control capacity of the aircraft, it becomes unstable or uncontrollable. The formula that is used to find moment is usually expressed as follows: Weight × Arm = Moment.

The CG is the point about which an aircraft will balance, and it is expressed in inches from datum. The CG is found by dividing the total moment by the total weight, and the formula is usually expressed as follows: Total Moment = CG (inches aft of datum) / Total Weight.

Lateral CG is also important (measured along the horizontal axis). Uneven distribution of weight on one side of the aircraft versus the other may cause controllability and/or performance issues.

1190. When loading cameras or other equipment on an sUAS, mount the items in a manner that

A—is visible to the visual observer or other crewmembers.
B—does not adversely affect the center of gravity.
C—can be easily removed without the use of tools.

Any mounted equipment should be balanced in a manner that does not adversely affect the CG or result in unsafe performance. (UA.IV.A.K1) — AC 107-2

1191. To ensure that the unmanned aircraft center of gravity (CG) limits are not exceeded, follow the aircraft loading instructions specified in the

A—Aircraft Weight and Balance Handbook.
B—Pilot's Operating Handbook or sUAS Flight Manual.
C—Aeronautical Information Manual (AIM).

Before any flight, verify that the unmanned aircraft is correctly loaded by determining the weight and balance condition. Review any available manufacturer weight and balance data and follow all restrictions and limitations. (UA.IV.A.K2) — FAA-H-8083-1

1192. What could be a consequence of operating a small unmanned aircraft above its maximum allowable weight?

A—Shorter endurance.
B—Increased maneuverability.
C—Faster speed.

Excessive weight reduces the flight performance in almost every respect, including a shorter endurance. In addition, operating above the maximum weight limitation can compromise the structural integrity of an unmanned aircraft. (UA.IV.A.K2) — AC 107-2

1193. When operating an aircraft, the remote PIC is responsible for using

A—the most current weight and balance data.
B—weight and balance data from the factory.
C—recent weight and balance data.

It is the responsibility of the remote PIC to use the most current weight and balance data when planning a flight and operating the sUAS. (UA.IV.A.K2) — FAA-H-8083-1

Answers

1190 [B]   1191 [B]   1192 [A]   1193 [A]

Chapter 4 **Loading and Performance**

1194. Which of the following is true regarding weight and balance of small unmanned aircraft?
A—CG cannot change during flight.
B—Lateral CG is not important to small unmanned aircraft operations.
C—Operations outside weight and balance limitations may result in loss of control.

Loading the aircraft outside of limitations (weight, balance, or both) may lead to moments that exceed the capabilities of the flight controls/engine(s), thus possibly leading to loss of control or other performance anomalies. (UA.IV.A.K1b) — FAA-H8083-1

1293. A small unmanned aircraft loaded with the most rearward center of gravity is
A—less stable at all speeds.
B—more stable at slow speeds.
C—more stable at fast speeds.

Operation with the CG outside the approved limits results in control difficulty. (UA.IV.A.K1a) — FAA-H-8083-25

Load Factor

In aerodynamics, **load** is the force or imposed stress that must be supported by an sUA structure in flight. The loads imposed on the wings or rotors in flight are stated in terms of **load factor**. In straight-and-level flight, the sUAS wings/rotors support a load equal to the sum of the weight of the sUAS plus its contents. This particular load factor is equal to 1 G, where "G" refers to the pull of gravity. However, centrifugal force is generated which acts toward the outside of the curve any time an sUAS is flying a curved path (turns, climbs, or descents).

Unmanned aircraft performance can be decreased due to an increase in load factor when the aircraft is operated in maneuvers other than straight and level flight. The load factor increases at a significant rate after a bank (turn) has reached 45° or 50°. The load factor for any aircraft in a coordinated level turn at 60° bank is 2 Gs. The load factor in an 80° bank is 5.75 Gs. See Figure 4-2. The wing must produce lift equal to these load factors if altitude is to be maintained. The remote PIC should be mindful of the increased load factor and its possible effects on the aircraft's structural integrity and the results of an increase in stall speed. These principles apply to both fixed-wing and rotor-wing designs, but in the case of rotor-wing unmanned aircraft, the weight/load must be supported by the lift generated by the propellers.

As with manned aircraft, an unmanned aircraft will stall when critical angle of attack of the wing or rotors/propeller is exceeded. This can occur when an unmanned aircraft is turned too sharply/tightly or pitched up too steeply or rapidly. Remote pilots of rotor type unmanned aircraft should use particular caution when descending in a vertical straight line. In some cases, the turbulent downward airflow can disrupt the normal production of lift by the propellers as well as cause problematic air circulation producing vortices. These phenomena are referred to as vortex ring state or settling with power, and when they occur the aircraft can wobble, descend rapidly, or become uncontrollable. Recovery from this state of flight requires forward or rearward motion—counterintuitively, the addition of power to arrest the descent only makes the situation worse. Due to the low-altitude operating environment, consideration should be given to ensure aircraft control is maintained and the aircraft is not operated outside its performance limits.

Figure 4-2. Load factor chart

Answers

1194 [C]   1293 [A]

Chapter 4 **Loading and Performance**

1195. When operating an unmanned aircraft, the remote pilot-in-command should consider that the load factor on the wings or rotors may be increased anytime

A—the aircraft is subjected to maneuvers other than straight and level flight.
B—the CG is shifted rearward to the aft CG limit.
C—the gross weight is reduced.

Unmanned aircraft performance can be decreased due to an increase in load factor when the aircraft is operated in maneuvers other than straight-and-level flight. (UA.IV.A.K1a) — FAA-H-8083-25

1196. (Refer to Figure 2.) If an sUAS weighs 10 pounds, what approximate weight would the sUAS structure be required to support during a 60° banked turn while maintaining altitude?

A—10.15 pounds.
B—30 pounds.
C—20 pounds.

Refer to Figure 2 and use the following steps:

1. Enter the chart at a 60° angle of bank and proceed upward to the curved reference line. From the point of intersection, move to the left side of the chart and read a load factor of 2 Gs.

2. Multiply the aircraft weight by the load factor: 10 × 2 = 20 lbs. Or, working from the table: 10 × 2.0 (load factor) = 20 lbs.

(UA.IV.A.K1a) — FAA-H-8083-25

1197. (Refer to Figure 2.) If an sUAS weighs 50 pounds, what approximate weight would the sUAS structure be required to support during a 30° banked turn while maintaining altitude?

A—60 pounds.
B—45 pounds.
C—30 pounds.

Referencing Figure 2, use the following steps:

1. Enter the chart at a 30° angle of bank and proceed upward to the curved reference line. From the point of intersection, move to the left side of the chart and read an approximate load factor of 1.2 Gs.

2. Multiply the aircraft weight by the load factor: 50 × 1.2 = 60 lbs. Or, working from the table: 50 1.154 (load factor) = 57.7 lbs.

(UA.IV.A.K1a) — FAA-H-8083-25

Answers (B) and (C) are incorrect because they are less than 50 pounds; load factor increases with bank for level flight.

1198. (Refer to Figure 2.) If an unmanned airplane weighs 33 pounds, what approximate weight would the airplane structure be required to support during a 30° banked turn while maintaining altitude?

A—34 pounds.
B—47 pounds.
C—38 pounds.

Referencing Figure 2, use the following steps:

1. Enter the chart at a 30° angle of bank and proceed upward to the curved reference line. From the point of intersection, move to the left side of the chart and read an approximate load factor of 1.2 Gs.

2. Multiply the aircraft weight by the load factor: 33 × 1.2 = 39.6 lbs. Or, working from the table: 33 × 1.154 (load factor) = 38.1 lbs.

(UA.IV.A.K1a) — FAA-H-8083-25

1199. The amount of excess load that can be imposed on the wing of an airplane depends upon the

A—position of the CG.
B—speed of the airplane.
C—abruptness at which the load is applied.

At slow speeds, the maximum available lifting force of the wing is only slightly greater than the amount necessary to support the weight of the sUAS. However, at high speeds, the capacity of the flight controls, or a strong gust, may increase the load factor beyond safe limits. (UA.IV.A.K1a) — FAA-H-8083-25

Answer (A) is incorrect because the position of the CG affects the stability of the sUAS, but not the total load the wings can support. Answer (C) is incorrect because abrupt control inputs do not limit load.

Answers

1195 [A]   1196 [C]   1197 [A]   1198 [C]   1199 [B]

Chapter 4 **Loading and Performance**

1200. Which basic flight maneuver increases the load factor on an sUAS as compared to straight-and-level flight?
A—Climbs.
B—Turns.
C—Stalls.

A change in speed during straight flight will not produce any appreciable change in load, but when a change is made in the sUAS flight path an additional load is imposed upon the structure. This is particularly true if a change in direction is made at high speeds with rapid, forceful control movements. (UA.IV.A.K1a) — FAA-H-8083-25

Answer (A) is incorrect because the load increases only as the angle of attack is changed, momentarily. Once the climb attitude has been set, the wings only carry the load produced by the weight of the aircraft. Answer (C) is incorrect because in a stall, the wings are not producing lift.

Stalls

An **airfoil** is a structure or body that produces a useful reaction to air movement. Airplane wings, helicopter rotor blades, and propellers are airfoils. The **chord line** is an imaginary straight line from the leading edge to the trailing edge of an airfoil. In aerodynamics, **relative wind** is the wind "felt" or experienced by an airfoil. It is created by the movement of air past an airfoil, by the motion of an airfoil through the air, or by a combination of the two. Relative wind is parallel to, and in the opposite direction of the flight path of the airfoil. The **angle of attack** is the angle between the chord line of the airfoil and the relative wind. Angle of attack is directly related to the generation of lift by an airfoil. See Figures 4-3 through 4-6.

As the angle of attack is increased (to increase lift), the air will no longer flow smoothly over the upper airfoil surface but instead will become turbulent or "burble" near the trailing edge. A further increase in the angle of attack will cause the turbulent area to expand forward. At an angle of attack of approximately 18° to 20° (for most airfoils), turbulence over the upper wing surface decreases lift so drastically that flight cannot be sustained and the airfoil stalls. See Figure 4-7. The angle at which a stall occurs is called the **critical angle of attack**. An unmanned aircraft can stall at any airspeed or any attitude, but will always stall at the same critical angle of attack. The critical angle of attack of an airfoil is a function of its design therefore does not change based upon weight, maneuvering, or density altitude. However, the airspeed (strength of the relative wind) at which a given aircraft will stall in a particular configuration will remain the same regardless of altitude.

Because air density decreases with an increase in altitude, an unmanned aircraft must have greater forward speed to encounter the same strength of relative wind as would be experienced with the thicker air at lower altitudes. An easier way to envision this concept is to imagine how many molecules of air pass over an airfoil per second—thicker air at lower altitudes has more air molecules for a given area than the thinner air at higher altitudes. In order to successfully keep an aircraft aloft, a minimum number of air molecules must pass over the airfoil per second. As fewer molecules are available to make the journey as altitude increases, the only way to ensure that the aircraft can stay aloft is to increase its forward speed, thus forcing more air molecules over the airfoil each second.

Answers
1200 [B]

Chapter 4 **Loading and Performance**

Figure 4-3. A typical airfoil cross-section

Figure 4-4. Chord line

Figure 4-5. Relative wind

Figure 4-6. Angle of attack

Figure 4-7. Flow of air over wing at various angles of attack

Remote Pilot Test Prep ASA **4–11**

Chapter 4 **Loading and Performance**

1201. The term "angle of attack" is defined as the angle

A—between the wing chord line and the relative wind.
B—between the airplane's climb angle and the horizon.
C—formed by the longitudinal axis of the airplane and the chord line of the wing.

The angle of attack is the acute angle between the relative wind and the chord line of the wing. (UA.IV.A.K1b) — FAA-H-8083-25

Answer (B) is incorrect because there is no specific aviation term for this. Answer (C) is incorrect because this is the definition of the angle of incidence.

1202. The angle of attack at which an airfoil stalls will

A—increase if the CG is moved forward.
B—remain the same regardless of gross weight.
C—change with an increase in gross weight.

When the angle of attack is increased to between 18° and 20° (critical angle of attack) on most airfoils, the airstream can no longer follow the upper curvature of the wing because of the excessive change in direction. The airfoil will stall if the critical angle of attack is exceeded. The airspeed at which stall occurs will be determined by weight and load factor, but the stall angle of attack is the same. (UA.IV.A.K1b) — FAA-H-8083-25

1203. A stall occurs when the smooth airflow over the unmanned aircraft's wing/propeller(s) is disrupted, and the lift degenerates rapidly. This is caused when the wing/propeller(s)

A—exceeds maximum allowable operating weight.
B—exceeds the maximum speed.
C—exceeds its critical angle of attack.

The airfoil will stall if the critical angle of attack is exceeded. (UA.IV.A.K1b) — FAA-H-8083-3

Answer (A) is incorrect because while exceeding the maximum allowable operating weight could compromise the structural integrity and decrease controllability, it does not necessarily result in a stall. Answer (B) is incorrect because while the remote pilot may not fly faster than 87 knots (100 mph) or the manufacturer recommended maximum speed, exceeding these do not necessarily result in a stall.

1204. An increase in load factor will cause an unmanned aircraft to

A—stall at a higher airspeed.
B—have a tendency to spin.
C—be more difficult to control.

Stall speed increases in proportion to the square root of the load factor. Thus, with a load factor of 4, an aircraft will stall at a speed which is double the normal stall speed. (UA.IV.A.K1b) — FAA-H-8083-25

Answer (B) is incorrect because an airplane's tendency to spin does not relate to an increase in load factors. Answer (C) is incorrect because an airplane's stability determines its controllability.

1314. In a 45° banking turn, a small unmanned aircraft will

A—be more susceptible to spinning.
B—stall at a higher airspeed.
C—stall at a lower airspeed.

Stall speed increases in proportion to the square root of the load factor. Thus, with a load factor of 4, an aircraft will stall at a speed which is double the normal stall speed. (UA.IV.A.K1b) — FAA-H-8083-25

Performance

Performance or operational information may be provided by the manufacturer in the form of pilot's operating handbook, owner's manual, or on the manufacturer's website. Follow all manufacturer recommendations for evaluating performance to ensure safe and efficient operation. Even when specific performance data is not provided, the remote PIC should be familiar with:

- The operating environment.
- All available information regarding the safe and recommended operation of the sUAS.
- Conditions that may impact the performance or controllability of the sUAS.

Even when operational data is not supplied by the manufacturer, the remote PIC can better understand the unmanned aircraft's capabilities and limitations by establishing a process for tracking malfunctions,

Answers

1201 [A]   1202 [B]   1203 [C]   1204 [A]   1314 [B]

Chapter 4 **Loading and Performance**

defects, and flight characteristics in various environments and conditions. Use this operational data to establish a baseline for determining performance, reliability, and risk assessment for your particular system.

The remote PIC is responsible for ensuring that every flight can be accomplished safely, does not pose an undue hazard, and does not increase the likelihood of a loss of positive control. Consider how your decisions affect the safety of flight. For example:

- If you attempt flight in windy conditions, the unmanned aircraft may require an unusually high power setting to maneuver. This action may cause a rapid depletion of battery power and result in a failure mode.
- If you attempt flight in wintery weather conditions, ice may accumulate on the unmanned aircraft's surface. Ice increases the weight and adversely affects performance characteristics of the small unmanned aircraft.

Due to the diversity and rapidly evolving nature of sUAS operations, individual remote PICs have flexibility to determine what equipage methods, if any, mitigate risk sufficiently to meet performance-based requirements, such as the prohibition against creating an undue hazard if there is a loss of aircraft control.

1205. According to 14 CFR Part 107, who is responsible for determining the performance of a small unmanned aircraft?

A—Remote pilot-in-command.
B—Manufacturer.
C—Owner or operator.

The remote PIC is responsible for ensuring that every flight can be accomplished safely, does not pose an undue hazard, and does not increase the likelihood of a loss of positive control. (UA.I.B.K4) — 14 CFR §107.12

1206. What effect does an uphill terrain slope have on launch performance?

A—Increases launch speed.
B—Increases launch distance.
C—Decreases launch distance.

The effect of runway slope on launch distance is due to the component of weight along the inclined path of the aircraft. An upslope would contribute a retarding force component, while a downslope would contribute an accelerating force component. In the case of an upslope, the retarding force component adds to drag and rolling friction to reduce the net accelerating force. (UA.IV.A.K2) — FAA-H-8083-25

Answer (A) is incorrect because runway slope has no effect on the launch speed. Answer (C) is incorrect because an upslope will increase the launch distance required.

1207. The most critical conditions of launch performance are the result of some combination of high gross weight, altitude, temperature, and

A—unfavorable wind.
B—obstacles surrounding the launch site.
C—powerplant systems.

The most critical conditions of launch performance are the result of some combination of high gross weight, altitude, temperature, and unfavorable wind. In all cases, the remote pilot must make an accurate prediction of takeoff distance from the performance data of the POH, regardless of the runway available, and strive for polished, professional launch procedures. (UA.III.B.K1b) — FAA-H-8083-25

1208. Maximum endurance is obtained at the point of minimum power to maintain the aircraft

A—in steady, level flight.
B—in a long range descent.
C—at its slowest possible indicated airspeed.

The maximum endurance condition is obtained at the point of minimum power required since this would require the lowest fuel flow or battery to keep the sUAS in steady, level flight. Maximum range condition occurs where the proportion between speed and power required is greatest. (UA.IV.A.K2) — FAA-H-8083-25

Answers

1205 [A]   1206 [B]   1207 [A]   1208 [A]

Chapter 4 **Loading and Performance**

1209. When range and economy of operation are the principle goals, the remote pilot must ensure that the sUAS will be operated at the recommended

A—specific endurance.
B—long-range cruise performance.
C—equivalent airspeed.

Total range is dependent on both fuel available and specific range. When range and economy of operation are the principle goals, the remote pilot must ensure that the sUAS is operated at the recommended long-range cruise condition. By this procedure, the sUAS will be capable of its maximum design-operating radius, or can achieve lesser flight distances with a maximum of fuel reserve at the destination. (UA.IV.A.K2) — FAA-H-8083-25

1210. What is the best source for sUAS performance data and information?

A—Manufacturer publications.
B—Pilot reports.
C—Estimates based upon similar systems.

The manufacturer is the best source of performance data and information, if available. (UA.IV.A.K2) — FAA-H-8083-25

Physiology

Remote pilots are not required to hold a medical certificate. However, no person may manipulate the flight controls of an sUAS or act as a remote PIC, VO, or direct participant in the operation of the sUA if he or she knows or has reason to know that he or she has a physical or mental condition that would interfere with the safe operation of the sUAS. Remote pilots must self-assess their fitness for flight. Pilot performance can be seriously degraded by a number of physiological factors. While some of the factors may be beyond the control of the pilot, awareness of cause and effect can help minimize any adverse effects. At any time a remote PIC determines that they or another crewmember is unfit to operate the sUAS or participate in its operation, the remote PIC should terminate the operation and/or follow contingency plans for such occasions (e.g., incapacitation).

Hyperventilation, a deficiency of carbon dioxide within the body, can be the result of rapid or extra deep breathing due to emotional tension, anxiety, or fear. Symptoms will subside after the rate and depth of breathing are brought under control. A pilot should be able to overcome the symptoms or avoid future occurrences of hyperventilation by talking aloud, breathing into a bag, or slowing the breathing rate.

The sUAS operating environment can be very extreme for crewmembers. It is not uncommon for sUAS operations to take place in hot, dry and dusty locations, which can lead to dehydration and/or heat stroke. Alternatively, sUAS also operate in cold or other conditions that leave crewmembers exposed to the elements that could lead to dehydration and hypothermia. **Dehydration** is the term given to a critical loss of water from the body. Causes of dehydration are environmental conditions, wind, humidity, and diuretic drinks (i.e., coffee, tea, alcohol, and caffeinated soft drinks). Some common signs of dehydration are headache, fatigue, cramps, sleepiness, and dizziness. To help prevent dehydration, drink two to four quarts of water every 24 hours.

Heatstroke is a condition caused by any inability of the body to control its temperature. Onset of this condition may be recognized by the symptoms of dehydration, but also has been known to be recognized only upon complete collapse.

Hypothermia is indicated by shivering, clumsiness, slurred speech, confusion, low energy, discoloration of the skin (red or blue), and loss of consciousness. Remote PICs should ensure that they and their fellow crewmembers are adequately prepared for the planned sUAS operation and the environment in

Answers
1209 [B]   1210 [A]

which this operation is set to take place. Some things to keep in mind are: providing ample water or other hydrating beverages, eye protection, sun protection, insect repellent, warm clothes or clothes suited for heat (whichever is appropriate), support equipment, and any other items deemed necessary for safety and comfort.

Stress is ever present in our lives and you may already be familiar with situations that create stress in aviation. However, sUAS operations may create stressors that differ from manned aviation. Such examples may include: working with an inexperienced crewmember, lack of standard crewmember training, interacting with the public and government officials, and understanding new regulatory requirements. Proper planning for the operation can reduce or eliminate stress, allowing you to focus more clearly on the operation.

Fatigue is frequently associated with pilot error. Some of the effects of fatigue include degradation of attention and concentration, impaired coordination, and decreased ability to communicate. These factors seriously influence the ability to make effective decisions. Physical fatigue results from sleep loss, exercise, or physical work. Factors such as stress and prolonged performance of cognitive work can result in mental fatigue. Fatigue falls into two broad categories: acute and chronic. **Acute fatigue** is short term and is a normal occurrence in everyday living. It is the kind of tiredness people feel after a period of strenuous effort, excitement, or lack of sleep. Rest after exertion and 8 hours of sound sleep ordinarily cures this condition. **Chronic fatigue** is characterized by extreme fatigue or tiredness that doesn't go away with rest, and can't be explained by an underlying medical condition. Chronic fatigue can also occur when there is not enough time for a full recovery from repeated episodes of acute fatigue.

Chronic stress results with longer-term stresses and/or the mismanagement thereof and can result in serious health conditions such as anxiety, high blood pressure, a weakened immune system, depression, confusion, mental errors, insomnia, and memory loss. The best way to cope with chronic stress is to remove stressors as much as practical, take part in physical activity, and/or seek out the advice or care of a healthcare provider.

Vision is the most important body sense for safe flight. Major factors that determine how effectively vision can be used are the level of illumination and the technique of scanning the sky for other aircraft. Atmospheric haze and fog reduces the ability to see traffic or terrain during flight, making all features appear to be farther away than they actually are. Caution is always advised in areas of reduced visibility or low light.

Additionally, the remote PIC and crewmembers should take into account the impact the environment may have on vision, such as location and angle of the sun, the color and texture of the local terrain features, as well as glare from water, buildings, or other objects. Particular caution is advised when operating near terrain features which may make it difficult to distinguish the sUAS from the surrounding environment or may make it difficult to ascertain proper depth perception (e.g., terrain colors similar to the sUA or a large area of trees which may make it more challenging to determine the distance between the unmanned aircraft and the foliage).

Chapter 4 **Loading and Performance**

1254. Who is responsible for determining whether a pilot is fit to fly for a particular flight, even though he or she holds a current medical certificate?

A—The FAA.
B—The medical examiner.
C—The pilot.

The pilot is responsible for determining whether he or she is fit to fly for a particular flight. (UA.V.E.K7) — FAA-H-8083-25

1255. You are a remote pilot-in-command for a co-op energy service provider. You plan to use your unmanned aircraft to inspect powerlines in the remote area 15 hours away from your home office. After the drive, fatigue impacts your abilities to complete your assignment on time. What kind of fatigue is this?

A—Chronic fatigue.
B—Acute fatigue.
C—Exhaustion.

Acute fatigue is short term and is a normal occurrence in everyday living. It is the kind of tiredness people feel after a period of strenuous effort, excitement, or lack of sleep. (UA.V.E.K5) — FAA-H-8083-25

1302. What can affect your performance?

A—Prescription medications.
B—Over-the-counter medications.
C—Over-the-counter and prescribed medications.

Virtually all medications have the potential for adverse side effects in some people. (UA.V.E.K3) — FAA-H-8083-25

1256. Fatigue can be recognized

A—easily by an experienced pilot.
B—as being in an impaired state.
C—by an ability to overcome sleep deprivation.

The fatigued pilot is an impaired pilot, and flying requires unimpaired judgment. (UA.V.E.K5) — FAA-H-8083-2

1257. Fatigue can be either

A—physiological or psychological.
B—physical or mental.
C—acute or chronic.

Fatigue can be either acute (short-term) or chronic (long-term). Acute fatigue, a normal occurrence of everyday living, is the tiredness felt after long periods of physical and mental strain, including strenuous muscular effort, immobility, heavy mental workload, strong emotional pressure, monotony, and lack of sleep. Chronic fatigue occurs when there is not enough time for a full recovery from repeated episodes of acute fatigue. (UA.V.E.K5) — FAA-H-8083-25

1258. Fatigue is one of the most treacherous hazards to flight safety

A—because it results in slow performance.
B—as it may not be apparent until serious errors are made.
C—as it may be a function of physical robustness or mental acuity.

Fatigue is one of the most treacherous hazards to flight safety as it may not be apparent to a pilot until serious errors are made. (UA.V.E.K5) — FAA-H-8083-25

1259. When a stressful situation is encountered in flight, an abnormal increase in the volume of air breathed in and out can cause a condition known as

A—hyperventilation.
B—aerosinusitis.
C—aerotitis.

An abnormal increase in the volume of air breathed in and out of the lungs flushes an excessive amount of carbon dioxide from the lungs and blood, causing hyperventilation. (UA.V.E.K4) — AIM ¶8-1-3

1260. Which would most likely result in hyperventilation?

A—Emotional tension, anxiety, or fear.
B—The excessive consumption of alcohol.
C—An extremely slow rate of breathing and insufficient oxygen.

Hyperventilation is most likely to occur during periods of stress or anxiety. (UA.V.E.K4) — AIM ¶8-1-3

Answers

1254 [C]   1255 [B]   1302 [C]   1256 [B]   1257 [C]   1258 [B]
1259 [A]   1260 [A]

1261. Which will almost always affect your ability to fly?

A—Over-the-counter analgesics and antihistamines.
B—Antibiotics and anesthetic drugs.
C—Prescription analgesics and antihistamines.

Pilot performance can be seriously degraded by both prescribed and OTC medications, as well as by the medical conditions for which they are taken. Flying is almost always precluded while using prescription analgesics since these drugs may cause side effects such as mental confusion, dizziness, headaches, nausea, and vision problems. Depressants, including antihistamines, lower blood pressure, reduce mental processing, and slow motor and reaction responses. (UA.V.E.K3) — FAA-H-8083-25

Answer (A) is incorrect because over-the-counter analgesics such as aspirin, Tylenol® and Advil®, and non-drowsy antihistamines (Claritin®, Allegra®, etc.) have few side effects when taken in the correct dosage. Answer (B) is incorrect because these drugs do not typically limit flying (but the medical conditions for which they are being taken may indeed limit flying activities).

1262. As a pilot, flying for long periods in hot summer temperatures increases the susceptibility of dehydration since the

A—dry air at altitude tends to increase the rate of water loss from the body.
B—moist air at altitude helps retain the body's moisture.
C—temperature decreases with altitude.

As a pilot, flying for long periods in hot summer temperatures or at high altitudes increases the susceptibility of dehydration since the dry air at altitude tends to increase the rate of water loss from the body. If this fluid is not replaced, fatigue progresses to dizziness, weakness, nausea, tingling of hands and feet, abdominal cramps, and extreme thirst. (UA.V.E.K1) — FAA-H-8083-25

1273. Which would most likely result in hyperventilation?

A—Insufficient oxygen.
B—Excessive carbon monoxide.
C—Insufficient carbon dioxide.

As hyperventilation blows off excessive carbon dioxide from the body, a pilot can experience symptoms of lightheadedness, suffocation, drowsiness, tingling of the extremities, and coolness and react to them with even greater hyperventilation. (UA.V.E.K4) — FAA-H-8083-25

Answer (A) is incorrect because insufficient oxygen is a symptom of hypoxia. Answer (B) is incorrect because excessive carbon monoxide will lead to carbon monoxide poisoning.

1263. When setting up the location of the control station and placement of crewmembers for an afternoon flight, which of the following would be most appropriate for ensuring that vision is not impaired by the environment?

A—The operation should be set up so that the remote PIC and crewmembers can face east.
B—The operation should be set up so that the remote PIC and crewmembers can face west.
C—The operation should be set up so that the remote PIC and crewmembers are facing any reflective objects in the area.

If the operation is to take place in the afternoon, the sun will be setting towards the west and could impair the vision of those participating in the sUAS operation. Thus, when practical, the operation should be set up to minimize the impact of the sun on being able to maintain visual line-of-sight with the unmanned aircraft. (UA.V.E.K6) — FAA-H-8083-25, 14 CFR §107.31

Answer (B) is incorrect because persons will have the sun in their eyes. Answer (C) is incorrect because it potentially will present glare or reflections into the eyes of participants.

1297. What can help a pilot mitigate stress?

A—Increasing stress tolerance.
B—Removing stress from personal life.
C—Breathing into a paper bag.

There are several techniques to help manage the accumulation of life stresses and prevent stress overload. For example, to help reduce stress levels, set aside time for relaxation each day or maintain a program of physical fitness. To prevent stress overload, learn to manage time more effectively to avoid pressures imposed by getting behind schedule and not meeting deadlines. (UA.V.E.K5) — FAA-H-8083-25

Answers

1261 [C]   1262 [A]   1273 [C]   1263 [A]   1297 [B]

Chapter 4 **Loading and Performance**

1264. When setting up the location of the control station and placement of crewmembers for a flight over snowy terrain, which of the following would be most appropriate for ensuring that vision is not impaired by the environment?

A—The operation should be set up so that the crewmembers are the most comfortable.
B—The operation should be set up so that the crewmembers will experience the minimum glare from the snow.
C—The operation should be set up so that the crewmembers face the direction in which the terrain most closely matches the color of the unmanned aircraft.

If the operation is to take place in a snow covered environment, awareness concerning how this may impact vision, such as glare or the ability to see and operate the unmanned aircraft against a featureless background. Thus, when practical, the operation should be set up to minimize the impact of the terrain on being able to maintain visual line-of-sight with the unmanned aircraft. (UA.V.E.K6) — FAA-H-8083-25, 14 CFR §107.31

Answer (A) is incorrect because while comfort is important, maintaining visual line-of-sight and positive control over the unmanned aircraft is more critical. Answer (C) is incorrect because it may make it difficult to keep the unmanned aircraft in sight, distinguished from the background, and/or may result in loss of depth perception.

1351. When preparing for a night flight, what should a small unmanned aircraft pilot be aware of after assembling and conducting a preflight of an aircraft while using a bright flashlight or work light?

A—Once adapted to darkness, a person's eyes are relatively immune to bright lights.
B—It takes approximately 30 minutes for a person's eyes to fully adapt to darkness.
C—The person should use a flashlight equipped with LED lights to facilitate their night vision.

When preparing for a night flight, a remote pilot should wait approximately 30 minutes for their eyes to adjust to darkness after exposure to bright light. (UA.V.E.K8) — FAA-H-8083-25

Maintenance and Inspection Procedures

Maintenance for sUAS includes scheduled and unscheduled overhaul, repair, inspection, modification, replacement, and system software upgrades for the unmanned aircraft itself and all components necessary for flight.

Manufacturers may recommend a maintenance or replacement schedule for the unmanned aircraft and system components based on time-in-service limits and other factors. Follow all manufacturer maintenance recommendations to achieve the longest and safest service life of the sUAS. If the sUAS or component manufacturer does not provide scheduled maintenance instructions, it is recommended that you establish your own scheduled maintenance protocol. For example:

- Document any repair, modification, overhaul, or replacement of a system component resulting from normal flight operations.
- Record the time-in-service for that component at the time of the maintenance procedure.
- Assess these records over time to establish a reliable maintenance schedule for the sUAS and its components.

During the course of a preflight inspection, you may discover that an sUAS component requires some form of maintenance outside of the scheduled maintenance period. For example, an sUAS component may require servicing (such as lubrication), repair, modification, overhaul, or replacement as a result

Answers
1264 [B]   1351 [B]

of normal or abnormal flight operations. Or, the sUAS manufacturer or component manufacturer may require an unscheduled system software update to correct a problem. In the event such a condition is found, do not conduct flight operations until the discrepancy is corrected.

In some instances, the sUAS or component manufacturer may require certain maintenance tasks be performed by the manufacturer or by a person or facility specified by the manufacturer; maintenance should be performed in accordance with the manufacturer's instructions. However, if you decide not to use the manufacturer or the personnel recommended by the manufacturer and you are unable to perform the required maintenance yourself, you should:

- Solicit the expertise of maintenance personnel familiar with the specific sUAS and its components.
- Consider using certificated maintenance providers, such as repair stations, holders of mechanic and repairman certificates, and persons working under the supervision of a mechanic or repairman.

If you or the maintenance personnel are unable to repair, modify, or overhaul an sUAS or component back to its safe operational specification, then it is advisable to replace the sUAS or component with one that is in a condition for safe operation. Complete all required maintenance before each flight—preferably in accordance with the manufacturer's instructions or, in lieu of that, within known industry best practices.

Careful recordkeeping can be highly beneficial for sUAS owners and operators. For example, recordkeeping provides essential safety support for commercial operators who may experience rapidly accumulated flight operational hours/cycles. Consider maintaining a hardcopy and/or electronic logbook of all periodic inspections, maintenance, preventative maintenance, repairs, and alterations performed on the sUAS. See Figure 5-6. Such records should include all components of the sUAS, including the:

- Small unmanned aircraft itself;
- Control station;
- Launch and recovery equipment;
- Data link equipment;
- Payload; and
- Any other components required to safely operate the sUAS.

Figure 4-8. A UAS logbook can be used to track remote pilot hours as well as sUAS maintenance

Chapter 4 Loading and Performance

1265. Which of the following sources of information should you consult first when determining what maintenance should be performed on an sUAS or its components?

A—Local pilot best practices.
B—14 CFR Part 107.
C—Manufacturer guidance.

The preferred source of information is the manufacturer's guidance about maintenance schedule and instructions. (UA.V.F.K1) — AC 107-2

1266. Under what condition should the operator of a small unmanned aircraft establish a scheduled maintenance protocol?

A—When the manufacturer does not provide a maintenance schedule.
B—When the FAA requires you to, following an accident.
C—Small unmanned aircraft systems do not require maintenance.

Follow all manufacturer maintenance recommendations to achieve the longest and safest service life of the sUAS. If the sUAS or component manufacturer does not provide scheduled maintenance instructions, it is recommended that you establish your own scheduled maintenance protocol. (UA.V.F.K1) — AC 107-2

1336. What action should the operator of an sUAS take if the manufacturer does not provide information about scheduled maintenance?

A—The operator should contact the FAA for a minimum equipment list.
B—The operator should establish a scheduled maintenance protocol.
C—The operator should contact the NTSB for component failure rates for their specific sUAS.

Follow all manufacturer maintenance recommendations to achieve the longest and safest service life of the sUAS. If the sUAS or component manufacturer does not provide scheduled maintenance instructions, it is recommended that you establish your own scheduled maintenance protocol. (UA.V.F.K1) — AC 107-2

1267. Scheduled maintenance should be performed in accordance with the

A—Manufacturer's suggested procedures.
B—Stipulations in 14 CFR Part 43.
C—Contractor requirements.

Follow all manufacturer maintenance recommendations to achieve the longest and safest service life of the sUAS. If the sUAS or component manufacturer does not provide scheduled maintenance instructions, it is recommended that you establish your own scheduled maintenance protocol. (UA.V.F.K1) — AC 107-2

1268. The responsibility for ensuring that an sUAS is maintained in an airworthy condition is primarily that of the

A—Remote pilot-in-command.
B—owner or operator.
C—mechanic who performs the work.

No person may operate a sUAS unless it is in a condition for safe operation. Prior to each flight, the remote PIC must check the sUAS to determine whether it is in a condition for safe operation. No person may continue flight of the sUA when he or she knows or has reason to know that the sUAS is no longer in a condition for safe operation. (UA.V.F.K2) — 14 CFR §107.15

1269. When should the battery for a small unmanned aircraft be replaced?

A—Once recharged more than 10 times in the preceding 30 days.
B—Per the guidelines of the sUAS manufacturer or the battery manufacturer, whichever is more restrictive.
C—Per the guidelines of the sUAS manufacturer or the battery manufacturer, whichever is least restrictive.

Follow all manufacturer maintenance recommendations to achieve the longest and safest service life of the sUAS. By abiding by the more restrictive limitation or component life cycle, the remote PIC will be assured of being in compliance of both the sUAS and battery manufacturer's guidelines. (UA.V.F.K1) — AC 107-2

Answers

| 1265 [C] | 1266 [A] | 1336 [B] | 1267 [A] | 1268 [A] | 1269 [B] |

Chapter 5
Operations

Introduction *5–3*

Communication Procedures *5–5*

   sUAS Frequencies *5–9*

Emergency Procedures *5–13*

   Lost Link *5–13*

   Flight Termination *5–14*

   Flyaways *5–14*

   Loss of GPS *5–14*

   Battery Fires *5–15*

Aeronautical Decision Making *5–17*

Introduction

Before each flight, the remote PIC must perform tasks to ensure that the sUAS is in a condition for safe operation. This preflight inspection should be conducted in accordance with the sUAS manufacturer's inspection procedures when available (usually found in the manufacturer's owner or maintenance manual) and/or an inspection procedure developed by the sUAS owner or operator.

Such inspections should focus on evaluating equipment for damage or other malfunction(s). The preflight check should be performed prior to each flight and include an appropriate UAS preflight inspection that is specific and scalable to the sUAS, the program, and the operation. This should encompass the entire system in order to determine a continual condition for safe operation prior to flight. If manufacturers do not provide a preflight checklist or guide, remote PICs should create their own guidelines to properly check all components critical to the safety and operation of flight.

An example of a common issue with sUAS is propeller damage or installation issues. Propeller blades can have nicks, cracks, bends, etc., that significantly degrade the structural integrity of the blade and could potentially impact the controllability and overall safety of the sUAS. Also, propeller installation must be done per the manufacturer guidelines. Failure to do so can lead to separation of the blade inflight, loss of control, damage to the sUAS, and/or injury to the user or other persons in the area.

Another important item to consider during the preflight inspection is the security of panels, doors, and other components as well as the security of attachments of object such as the camera, antennae, and the battery. Batteries should be inspected for damage or malfunctions. If a battery is "bloated" or looks abnormal in anyway, it should not be used or charged. A good practice is to turn on the engine(s)/motor(s) to ensure they are working properly followed by a brief, low altitude test flight to verify controllability, radio link, and system integrity.

At minimum, the preflight inspection should include a visual or functional check of the following items:

1. Visual condition inspection of the sUAS components.
2. Airframe structure (including undercarriage), all flight control surfaces, and linkages.
3. Registration markings, for proper display and legibility.
4. Moveable control surfaces, including airframe attachment points.
5. Servo motor(s), including attachment point(s).
6. Propulsion system, including powerplants, propellers, rotors, ducted fans, etc.
7. Verify all systems (e.g., aircraft and control unit) have an adequate energy (fuel/battery) supply for the intended operation and are functioning properly.
8. Avionics, including control link transceiver, communication/navigation equipment, and antennas.
9. Calibrate sUAS compass prior to all flights.
10. Control link transceiver, communication/navigation data link transceiver, and antennas.
11. Display panel, if used, is functioning properly.
12. Ground support equipment, including takeoff and landing systems, for proper operation.
13. Control link correct functionality is established between the aircraft and the CS.
14. Correct movement of control surfaces using the CS.
15. Onboard navigation and communication data links.
16. Flight termination system, if installed.
17. Fuel, for correct type and quantity; and/or
18. Battery levels for the aircraft and CS.

Chapter 5 **Operations**

19. All equipment (cameras, etc.) is securely attached.
20. Verify communication with sUAS and that the sUAS has acquired GPS location (if applicable to the operation and/or aircraft).
21. Start the sUAS propellers to inspect for any imbalance or irregular operation.
22. Verify all controller operations for accuracy and display of heading and altitude (if available).
23. If required by flight path walk through, verify any noted obstructions that may interfere with the sUAS.
24. At a controlled low altitude, fly within range of any interference and recheck all controls and stability.
25. Confirm any and all software, controller, or aircraft settings to ensure they have been properly set for the impending flight or mission.

1211. During the preflight inspection who is responsible for determining the aircraft is safe for flight?
A—The remote pilot-in-command.
B—The owner or operator.
C—The certificated mechanic who performed the annual inspection.

The remote PIC of an sUAS is responsible for determining whether that aircraft is in condition for safe flight. (UA.I.B.K20) — FAA-H-8083-25

1212. How often is the remote PIC required to inspect the sUAS to ensure that it is in a condition for safe operation?
A—Annually.
B—Monthly.
C—Before each flight.

The remote PIC must inspect the sUAS before each flight. (UA.I.B.K20) — 14 CFR §107.49

1213. How should an sUAS preflight inspection be accomplished for the first flight of the day?
A—Quick walk around with a check of gas and oil.
B—Thorough and systematic means recommended by the manufacturer.
C—Any sequence as determined by the pilot-in-command.

The preflight inspection should be a thorough and systematic means by which the remote PIC determines that the sUAS is ready for safe flight. Most POH or UAS flight manuals contain a section on preflight inspection that should be used for guidance in this. (UA.I.B.K20) — FAA-H-8083-25

1214. During your preflight inspection, you discover that the casing of your sUAS battery has expanded beyond its normal dimensions. What action should you take?
A—Throw it away with your household trash.
B—Use it as long as it will still hold a charge.
C—Follow the manufacturer's guidance.

Your first action should be to seek out the manufacturer's guidance about replacement or disposal. Do not use damaged batteries, as they may self-ignite during flight or if charged. (UA.I.B.K20) — AC 107-2

1215. While preparing your sUAS for flight, you notice that one of the propeller blades has a nick. What action should you take?
A—If the nick is less than ¼ the length of the blade, it is safe to operate without replacement.
B—Remove and replace the propeller; consult manufacturer guidelines for repair, if any.
C—Repair by filing the nick to a smooth curve or with adhesive approved for use on the propeller material.

When in doubt, remove and replace any damaged part. If repair is allowed, it should be outlined by the manufacturer. Remote PICs should consult with the manufacturer about such repair. (UA.I.B.K20) — AC 107-2

Answers

1211 [A]   1212 [C]   1213 [B]   1214 [C]   1215 [B]

1216. In which of the following scenarios is a remote PIC not required to perform a preflight inspection of their sUAS?

A—If the subsequent flight occurs immediately following a flight before which an inspection was made.
B—Preflight inspections are only required for the first flight of the day, so any other flight does not require such an inspection.
C—Preflight inspections are required before each flight, thus there is no scenario that precludes such an inspection.

The remote PIC must inspect the sUAS before each flight. (UA.I.B.K20) — 14 CFR §107.49

Communication Procedures

The FAA requires that the remote PIC and other crewmembers coordinate to:

1. Scan the airspace in the operational area for any potential collision hazard; and
2. Maintain awareness of the position of the sUAS through direct visual observation.

To achieve this goal, the remote PIC should:

- Foster an environment where open communication is encouraged and expected among the entire crew to maximize team performance.
- Establish effective communication procedures prior to flight.
- Select an appropriate method of communication, such as the use of hand-held radio or other effective means that would not create a distraction and allows all crewmembers to understand each other.
- Inform the crew as conditions change about any needed adjustments to ensure a safe outcome of the operation.

One way to accomplish effective communications procedures is to have a VO maintain visual contact with the sUA and maintain awareness of the surrounding airspace, and then communicate flight status and any hazards to the remote PIC and person manipulating the controls so that appropriate action can be taken. The remote PIC should evaluate which method is most appropriate for the operation and should be determined prior to flight.

Aviation has a language all its own to facilitate communication between all participants. These participants include both ATC and pilots, often communicating in a busy and noisy environment. The most important component to effective communications is understanding between the parties involved. Brevity is important, and contacts should be kept as brief as possible. Basic communication procedures include:

- Listen before you transmit.
- Think before keying your transmitter.
- Place the microphone (mic) close to your lips and after pressing the mic button, speak in a normal, conversational tone.
- Be alert both to sounds as well as a lack of sounds, which could indicate lost or broken communications.

Answers

1216 [C]

Chapter 5 **Operations**

Character	Telephony	Phonic (Pronunciation)
A	Alfa	(AL-FAH)
B	Bravo	(BRAH-VOH)
C	Charlie	(CHAR-LEE) or (SHAR-LEE)
D	Delta	(DELL-TAH)
E	Echo	(ECK-OH)
F	Foxtrot	(FOKS-TROT)
G	Golf	(GOLF)
H	Hotel	(HOH-TEL)
I	India	(IN-DEE-AH)
J	Juliett	(JEW-LEE-ETT)
K	Kilo	(KEY-LOH)
L	Lima	(LEE-MAH)
M	Mike	(MIKE)
N	November	(NO-VEM-BER)
O	Oscar	(OSS-CAH)
P	Papa	(PAH-PAH)
Q	Quebec	(KEH-BECK)
R	Romeo	(ROW-ME-OH)
S	Sierra	(SEE-AIR-RAH)
T	Tango	(TANG-GO)
U	Uniform	(YOU-NEE-FORM) or (OO-NEE-FORM)
V	Victor	(VIK-TAH)
W	Whiskey	(WISS-KEY)
X	Xray	(ECKS-RAY)
Y	Yankee	(YANG-KEY)
Z	Zulu	(ZOO-LOO)
1	One	(WUN)
2	Two	(TOO)
3	Three	(TREE)
4	Four	(FOW-ER)
5	Five	(FIFE)
6	Six	(SIX)
7	Seven	(SEV-EN)
8	Eight	(AIT)
9	Nine	(NIN-ER)
0	Zero	(ZEE-RO)

Figure 5-1. Phonetic alphabet

The **phonetic alphabet** is used in aviation communications by both ATC facilities and pilots. Use the phonetic equivalents for single letters and to spell out groups of letters or difficult words during adverse communications conditions. See Figure 5-1.

Figures indicating hundreds and thousands in round numbers as used in weather reports or for altitudes should include both the first number of the hundred/thousand and then followed by the quantity descriptor(s). For example, "500" should be spoken "fife hundred." Another example, "4,500" should be annunciated "four thousand five hundred." The number nine is spoken "niner" and the number five is spoken "fife" to further help alleviate confusion over the radio waves and to avoid confusion among languages ("nine" sounds like the German word for no: "nein").

The three digits for course, heading or wind direction should be magnetic and spoken individually. The word "true" should be added when it applies. For example, magnetic heading 360 would be spoken "three six zero."

Speed should be followed by the words "knots" or "mile per hour." For example, the speed 87 knots is spoken "eighty-seven knots."

Time is measured in relation to the rotation of the Earth. A day is defined as the time required for the earth to make one complete revolution of 360°. Since the day is divided into 24 hours, it follows that the earth revolves at the rate of 15° each hour. Thus, lines of longitude may be expressed as 90° apart, the first of which is 6 hours west of Greenwich. Twenty-four time zones have been established. Each time zone is approximately 15° of longitude in width, with the first zone centered on the meridian of Greenwich. For most aviation operations, time is expressed in terms of the 24-hour clock (for example, 8 a.m. is expressed as 0800; 2 p.m. is 1400; 11 p.m. is 2300) and may be either local or Coordinated Universal Time (UTC). UTC is the time at the prime meridian and is represented in aviation operations by the letter "Z," referred to as "Zulu time" and is not adjusted for daylight savings time. For example, 1500Z would be spoken as "one five zero zero Zulu."

Initial transmissions to ATC should contain the following elements:
- Who you are—aircraft's complete call sign.
- Where you are located (either in reference to an airport, geographical location, or point on an airport).
- What you want to do or need to do—you should think about what you want to say before communicating it.

Call signs should be spoken in their entirety the first time. Never abbreviate on initial contact or any time other aircraft call signs have similar numbers/sounds or identical letters/numbers. Standard phraseology should be used at all times. See Figure 5-2.

When ATC authorization is required (at or near an airport with a control tower and/or when operating within controlled airspace), such permission must be requested and granted before any operation in that airspace. When ATC authorization is not required (at or near an airport without a control tower and/or when operating within uncontrolled airspace), remote PICs should monitor the CTAF to stay aware of manned aircraft communications and operations. Manned pilots will self-announce their position and intentions on the CTAF, consistent with recommended traffic advisory procedures. It is helpful to announce sUAS operations on the CTAF to increase local pilots' situational awareness, as well as potentially increase the safe interaction among manned and unmanned aircraft. Use standard phraseology at all times so as not to confuse manned pilots or other operators on the frequency.

Automatic Terminal Information Service (ATIS) is a continuous broadcast of non-control information in selected high-activity terminal areas. ATIS frequencies are listed in the *Chart Supplement U.S.* To relieve frequency congestion, pilots are urged to listen to ATIS, and on initial contact, to advise controllers that the information has been received by repeating the alphabetical code word appended to the broadcast. For example: "information Sierra received."

At airports with operating **air traffic control towers (ATCT)**, approval must be obtained prior to advancing an aircraft onto the movement area. Ground control frequencies are provided to reduce

"Acknowledge"	Let me know that you have received my message.
"Advise intentions"	Tell me what you plan to do.
"Affirmative"	Yes.
"Final"	Commonly used to mean that an aircraft is on the final approach course or is aligned with a landing area.
"Hold for"	(takeoff clearance, release, landing/taxiing aircraft, etc.) Stay in place where you are currently located.
"Hold short"	November 477ZA, runway four, taxi via Echo, hold short runway two five at taxiway Delta.
"How do you hear me?"	A question relating to the quality of the transmission or to determine how well the transmission is being received.
"Immediately"	Used by ATC or pilots when such action compliance is required to avoid an imminent situation.
"Line up and wait"	Used by ATC to inform a pilot to taxi onto the departure runway in takeoff position and line up and wait. *It is not authorization for takeoff.* It is used when takeoff clearance cannot immediately be issued because of traffic or other reasons.
"Negative"	"No" or "permission not granted" or "that is not correct."
"Read back"	Repeat my message back to me.
"Roger"	I have received all of your last transmission. *Should not be used to answer a question requiring a yes or no answer.*
"Stand by"	Means the controller or pilot must pause for a few seconds, usually to attend to other duties of a higher priority. Also means to wait, as in "stand by for clearance." The caller should reestablish contact if a delay is lengthy. "Stand by" is not an approval or denial.
"Unable"	Indicates inability to comply with a specific instruction, request, or clearance.
"Verify"	Request confirmation of information (for example, "verify assigned altitude").
"WILCO"	I have received your message, understand it, and will comply with it.
"Without delay"	With a sense of urgency, proceed with approved instructions in a rapid manner.

Figure 5-2. Standard aviation phraseology

Chapter 5 **Operations**

congestion on the tower frequency. They are used for issuance of taxi information, clearances, and other necessary contacts. If instructed by ground control to "taxi to" a particular runway, the pilot must stop prior to crossing any runway. A clearance must be obtained prior to crossing any runway. Aircraft arriving at an airport where a control tower is in operation should not change to ground control frequency until directed to do so by ATC.

The key to operating at an airport without an operating control tower is selection of the correct CTAF, which is identified in the *Chart Supplement U.S.* and on the Sectional Chart. CTAF is the frequency on which pilots (manned and unmanned) announce their intentions, location, or other pertinent information and monitor the intentions, location, etc. conveyed by other pilots in the area. If the airport has a part-time ATCT, the CTAF is usually a tower frequency. Where there is no tower, UNICOM, (if available) is usually the CTAF. UNICOM is limited to the necessities of safe and expeditious operation of private aircraft pertaining to runways and wind conditions, types of fuel available, weather, and dispatching. UNICOM may also transmit information concerning ground transportation, food, lodging and services available during transit. When no tower, FSS, or UNICOM is available, use the MULTICOM frequency 122.9 for self-announce procedures.

Often, there is more than one airport using the same frequency. To avoid confusion, be sure to state the airport name, followed by the term "traffic" (addressing other aircraft in the area) as part of the beginning and end of the transmission. For example, "Manatee traffic, unmanned aircraft XYZ is operating at 200 AGL approximately 3 NM south of the airport, Manatee traffic." See Figure 5-3.

	Facility at Airport	Frequency Use	Communication/Broadcast Procedures		
			Outbound	*Inbound*	*Practice Instrument Approach*
1	UNICOM (No Tower or FSS)	Communicate with UNICOM station on published CTAF frequency (122.7, 122.8, 122.725, 122.975, or 123.0). If unable to contact UNICOM station, use self-announce procedures on CTAF.	Before taxiing and before taxiing on the runway for departure.	10 miles out. Entering downwind, base, and final. Leaving the runway.	
2	No Tower, FSS, or UNICOM	Self-announce on MULTICOM frequency 122.9.	Before taxiing and before taxiing on the runway for departure.	10 miles out. Entering downwind, base, and final. Leaving the runway.	Departing final approach fix (name) or on final approach segment inbound.
3	No Tower in operation, FSS open	Communicate with FSS on CTAF frequency.	Before taxiing and before taxiing on the runway for departure.	10 miles out. Entering downwind, base, and final. Leaving the runway.	Approach completed/terminated.
4	FSS closed (No Tower)	Self-announce on CTAF.	Before taxiing and before taxiing on the runway for departure.	10 miles out. Entering downwind, base, and final. Leaving the runway.	
5	Tower or FSS not in operation	Self-announce on CTAF.	Before taxiing and before taxiing on the runway for departure.	10 miles out. Entering downwind, base, and final. Leaving the runway.	

Figure 5-3. Summary of recommended communications procedures

Although it is unlikely that ATC will be able to track unmanned aircraft in the near future, they may issue information about traffic that is in the vicinity of sUAS operations. Traffic advisories given by ATC will refer to the other aircraft by azimuth in terms of the 12-hour clock, with twelve o'clock being the direction of flight (track), not aircraft heading. Each hourly position is equal to 30°. For example, an aircraft heading 090° is advised of traffic at the three o'clock position. The remote PIC (and any VO or crew) should look 90° to the right of the direction of flight of the sUAS, or to the south of the area of operation/

sUA. Remote pilots should be aware that traffic information is based upon the track observed on radar, thus if traffic advisories about your operation are conveyed to manned aircraft, they may indicate a slight difference in the perceived location of observed aircraft and the actual location of such aircraft. See Figure 5-4.

Figure 5-4. Traffic advisories are issued based on direction of flight, not the aircraft heading

sUAS Frequencies

Most sUAS use radio frequencies to establish the data link between the control station and the small unmanned aircraft.

Considerations for radio frequencies used in sUAS operations include:

- Frequency interference.
- Line of sight/obstructions.

The most commonly used sUAS frequencies are 2.4 GHz and 5.8 GHz. These unlicensed radio frequency bands are regulated by the Federal Communications Commission (FCC). These frequencies are also used for computer wireless networks. Therefore, frequency interference can cause problems when operating an unmanned aircraft in areas with many wireless signals (e.g., near dense housing or office buildings). Lost links and flyaways are some of the reported problems with sUAS frequency implications. To avoid frequency interference many modern sUAS operate using a 5.8 GHz system to control the sUAS, and a 2.4 GHz system to transmit video and photos to the ground. Consult the sUAS operating manual and manufacturers recommended procedures before conducting sUAS operations

Both sUAS radio frequency bands (2.4 GHz and 5.8 GHz) are considered line-of-sight. Be aware that the command and control link between the control station and the sUAS might not work properly when barriers are between the control station and the unmanned aircraft.

Radio transmissions, such as those used to control an sUA and to downlink real-time video, must use frequency bands that are approved for use by the operating agency. The FCC authorizes civil operations. Some operating frequencies are unlicensed and can be used freely (e.g., 900 MHz, 2.4 GHz, and 5.8 GHz) without FCC approval. All other frequencies require a user-specific license for all civil users, except federal agencies, to be obtained from the FCC. For further information, visit **fcc.gov/licensing-databases/licensing**. It is recommended that the remote PIC utilize a frequency spectrum analyzer prior to operation to ensure that there are no potential interfering transmissions in the area.

1217. Inbound to an airport with no tower, FSS, or UNICOM in operation, a pilot should self-announce on MULTICOM frequency

A—123.0.
B—122.9.
C—122.7.

Where there is no tower or UNICOM station on the airport, use MULTICOM frequency 122.9 for self-announce procedures. (UA.V.A.K4) — AIM ¶4-1-9

1279. The aircraft call sign N169US will be spoken in this way:

A—November one six niner uniform sierra.
B—November one six niner unmanned system.
C—November one hundred sixty nine uniform sierra.

Aircraft call signs should be spoken in their entirety, using the phonetic alphabet. Numbers are spoken individually. (UA.V.A.K7) — AIM ¶4-2-3

Answers

1217 [B]   1279 [A]

Chapter 5 **Operations**

1218. When flying HAWK N666CB, the proper phraseology for initial contact with Whitted ATC tower is

A—"Whitted Tower, HAWK SIX SIX SIX CHARLIE BRAVO, five NM west of the airport, request permission to enter Class D airspace for unmanned aircraft operations below four hundred AGL, three NM west of the airport"
B—"Whitted, HAWK SIX SIX SIX CEE BEE, requesting to operate within Class D, west of the field"
C—"Whitted tower, Triple Six Charlie Bravo, five NM west, operating in Class D below four hundred AGL west of the airport"

The term initial radio contact, or initial callup, means the first radio call you make to a given facility, or the first call to a different controller or Flight Service specialist within a facility. Use the following format:

1. *Name of facility being called;*
2. *Your full aircraft identification as filed in the flight plan;*
3. *Type of message to follow or your request if it is short, and*
4. *The word "over," if required (typically omitted, except for communications via a remote communication outlet or in cases when it is necessary to confirm the end of a transmission). Example: "New York Radio, Mooney Three One One Echo, over."*

When the aircraft manufacturer's name or model is stated, the prefix "N" is dropped. The first two characters of the call sign may be dropped only after ATC calls you by your last three letters/numbers. (UA.V.A.K8) — AIM ¶4-2-3

1219. The correct method of stating 4,500 feet MSL to ATC is

A—"FOUR THOUSAND FIVE HUNDRED."
B—"FOUR POINT FIVE."
C—"FORTY-FIVE HUNDRED FEET MSL."

Up to but not including 18,000 feet MSL, state the separate digits of the thousands, plus the hundreds, if appropriate. Example: "4,500—four thousand, five hundred." (UA.V.A.K8) — AIM ¶4-2-9

1233. What is the best way for the remote PIC to minimize the risk of radio frequency interference during sUAS operations?

A—Never transmit on aviation frequency ranges during flight operations.
B—Monitor frequency use with a spectral analyzer.
C—Avoid the use of cellphones in the vicinity of the control station.

Remote PICs should monitor the appropriate aviation frequency such as CTAF during flight operations and make announcements concerning sUAS operations as appropriate. Some sUAS require the use of cellphone or tablet computers for operation, therefore are acceptable for use in most cases. The best way to avoid frequency interference is to check local frequency spectrum use prior to flight and continue to monitor such use during flight by utilizing a frequency spectrum analyzer. (UA.V.A.K1) — AC 107-2

1220. (Refer to Figure 20, area 3.) What is the recommended communications procedure for a landing at Currituck County Airport?

A—Transmit intentions on 122.9 MHz when 10 miles out and give position reports in the traffic pattern.
B—Contact Elizabeth City FSS for airport advisory service.
C—Contact New Bern FSS for area traffic information.

Where there is no tower, Flight Service, or UNICOM station on the airport, use MULTICOM frequency 122.9 for self-announce procedures. Such airports will be identified in the appropriate aeronautical information publications. (UA.V.A.K1) — AIM ¶4-1-9

1221. When should pilots state their position on the airport when calling the tower for takeoff?

A—When visibility is less than 1 mile.
B—When parallel runways are in use.
C—When departing from a runway intersection.

Pilots should state their position on the airport when calling the tower for takeoff from a runway intersection. (UA.V.A.K1) — AIM ¶4-3-10

Answers

1218 [A]   1219 [A]   1233 [B]   1220 [A]   1221 [C]

Chapter 5 **Operations**

1222. As standard operating practice, all inbound and local traffic approaching or near an airport without a control tower should continuously monitor the appropriate facility from a distance of

A—25 miles.
B—20 miles.
C—10 miles.

Pilots of inbound traffic should monitor and communicate as appropriate on the designated CTAF from 10 miles to landing. Pilots of departing aircraft should monitor/communicate on the appropriate frequency from start-up, during taxi, and until 10 miles from the airport unless the regulations or local procedures require otherwise. (UA.V.A.K1) — AIM ¶4-1-9

1223. Absence of the sky condition and visibility on an ATIS broadcast indicates that

A—weather conditions are at or above VFR minimums.
B—the sky condition is clear and visibility is unrestricted.
C—the ceiling is at least 5,000 feet and visibility is 5 miles or more.

The absence of a sky condition or ceiling and/or visibility on ATIS indicates a ceiling of 5,000 feet or above and visibility of 5 miles or more. (UA.V.A.K5) — AIM ¶4-1-13

1224. (Refer to Figure 22 area 2; and Figure 31.) At Coeur D'Alene, which frequency should be used as a Common Traffic Advisory Frequency (CTAF) to monitor airport traffic?

A—122.05 MHz.
B—135.075 MHz.
C—122.8 MHz.

CTAF is a frequency designed for the purpose of carrying out airport advisory practices and/or position reporting at an uncontrolled airport (which may also occur during hours when a tower is closed). The CTAF may be a UNICOM, MULTICOM, FSS, or tower frequency and is identified in the appropriate aeronautical publications. A solid dot with the letter "C" inside indicates CTAF. When the control tower operates part time and a UNICOM frequency is provided, use the UNICOM frequency. (UA.V.A.K2) — AIM ¶4-1-9

1330. (Refer to Figure 21, Area 1.) After receiving authorization from ATC to operate a small UA near Minot International airport (MOT) while the control tower is operational, which radio communication frequency could be used to monitor manned aircraft and ATC communications?

A—UNICOM 122.95
B—ASOS 118.725
C—CT-118.2

Minot International airport (MOT) is in Class D airspace, depicted by the dashed blue lines. You should monitor the control tower frequency 118.2 to hear manned aircraft and ATC communications operating in this vicinity. (UA.V.A.K1) — Sectional Chart Legend

Answer (A) is incorrect because the UNICOM frequency will only provide airport activity information when the control tower is not operating. Answer (B) is incorrect because the ASOS frequency will provide weather information for that airport but not activity information.

1225. (Refer to Figure 26, area 2.) What is the recommended communication procedure when operating in the vicinity of Cooperstown Airport?

A—Broadcast intentions when 10 miles out and monitor transmissions on the CTAF/MULTICOM frequency, 122.9 MHz.
B—Contact UNICOM when 10 miles out on 122.8 MHz.
C—Circle the airport in a left turn prior to entering traffic monitoring transmissions on 122.9.

MULTICOM frequency is always 122.9 MHz, and the correct procedure is to broadcast intentions when 10 miles from the airport. (UA.V.A.K2) — AIM ¶4-1-9

Answers

1222 [C] 1223 [C] 1224 [C] 1330 [C] 1225 [A]

Chapter 5 **Operations**

1308. The Common Traffic Advisory Frequency (CTAF) is used for manned aircraft to

A—announce ground and flight intentions.
B—request air traffic control clearance.
C—request fuel services.

CTAF is designed for the purpose of carrying out airport advisory practices and/or position reporting at an uncontrolled airport (which may also occur during hours when a tower is closed). The CTAF may be a UNICOM, MULTICOM, FSS, or tower frequency and is identified in the appropriate aeronautical publications. On the sectional chart, a solid dot with the letter "C" inside indicates CTAF. When the control tower operates part time and a UNICOM frequency is provided, use the UNICOM frequency. (UA.V.A.K2) — AIM ¶4-1-9

1226. Automatic Terminal Information Service (ATIS) is the continuous broadcast of recorded information concerning

A—pilots of radar-identified aircraft whose aircraft is in dangerous proximity to terrain or to an obstruction.
B—nonessential information to reduce frequency congestion.
C—noncontrol information in selected high-activity terminal areas.

ATIS is the continuous broadcast of recorded non-control information in selected high-activity terminal areas. (UA.V.A.K5) — AIM ¶4-1-13

1227. What services will a FSS provide?

A—Fuel pricing.
B—Assistance during an emergency.
C—Clearance to taxi for takeoff.

FSS is an air traffic facility that provides pilot briefings, enroute communications, and VFR search-and-rescue services, assists lost aircraft and aircraft in emergency situations, relays ATC clearances, originates Notices to Air Missions, broadcasts aviation weather and NAS information, receives and processes IFR flight plans, and monitors NAVAIDs. In addition, FSS takes weather observations, issues airport advisories, advises customs and immigration of transborder flights, and provides En Route Flight Advisory Service (Flight Watch) (in Alaska only). (UA.V.A.K1) — AIM ¶4-1-3

1230. An ATC radar facility issues the following advisory to a pilot flying on a heading of 090°: "UNMANNED AIRCRAFT OPERATIONS THREE O'CLOCK, 2 MILES, WESTBOUND..." Where should the remote PIC (also visual observer and crew, if applicable) look for this traffic in reference to the small unmanned aircraft?

A—North.
B—South.
C—West.

Traffic information will be given in azimuth from the aircraft in terms of the 12-hour clock. Thus, each hour would constitute an angle of 30°. Picture a clock in your lap; three o'clock is to your right, nine o'clock is to your left, twelve o'clock is straight ahead, and six o'clock is behind you. If an aircraft is proceeding on a heading of 090° (east), traffic located at the three o'clock position would be 90° right of the nose, south of the aircraft. If the sUAS is being operated to the south of the aircraft, the aircraft itself is to the north of the operation. (UA.V.A.K8) — AIM ¶4-1-15

1231. An ATC radar facility issues the following advisory to a manned aircraft pilot flying north in a calm wind: "UNMANNED AIRCRAFT OPERATIONS AT NINE O'CLOCK, 2 MILES..." Where should the remote PIC (also visual observer and crew, if applicable) look for this traffic?

A—East.
B—North.
C—West.

An aircraft flying north in calm wind would be heading 360°. When advised of traffic at the nine o'clock position, the pilot should look 90° left of the nose, to the west but the remote PIC and sUAS need to look to the east as they are to the west of the manned aircraft. (UA.V.A.K8) — AIM ¶4-1-15

Answers

1308 [A]   1226 [C]   1227 [B]   1230 [A]   1231 [A]

1232. A visual observer notices a manned aircraft approaching the area in which sUAS operations are taking place, flying just north of the area from west to east. What call could the remote PIC/visual observer make on CTAF to alert the manned pilot?

A—Zephyrhills traffic, unmanned aircraft Xray Yankee Zulu, operating five NM south of the airport at or below 400 AGL, located at the three o'clock position of the Cessna just north of our position, Zephyrhills traffic.

B—Zephyrhills traffic, unmanned aircraft at three o'clock of manned aircraft in the area, Zephyrhills traffic.

C—Zephyrhills traffic, unmanned aircraft Xray Yankee Zulu to Cessna in the area, look for us at your three o'clock position, we are about a mile south.

Using standard phraseology, remote PICs/crew should clearly communicate the position of the sUAS operation in relation to a known geographic location and any other information that may help the manned aircraft be aware of and avoid conflicting with the sUAS. (UA.V.A.K8) — AIM ¶4-1-15, AC 107-2

Emergency Procedures

Follow any manufacturer guidance for appropriate response procedures in abnormal or emergency situations prior to flight. In case of an inflight emergency, the remote PIC is permitted to deviate from any rule of Part 107 to the extent necessary to meet that emergency. FAA may request a written report explaining the deviation. Review emergency actions during preflight planning and inform crewmembers of their responsibilities.

The remote PIC must be prepared to respond to abnormal and emergency situations during sUAS operations. Refer to the manufacturer's guidance for appropriate procedures in the following situations:

- Abnormal situations, such as lost link, alternate landing/recovery sites, loss of GPS, loss of video link, avoidance of proximate manned or unmanned aircraft, and flight termination (controlled flight to the ground).
- Emergency situations, such as flyaways, loss of control link, avoidance of manned or unmanned aircraft in imminent danger of colliding with the sUAS, and battery fires.

Lost Link

Without an onboard pilot, sUAS crewmembers rely on the command and control link to operate the aircraft. For example, an uplink transmits command instructions to the aircraft and a downlink transmits the status of the aircraft and provides situational awareness to the remote PIC or person manipulating the controls. **Lost link** is an interruption or loss of the control link between the control station and the unmanned aircraft, preventing control of the aircraft. As a result, the unmanned aircraft may perform pre-set lost link procedures. Such procedures ensure that the unmanned aircraft:

- Remains airborne in a predictable or planned maneuver, allowing time to re-establish the communication link.
- Autolands, if available, after a predetermined length of time or terminates the flight when the power source is depleted.

A lost link is an abnormal situation, but not an emergency. A lost link is not considered a flyaway.

Answers

1232 [A]

Follow the manufacturer's recommendations for programming lost link procedures prior to the flight. Examples of lost link procedures may include, when applicable:

- A lost link sUA flies at an altitude (set by the remote PIC prior to flight) that avoids obstacles in the area or may fly a route predefined by the remote PIC.
- Communications procedures to notify crewmembers or other pertinent personnel of the loss of link.

Plan contingency measures in the event recovery of the sUAS is not feasible.

Remote PICs should conduct a thorough preflight briefing with crewmembers to discuss all lost link procedures including crewmember responsibilities and all contingency plans for abnormal and emergency situations. Contingency planning should include an alternate landing/recovery site to be used in the event of an abnormal condition that requires a precautionary landing away from the original launch location. Incorporate the means of communication with ATC throughout the descent and landing (if required for the flight operation) as well as a plan for ground operations and securing/parking the aircraft on the ground. This includes the availability of control stations capable of launch/recovery, communication equipment, and an adequate power source to operate all required equipment. Take into consideration all airspace constructs and minimize risk to other aircraft by avoiding persons, congested areas, and other aircraft to the maximum extent possible.

Flight Termination

Flight termination is the intentional and deliberate process of performing controlled flight to the ground. Flight termination may be part of lost link procedures, or it may be a contingency that you elect to use if further flight of the aircraft cannot be safely achieved, or if other potential hazards exist that require immediate discontinuation of flight. Execute flight termination procedures if you have exhausted all other contingencies. **Flight termination points (FTPs)**, if used, or alternative contingency planning measures must:

- Be located within power-off glide distance (fixed wing) or low-power rapid descent (rotor wing) of the aircraft during all phases of flight;
- Be based on the assumption of an unrecoverable system failure;
- Take into consideration altitude, winds, and other factors; and
- Take into consideration obstacles, persons, congested areas, and other aircraft operations.

Flyaways

A flyaway often begins as a lost link—an interruption or loss of the control link prevents control of the aircraft. As a result, the unmanned aircraft is not operating in a predicable or planned manner. However, in a flyaway, the pre-set lost link procedures are not established or are not being executed by the unmanned aircraft, creating an emergency situation. In rare instances, software or hardware malfunctions may induce a flyaway. If a flyaway occurs while operating in airspace that requires authorization, notify ATC as outlined in the authorization.

Loss of GPS

GPS tools can be a valuable resource for flight planning and situational awareness during sUAS operation. However, as with manned aviation, remote PICs in sUAS operations must avoid overreliance on automation and must be prepared to operate the unmanned aircraft manually, if necessary.

- Prior to flight, check NOTAMs for any known GPS service disruptions in the planned location of the sUAS operation. Most sUAS have the ability to operate without significant degradation of control if GPS signals are not available or are lost in flight (contingency planning should include such scenarios).
- Make a plan of action to prevent or minimize damage in the event of equipment malfunction or failure.

Battery Fires

Battery fires pose a significant hazard to sUAS. Because sUAS often utilize high energy density, rechargeable batteries, the risk for battery malfunction or failure are real concerns for sUAS operations. The charge/discharge cycle involves significant changes in temperature which can stress internal components of the battery. Before each flight, batteries should be inspected for any obvious damage, bloating or deformation, and excessive heat.

Both lithium metal and lithium-ion batteries are:
- Highly flammable;
- Capable of self-ignition when a battery short circuits or is overcharged, heated to extreme temperatures, mishandled, or otherwise defective; and
- Subject to thermal runaway.

Thermal runaway usually occurs during a rapid discharge event such as a short or structural failure within in battery cell. During thermal runaway, lithium batteries generate sufficient heat to cause adjacent cells to also go into thermal runaway. Once in thermal runaway, the battery may hiss (release gas), smoke, catch fire, or explode. Fires with these types of batteries are very difficult to extinguish. Because lithium can react with water, it is inadvisable to use water to aid in extinguishing the fire. Type D fire extinguishers, designed for chemical and combustible metal fires are recommended to assist in fire suppression. Covering the battery in sand can also help smother the fire. Batteries should be charged and stored in battery bags specifically designed to contain battery failures. As with any component, follow manufacturer guidelines and cautions prior to and during use.

Ensure careful storage of spare (uninstalled) lithium batteries. Take the following precautions to prevent a battery fire:
- Prevent short circuits by placing each individual battery in the original retail packaging, a separate plastic bag, a protective pouch, or by insulating exposed terminals with tape.
- Do not allow spare batteries to come in contact with metal objects, such as coins, keys, or jewelry.
- Take steps to prevent objects from crushing, puncturing, or applying pressure on the battery.

When preparing to conduct sUAS operations, do not charge or use any battery with signs of damage or defect. For example, check carefully for small nicks in the battery casing and be alert for signs of bubbling or warping during charging. Once the battery is installed and the sUAS takes flight, the remote PIC or ground crew might not observe a battery fire until it is too late to land the aircraft safely. If a battery fire occurs, follow any manufacturer guidance for response procedures. Following flight, allow the battery to cool prior to charging or storing (allow it to return to room temperature).

When disposing of a used or damaged battery, follow the manufacturer and local trash collection guidelines, as these types of devices are typically considered hazardous materials and should not be treated as regular trash for disposal.

1234. Damaged lithium batteries can cause
A—an inflight fire.
B—a change in aircraft center of gravity
C—increased endurance.

Both lithium metal and lithium-ion batteries are highly flammable and capable of self-ignition when a battery short circuits or is overcharged, heated to extreme temperatures, mishandled, or otherwise defective. (UA.V.C.K2c) — SAFO 10017

Answers
1234 [A]

1334. What precautions should a remote PIC take to prevent possible inflight emergencies when using lithium-based batteries?

A—Store the batteries in a freezer to allow proper recharging.
B—Follow the manufacturer's recommendations for safe battery handling.
C—Allow the battery to charge until it reaches a minimum temperature of 100°C.

Lithium-based batteries are highly flammable and capable of ignition. A battery fire could lead to an inflight emergency by causing a loss of control of the sUA. Lithium battery fires can occur when a battery short-circuits, is improperly charged, is heated to extreme temperatures, is damaged as a result of a crash, is mishandled, or is simply defective. The remote PIC should follow the manufacturer's recommendations to help ensure safe battery handling and usage. (UA.V.C.K2) — AC 107-2

1235. Which of the following lithium batteries should not be used?

A—A partially discharged battery that is warm from recent prior use.
B—A new battery that has only been charged once, several charging cycles are required prior to normal use.
C—A battery with a bulge on one of the sides of its case.

Damaged batteries should never be used or charged. Lithium batteries do normally get warm during discharge. Avoid the use of hot batteries. New batteries should be treated per manufacturing instructions, but do not normally need several charge cycles to use. (UA.V.C.K2) — SAFO 10017

1236. What is the proper response by the remote PIC if experiencing a lost link situation?

A—Notify all available crew and ATC (if applicable) while executing the briefed lost link procedure.
B—Wait for the unit to reestablish link while notifying local law enforcement of possible dangers to nonparticipants.
C—Turning the control station off and then back on to attempt the reestablishment of the link.

All participants in the sUAS operation and ATC (if operating within or near controlled airspace) should be notified of the lost link situation. In most cases this is not considered an emergency however, if at anytime it appears that lost link may result in a flyaway or other type of dangerous situation, an emergency should be declared. There is no obligation to contact local law enforcement. It is never recommended to turn off the control station when the sUA engines are running or if it is in flight. (UA.V.C.K3) — AC 107-2, 14 CFR §107.21

1237. Which of the following events is considered a flyaway?

A—Loss of link between the remote PIC and the unmanned aircraft.
B—Loss of communication link between the Remote PIC and ATC.
C—Unmanned aircraft does not respond to control inputs and does not execute known lost link maneuvers.

A flyaway is when the sUAS becomes uncontrollable and does not operate in a manner that would be expected in a normal or lost link flight situation. (UA.V.C.K3) — 14 CFR Part 107

1238. What action should be taken by the remote PIC during a sUAS flyaway event?

A—Immediately notify the NTSB.
B—Immediately notify any/all crewmembers, bystanders, and ATC (if applicable).
C—Immediately notify any/all crewmembers, local law enforcement personnel, and bystanders.

During a flyaway event, sUAS may not react in ways that can be expected or predicted, thus this is an emergency situation. The remote PIC should immediately communicate this emergency to crewmembers and ATC (if applicable) as well as any persons in the immediate area so as to minimize risk for injury. There is no obligation to contact the NTSB or law enforcement during a flyaway, (UA.V.C.K3) — 14 CFR §§107.19 and 107.21

1239. A common cause of sUAS flyaway events is

A—frequency interference.
B—loss of GPS signals.
C—persons standing close to the control station antenna.

Frequency interference is one of the most common causes of flyaways; therefore remote PICs should assess the risk of such interference prior to and during flight. Extra caution is necessary when operating in the vicinity of other sUAS. The loss of GPS may degrade

Answers

1334 [B] 1235 [C] 1236 [A] 1237 [C] 1238 [B] 1239 [A]

the sUAS capabilities slightly but should not cause a flyaway. It is not unusual for people to stand near the control station; it is highly unlikely for this to cause a flyaway. (UA.V.C.K3) — AC 107-2

1240. Upon GPS signal loss, the remote pilot should immediately

A—contact ATC and declare an emergency.
B—perform the planned lost link contingency procedure.
C—operate the sUAS normally, noting to account for any mode or control changes that occur if GPS is lost.

Most sUAS are designed to fly normally with minimal impact on features or controllability if GPS signals are degraded or lost. Loss of GPS is not an emergency and is not considered to be a loss of link between the unmanned aircraft and the control station. If the failure of GPS does result in a flyaway or other dangerous situation, it should be treated as an emergency. (UA.V.C.K4) — AC 107-2

1241. What action should the remote PIC take upon GPS signal loss?

A—Perform the planned flyaway emergency procedure.
B—Follow normal sUAS operational procedures, noting any mode or control changes that normally occur if GPS is lost.
C—Land the unmanned aircraft immediately prior to loss of control.

Most sUAS are designed to fly normally with minimal impact on features or controllability if GPS signals are degraded or lost. Loss of GPS is not an emergency and is not considered to be a flyaway situation nor does it require the sUAS operation to be terminated (unless specified by the manufacturer). If the failure of GPS does result in a flyaway or other dangerous situation, it should be treated as an emergency. (UA.V.C.K4) — AC 107-2

Aeronautical Decision Making

A remote PIC should use a variety of different resources to safely operate an sUAS and needs to be able to manage these resources effectively. An sUAS operation may involve one individual or a team of crewmembers, as follows:

- The remote PIC who holds a current Remote Pilot Certificate with an sUAS Rating and has the final authority and responsibility for the operation and safety of the sUAS;
- A person manipulating the controls operates the sUAS under direct supervision of the remote PIC;
- A VO acts as a flight crewmember to help see and avoid air traffic or other objects in the sky, overhead, or on the ground; and/or
- Other persons associated with the operation of the sUAS acting as part of the designated crew.

A culture of safety must be established with all commercial sUAS operations. Many techniques from manned aircraft operations apply to the operation of unmanned aircraft. Examples include situational awareness, risk-based **aeronautical decision making (ADM)**, **crew resource management (CRM)**, and **safety management systems (SMS)**.

The remote PIC attains situational awareness by obtaining as much information as possible prior to a flight and becoming familiar with the performance capabilities of the sUAS, weather conditions, surrounding airspace, privacy issues, and ATC requirements. Sources of information include a weather briefing, ATC, FAA, local pilots, local laws and ordinances, as well as landowners.

Technology, such as GPS, mapping systems, and computer applications, can assist in collecting and managing information to improve your situational awareness and risk-based ADM. ADM is a systematic

Answers

1240 [C]   1241 [B]

approach to the mental process used by pilots to consistently determine the best course of action in response to a given set of circumstances.

CRM is the effective use of all available resources—human, hardware, and information—prior to and during flight to ensure a successful outcome of the operation. The remote PIC must integrate CRM techniques into all phases of the sUAS operation. Many of these techniques traditionally used in manned aircraft operations are also applicable for sUAS, such as the ability to:

- Delegate operational tasks and manage crewmembers;
- Recognize and address hazardous attitudes;
- Establish effective team communication procedures; and
- Be open to questions and concerns of any and all crewmembers.

Risk management is part of the decision-making process which relies on situational awareness, problem recognition, and good judgment to reduce risks associated with each flight. Sound risk management skills will help prevent and break the final "link" in the accident chain.

An SMS is a formal, top-down business-like approach to managing safety risk, which includes a systemic approach to managing safety, including the necessary organizational structures, accountabilities, policies, and procedures.

The remote PIC identifies, delegates, and manages tasks for each sUAS operation. Tasks can vary greatly depending on the complexity of the sUAS operation. Supporting crewmembers can help accomplish those tasks and ensure the safety of flight. For example, VOs and other ground crew can provide valuable information about traffic, airspace, weather, equipment, and aircraft loading and performance. The remote PIC:

- Assesses the operating environment (airspace, surrounding terrain, weather, hazards, etc.).
- Determines the appropriate number of crewmembers that are needed to safely conduct a given operation. The remote PIC must ensure sufficient crew support so that no one on the team becomes over-tasked, which increases the possibility of an incident or accident.
- Informs participants of delegated tasks and sets expectations.
- Manages and supervises the crew to ensure that everyone completes their assigned tasks.

Hazardous attitudes can affect unmanned operations if the remote PIC is not aware of the hazards, leading to situations such as:

- Falling behind in the progress of the aircraft/situation;
- Operating without adequate fuel/battery reserve;
- Loss of positional or situational awareness;
- Operating outside the unmanned aircraft flight envelope; and
- Failure to complete all flight planning tasks, preflight inspections, and checklists.

Operational pressure is a contributor to becoming subject to these pitfalls. Studies have identified five hazardous attitudes that can interfere with the ability to make sound decisions and properly exercise authority: anti-authority, impulsivity, invulnerability, "machoism," and resignation. See Figure 5-5. Remote PICs should be alert to recognize hazardous attitudes (in themselves or in other crewmembers), bring attention to and label actions deemed to be hazardous, and correct the behavior.

Identifying associated hazards is the first step to mitigating the hazardous attitude. Analyzing the likelihood and severity of the hazards occurring establishes the probability of risk. In most cases, risk management steps can be taken to mitigate, even eliminate, those risks. Actions such as using VOs, completing a thorough preflight inspection, planning for weather, familiarity with the airspace, proper aircraft loading, and performance planning can mitigate identified risks. Take advantage of information from a weather briefing, ATC, the FAA, local pilots, and landowners. Technology can aid in decision making and improve situational awareness. Being able to collect the information from these resources and manage the information is key to situational awareness and could have a positive effect on your decision making.

It is also beneficial for remote PICs to assess risk for each mission or type of operation. Guidance on how to conduct such an evaluation is available from the U.S. Geological Survey and can be found in the reader resources at **asa2fly.com/TPUAS**. This can focus attention on actions or parts of the mission that may entail the highest risk and therefore can be actively mitigated with proper planning, ADM, and CRM.

Attitude	Motto	Indicators
Anti-authority	"Don't tell me what to do."	The person does not like or may resent anyone telling him or her what to do. The person may regard rules, regulations, and procedures as silly or unnecessary. (Note: it is always your prerogative to question authority if you feel it is in error.)
Impulsivity	"Do it quickly."	The person frequently feels the need to do something, anything, immediately. He or she does not stop to think about the best alternative and does the first thing that comes to mind.
Invulnerability	"It won't happen to me."	The person falsely believes that accidents happen to others, but never to him or her. The person knows accidents can happen and that anyone can be affected. However, the person never really feels or believes that he or she will be personally involved. Such people are more likely than others to take chances and increase risk.
Machoism	"I can do it—I'll show them."	The person tries to prove that he or she is better than anyone else. The person takes risks to impress others. (Note: While this pattern is thought to be a male characteristic, females are equally susceptible.)
Resignation	"What's the use?"	The person does not believe his or her actions make a difference in what happens. The person attributes outcomes to good or bad luck. He or she leaves the action to others, for better or worse. Sometimes, the person even goes along with unreasonable requests just to be a "nice guy."

Figure 5-5. Hazardous attitudes

Chapter 5 Operations

1242. The effective use of all available resources—human, hardware, and information—prior to and during flight to ensure the successful outcome of the operation is called

A—risk management.
B—crew resource management.
C—safety management system.

CRM is the effective use of all available resources—human, hardware, and information—prior to and during flight to ensure a successful outcome of the operation. (UA.V.D.K2) — AC 107-2

Answer (A) is incorrect because risk management is part of the decision-making process which relies on situational awareness, problem recognition, and good judgment to reduce risks associated with each flight. Answer (C) is incorrect because an SMS is a formal, top-down business-like approach to managing safety risk, which includes a systemic approach to managing safety, including the necessary organizational structures, accountabilities, policies, and procedures.

1243. When adapting crew resource management (CRM) concepts to the operation of a small unmanned aircraft, CRM must be integrated into

A—the communications only.
B—the flight portion only.
C—all phases of the operation.

CRM is the effective use of all available resources—human, hardware, and information—prior to and during flight to ensure a successful outcome of the operation. The remote PIC must integrate crew resource management techniques into all phases of the sUAS operation. (UA.V.D.K2) — FAA-H-8083-25

1244. Safety is an important element for a remote pilot to consider prior to operating an unmanned aircraft system. To prevent the final "link" in the accident chain, a remote pilot must consider which methodology?

A—Crew resource management.
B—Safety management system.
C—Risk management.

Risk management is the part of the decision making process that relies on situational awareness, problem recognition, and good judgment to reduce the risks associated with each flight. (UA.V.D.K5) — FAA-H-8083-25

Answers (A) and (B) are incorrect because CRM and SMS will incorporate risk management as part of their process.

1245. A local TV station has hired a remote pilot to operate their small unmanned aircraft to cover breaking news stories. The remote pilot has had multiple near misses with obstacles on the ground and two small unmanned aircraft accidents. What would be a solution for the news station to improve their operating safety culture?

A—The news station should implement a policy of no more than five crashes/incidents within 6 months.
B—The news station does not need to make any changes; there are times that an accident is unavoidable.
C—The news station should recognize hazardous attitudes and situations and develop standard operating procedures that emphasize safety.

A culture of safety must be established with all commercial sUAS operations. This safety culture may use a number of techniques including situational awareness, risk-based ADM, CRM, and SMS. (UA.V.D.K4) — FAA-H-8083-25

1246. Identify the hazardous attitude or characteristic a remote pilot-in-command displays while taking risks in order to impress others?

A—Impulsivity.
B—Invulnerability.
C—Machoism.

Machoism, as a hazardous attitude, has the motto "I can do it, I'll show them." The person tries to prove that he or she is better than anyone else and takes risks to impress others. (UA.V.D.K4) — FAA-H-8083-25

1247. You have been hired as a remote pilot-in-command by a local TV news station to film breaking news with a small unmanned aircraft. You expressed a safety concern and the station manager has instructed you to "fly first, ask questions later." What type of hazardous attitude does this attitude represent?

A—Invulnerability.
B—Impulsivity.
C—Machoism.

Impulsivity, as a hazardous attitude, has the motto "Do it quickly." The person frequently feels the need to do something, anything, immediately. He or she does not stop to think about the best alternative and does the first thing that comes to mind. (UA.V.D.K4) — FAA-H-8083-25

Answers

1242 [B] 1243 [C] 1244 [C] 1245 [C] 1246 [C] 1247 [B]

1248. What antidotal phrase can help reverse the hazardous attitude of "anti-authority"?

A—Rules do not apply in this situation.
B—I know what I am doing.
C—Follow the rules.

The anti-authority (don't tell me!) attitude is found in people who do not like anyone telling them what to do. The antidote for this attitude is: follow the rules, they are usually right. (UA.V.D.K4) — FAA-H-8083-25

1249. Hazardous attitudes occur to every pilot to some degree at some time. What are some of these hazardous attitudes?

A—Poor risk management and lack of stress management.
B—Anti-authority, impulsivity, macho, resignation, and invulnerability.
C—Poor situational awareness, snap judgments, and lack of a decision making process.

ADM addresses the following five hazardous attitudes: anti-authority (don't tell me!), impulsivity (do something quickly!), invulnerability (it won't happen to me!), machoism (I can do it!), and resignation (what's the use?). (UA.V.D.K4) — FAA-H-8083-25

1250. Risk management, as part of the aeronautical decision making (ADM) process, relies on which features to reduce the risks associated with each flight?

A—Application of stress management and risk element procedures.
B—Situational awareness, problem recognition, and good judgment.
C—The mental process of analyzing all information in a particular situation and making a timely decision on what action to take.

Risk management is the part of the decision-making process which relies on situational awareness, problem recognition, and good judgment to reduce risks associated with each flight. (UA.V.D.K1) — FAA-H-8083-25

1251. To avoid missing important steps, always use the

A—appropriate checklists.
B—placarded airspeeds.
C—airworthiness certificate.

To avoid missing important steps, always use the appropriate checklists whenever they are available. Consistent adherence to approved checklists is a sign of a disciplined and competent pilot. (UA.V.D.K1) — FAA-H-8083-25

1252. An extreme case of a pilot getting behind the aircraft can lead to the operational pitfall of

A—loss of situational awareness.
B—loss of workload.
C—internal stress.

"Getting behind the aircraft," or falling behind in the progress of a flight, can result in not knowing where you are, an inability to recognize deteriorating circumstances, and/or the misjudgment of the rate of deterioration. (UA.V.D.K3) — FAA-H-8083-25

1253. Which statement is not correct concerning crew resource management in sUAS operations?

A—Crewmembers cannot, under any circumstances, challenge the decisions of the Remote PIC.
B—Individuals who are exhibiting signs of hazardous attitudes should be approached about the issue.
C—The remote PIC and all crewmembers should communicate any observed hazards or concerns to one another.

Crewmembers should express any and all concerns about decisions of the remote PIC or other crewmembers at any time. Clearly, the remote PIC is in charge, but that does not always make them right or invulnerable to errors, omissions, or other potentially hazardous instances. (UA.V.D.K2) — FAA-H-8083-25

Answers (B) and (C) are incorrect because these are of favorable CRM interactions.

Answers

| 1248 [C] | 1249 [B] | 1250 [B] | 1251 [A] | 1252 [A] | 1253 [A] |

Chapter 5 **Operations**

1284. A remote pilot-in-command and a visual observer define their roles and responsibilities prior to and during the operation of a small unmanned aircraft. This is a good use of

A—crew resource management.
B—authoritarian resource management.
C—single-pilot resource management.

CRM is the effective use of all available resources—human, hardware, and information—prior to and during flight to ensure a successful outcome of the operation. (UA.V.D.K2) — FAA-H-8083-25

1291. What antidotal phrase can help reverse the hazardous attitude of impulsivity?

A—It could happen to me.
B—Do it quickly to get it over with.
C—Not so fast, think first.

Impulsivity (do something quickly!) is the attitude of people who frequently feel the need to do something, anything, immediately. They do not stop to think about what they are about to do, they do not select the best alternative, and they do the first thing that comes to mind. The antidote for this attitude is: Not so fast. Think first. (UA.V.D.K4) — FAA-H-8083-25

1299. What is the best way to mitigate risk?

A—SMS plan.
B—Weekly meetings.
C—Establishing an operational procedure guideline.

To fly safely, the pilot needs to assess the degree of risk and determine the best course of action to mitigate the risk. (UA.V.D.K1) — FAA-H-8083-25

1315. The accurate perception and understanding of all the risk element factors and conditions is

A—situational awareness.
B—judgment.
C—aeronautical decision making.

Situational awareness is the accurate perception and understanding of all the factors and conditions within the five fundamental risk elements (flight, pilot, aircraft, environment, and type of operation that comprise any given aviation situation) that affect safety before, during, and after the flight. (UA.V.D.K3) — FAA-H-8083-25

1337. Aeronautical decision making (ADM) can be described as the pilot's ability for

A—sound judgment and good decision making.
B—making quick decisive actions.
C—interpreting dangerous situations.

ADM provides a structured, systematic approach to analyzing changes that may occur during a flight and how these changes might affect the safe outcome of that flight. The ADM process addresses all aspects of decision making for the crew and identifies the steps involved in good decision making. (UA.V.D.K1) — FAA-H-8083-25

Answers

1284 [A]   1291 [C]   1299 [C]   1315 [A]   1337 [A]

Cross-Reference A
Question Number and Page Number

This cross-reference lists all of the questions in this book in sequential order. Use this list in combination with Cross-Reference B to find specific questions to aid your studies. For more information about the questions included in ASA Test Preps, please see pages vi–vii and xiv.

Question Number	Page Number	Question Number	Page Number	Question Number	Page Number	Question Number	Page Number
1001	1–4	1042	1–20	1084	2–11	1125	2–26
1002	1–4	1043	1–21	1085	2–11	1126	2–26
1003	1–4	1044	1–21	1086	2–13	1127	2–26
1004	1–4	1045	1–21	1087	2–13	1128	2–26
1005	1–5	1046	1–22	1088	2–13	1129	2–26
1006	1–5	1047	1–23	1089	2–14	1130	2–28
1007	1–5	1048	1–23	1090	2–14	1131	2–28
1008	1–5	1049	1–23	1091	2–14	1132	2–29
1009	1–5	1050	1–25	1092	2–14	1133	2–29
1010	1–5	1051	1–25	1093	2–14	1134	2–29
1011	1–5	1052	1–25	1094	2–15	1135	3–3
1012	1–7	1053	1–26	1095	2–15	1136	3–3
1013	1–7	1054	1–26	1096	2–16	1137	3–4
1014	1–7	1055	1–26	1097	2–16	1138	3–4
1015	1–7	1056	1–28	1098	2–16	1139	3–4
1016	1–8	1057	1–28	1099	2–16	1140	3–5
1017	1–8	1058	1–28	1100	2–17	1141	3–5
1018	1–8	1059	1–29	1101	2–17	1142	3–6
1019	1–8	1060	1–29	1102	2–17	1143	3–6
1020	1–9	1061	1–29	1103	2–17	1144	3–6
1021	1–10	1062	1–29	1104	2–17	1145	3–7
1022	1–10	1063	1–30	1105	2–18	1146	3–7
1023	1–10	1064	1–31	1106	2–18	1147	3–7
1024	1–10	1065	1–32	1107	2–18	1148	3–7
1025	1–10	1066	1–32	1108	2–19	1149	3–8
1026	1–11	1067	2–4	1109	2–19	1150	3–8
1027	1–12	1068	2–4	1110	2–19	1151	3–9
1028	1–12	1070	2–5	1111	2–21	1152	3–9
1029	1–12	1071	2–5	1112	2–21	1153	3–11
1030	1–12	1072	2–5	1113	2–21	1154	3–11
1031	1–13	1073	2–5	1114	2–21	1155	3–11
1032	1–13	1074	2–6	1115	2–21	1156	3–11
1033	1–14	1075	2–6	1116	2–24	1157	3–11
1034	1–14	1076	2–6	1117	2–24	1158	3–12
1035	1–15	1077	2–10	1118	2–25	1159	3–12
1036	1–17	1078	2–10	1119	2–25	1160	3–12
1037	1–17	1079	2–11	1120	2–25	1161	3–12
1038	1–18	1080	2–11	1121	2–25	1162	3–12
1039	1–19	1081	2–11	1122	2–25	1163	3–12
1040	1–26	1082	2–11	1123	2–25	1164	3–13
1041	1–20	1083	2–11	1124	2–26	1165	3–13

Cross-Reference A Question Number and Page Number

Question Number	Page Number	Question Number	Page Number	Question Number	Page Number	Question Number	Page Number
1166	3–14	1215	5–4	1264	4–18	1314	4–12
1167	3–15	1216	5–5	1265	4–20	1315	5–22
1168	3–15	1217	5–9	1266	4–20	1316	1–12
1169	3–15	1218	5–10	1267	4–20	1317	1–25
1170	3–15	1219	5–10	1268	4–20	1318	1–28
1171	3–15	1220	5–10	1269	4–20	1319	1–29
1172	3–15	1221	5–10	1270	1–22	1320	1–23
1173	3–16	1222	5–11	1271	3–9	1321	2–12
1174	3–16	1223	5–11	1272	3–4	1322	1–21
1175	3–16	1224	5–11	1273	4–17	1323	1–22
1176	3–16	1225	5–11	1274	1–27	1324	1–13
1177	3–16	1226	5–12	1275	1–30	1325	1–30
1178	3–17	1227	5–12	1276	2–6	1326	2–10
1179	3–23	1228	2–10	1277	3–7	1327	2–12
1180	3–23	1229	2–19	1278	3–5	1328	2–12
1181	3–23	1230	5–12	1279	5–9	1329	3–9
1182	3–23	1231	5–12	1280	1–5	1330	5–11
1183	3–23	1232	5–13	1281	1–30	1331	2–15
1184	3–23	1233	5–10	1282	2–12	1332	2–18
1185	3–23	1234	5–15	1283	3–13	1333	2–18
1186	4–4	1235	5–16	1284	5–22	1334	5–16
1187	4–5	1236	5–16	1285	3–8	1336	4–20
1188	4–5	1237	5–16	1286	3–6	1337	5–22
1189	4–5	1238	5–16	1287	3–13	1338	2–13
1190	4–7	1239	5–16	1288	3–9	1339	2–17
1191	4–7	1240	5–17	1289	3–9	1340	2–10
1192	4–7	1241	5–17	1290	3–17	1341	2–13
1193	4–7	1242	5–20	1291	5–22	1342	1–6
1194	4–8	1243	5–20	1292	3–24	1343	1–15
1195	4–9	1244	5–20	1293	4–8	1344	1–16
1196	4–9	1245	5–20	1295	2–12	1345	1–16
1197	4–9	1246	5–20	1296	2–15	1346	1–16
1198	4–9	1247	5–20	1297	4–17	1347	1–16
1199	4–9	1248	5–21	1298	3–14	1348	1–19
1200	4–10	1249	5–21	1299	5–22	1349	1–19
1201	4–12	1250	5–21	1300	4–4	1350	2–6
1202	4–12	1251	5–21	1301	2–14	1351	4–18
1203	4–12	1252	5–21	1302	4–16	1352	1–19
1204	4–12	1253	5–21	1303	2–29	1353	1–19
1205	4–13	1254	4–16	1304	1–13	1354	1–25
1206	4–13	1255	4–16	1305	2–12	1355	1–25
1207	4–13	1256	4–16	1306	1–30	1356	1–15
1208	4–13	1257	4–16	1307	2–12	1357	1–17
1209	4–14	1258	4–16	1308	5–12	1358	2–13
1210	4–14	1259	4–16	1309	2–15	1360	2–10
1211	5–4	1260	4–16	1310	3–9	1361	1–19
1212	5–4	1261	4–17	1311	3–24	1362	2–18
1213	5–4	1262	4–17	1312	2–29		
1214	5–4	1263	4–17	1313	2–5		

Cross-Reference B
Airman Knowledge Test Report Codes and Question Numbers

When you take the applicable FAA Knowledge Exam required for an airman certificate or rating, you will receive an Airman Knowledge Test Report (AKTR). This test report will list the Airman Certification Codes (ACS) for questions you have answered incorrectly. Match the codes given on your AKTR to the ones listed in this cross-reference. Use Cross-Reference A in this book to find the page number for the question numbers listed below. You can reference the ACS specific to the certificate or rating to determine the subject you missed on the test: **faa.gov/training_testing/testing/acs/**

Your instructor is required to provide instruction on each of the areas of deficiency listed on your AKTR and give you an endorsement for this instruction. The AKTR must be presented to the examiner conducting your practical test. During the oral portion of the practical test, the examiner is required to evaluate the noted areas of deficiency.

If you received a code on your AKTR that is not listed in this cross-reference, email ASA at **cfi@asa2fly.com**. We will provide the definition so you can review that subject area.

ACS Code	Question Numbers
UA.I.A.K1	1002, 1003, 1006, 1007, 1280, 1342
UA.I.A.K2	1004, 1005
UA.I.A.K3	1026
UA.I.A.K4	1027, 1028, 1029, 1030, 1316
UA.I.A.K5	1031, 1032, 1064, 1304, 1324
UA.I.B.K1	1001, 1033, 1034, 1035, 1343, 1356
UA.I.B.K2	1036, 1186
UA.I.B.K3	1015
UA.I.B.K4	1016, 1017, 1018, 1019, 1024, 1025, 1205
UA.I.B.K4a	1021, 1022
UA.I.B.K5	1008, 1009, 1010, 1011
UA.I.B.K6b	1056, 1057, 1058, 1318
UA.I.B.K7	1053, 1054, 1055
UA.I.B.K8	1059, 1060, 1061, 1062, 1281, 1319
UA.I.B.K9	1039
UA.I.B.K10	1041, 1042
UA.I.B.K11	1023
UA.I.B.K12	1020
UA.I.B.K14	1047, 1048, 1049, 1091, 1131, 1303, 1312, 1320
UA.I.B.K20	1037, 1211, 1212, 1213, 1214, 1215, 1216
UA.I.B.K21a	1044, 1045, 1322
UA.I.B.K21b	1043, 1270, 1323
UA.I.B.K21c	1151

Cross-Reference B Airman Knowledge Test Report Codes and Question Numbers

ACS Code	Question Numbers
UA.I.B.K21d	1046, 1152
UA.I.B.K22	1014
UA.I.B.K25	1348, 1349, 1352, 1353, 1361
UA.I.B.K28	1357
UA.I.C.K1	1275, 1306
UA.I.C.K2	1063, 1325
UA.I.C.K3	1012
UA.I.C.K4	1013
UA.I.D.K1	1065, 1066
UA.I.E.K1	1050, 1317
UA.I.E.K3a	1051
UA.I.E.K3c	1354
UA.I.E.K3d	1052
UA.I.E.K6	1274
UA.I.E.K12	1355
UA.I.E.K13	1040
UA.I.F.K1	1345
UA.I.F.K2	1344
UA.I.F.K3	1347
UA.I.F.K5	1346
UA.II.A.K1a	1077, 1228, 1326, 1360
UA.II.A.K1b	1078, 1305, 1340
UA.II.A.K1c	1081, 1082, 1094, 1282, 1307, 1327, 1338
UA.II.A.K1d	1075, 1093, 1295, 1328
UA.II.A.K1e	1083, 1085, 1108, 1321
UA.II.A.K2	1086, 1087, 1106, 1296, 1309, 1358
UA.II.A.K3	1072, 1073, 1090, 1101, 1111, 1229, 1301, 1350
UA.II.A.K4	1074
UA.II.B.K1	1271, 1288, 1289, 1310, 1329
UA.II.B.K2	1079, 1080, 1084, 1089, 1095, 1107
UA.II.B.K4	1076, 1100
UA.II.B.K4a	1130
UA.II.B.K4g	1132, 1133
UA.II.B.K5	1068, 1070, 1071, 1276, 1313
UA.III.A.K1	1178, 1311
UA.III.A.K2	1180, 1181, 1292
UA.III.A.K3	1182, 1183, 1184, 1185

Cross-Reference B Airman Knowledge Test Report Codes and Question Numbers

ACS Code	Question Numbers
UA.III.A.K5	1179
UA.III.B.K1	1135
UA.III.B.K1a	1173, 1174, 1175, 1176, 1177, 1290
UA.III.B.K1b	1140, 1141, 1207, 1278
UA.III.B.K1c	1136, 1137, 1138, 1139, 1145, 1146, 1147, 1148, 1149, 1150, 1285
UA.III.B.K1d	1142, 1143, 1144, 1272, 1277, 1286
UA.III.B.K1e	1153, 1154, 1155, 1156, 1157, 1158, 1159, 1160, 1161, 1162, 1163, 1283, 1287
UA.III.B.K1g	1164, 1165, 1166, 1298
UA.III.B.K1i	1167, 1168, 1169, 1170, 1171, 1172
UA.IV.A.K1	1190
UA.IV.A.K1a	1195, 1196, 1197, 1198, 1199, 1200, 1293
UA.IV.A.K1b	1194, 1201, 1202, 1203, 1204, 1300, 1314
UA.IV.A.K2	1187, 1189, 1191, 1192, 1193, 1206, 1208, 1209, 1210
UA.V.A.K1	1220, 1221, 1222, 1227, 1233, 1330
UA.V.A.K2	1224, 1225, 1308
UA.V.A.K4	1217
UA.V.A.K5	1223, 1226
UA.V.A.K7	1279
UA.V.A.K8	1218, 1219, 1230, 1231, 1232
UA.V.B.K3	1116, 1121, 1122, 1123, 1124, 1125, 1126, 1127, 1128, 1129
UA.V.B.K4	1112, 1113, 1114, 1117, 1118, 1119, 1120
UA.V.B.K5	1115
UA.V.B.K6a	1088, 1092, 1096, 1097, 1098, 1099, 1102, 1103, 1104, 1105, 1109, 1110, 1188, 1331, 1332, 1339, 1341, 1362
UA.V.B.K6b	1067, 1333
UA.V.B.K7	1134
UA.V.C.K2	1038, 1235, 1334
UA.V.C.K2c	1234
UA.V.C.K3	1236, 1237, 1238, 1239
UA.V.C.K4	1240, 1241
UA.V.D.K1	1250, 1251, 1299, 1337
UA.V.D.K2	1242, 1243, 1253, 1284
UA.V.D.K3	1252, 1315
UA.V.D.K4	1245, 1246, 1247, 1248, 1249, 1291
UA.V.D.K5	1244
UA.V.E.K1	1262
UA.V.E.K3	1261, 1302

Cross-Reference B Airman Knowledge Test Report Codes and Question Numbers

ACS Code	Question Numbers
UA.V.E.K4	1259, 1260, 1273
UA.V.E.K5	1255, 1256, 1257, 1258, 1297
UA.V.E.K6	1263, 1264
UA.V.E.K7	1254
UA.V.E.K8	1351
UA.V.F.K1	1265, 1266, 1267, 1269, 1336
UA.V.F.K2	1268

Tests are hard.
Studying doesn't need to be.

Millions of pilots and mechanics chose ASA and passed their tests the first time.

asa2fly.com/TestPrep

Remote pilot operations.

Whether you use your drone for business or recreation, ASA has the resources to teach you the essentials of safe and effective uncrewed aircraft operations. From textbooks to logbooks, you can count on ASA's experience in aviation training to provide the information necessary to become a successful aviator.

asa2fly.com/UAS

— Since 1940 —

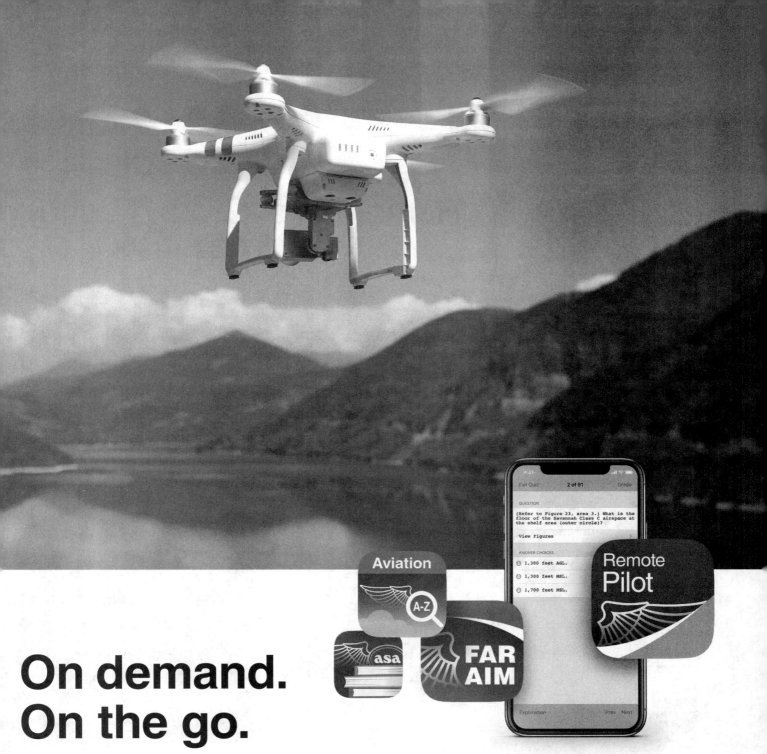

On demand.
On the go.

ASA apps have been helping students study and prepare for FAA knowledge exams for more than 10 years. Supplement your test preparation with the Remote Pilot Prepware app, stay up to date with current regulations using the FAR/AIM app, and learn aviation language with the Aviation Dictionary app.

Available for Apple and Android operating systems.

asa2fly.com/Apps

— Since 1940 —

Read, watch, practice, prepare.

Pass your FAA Part 107 Knowledge Exam with this convenient and comprehensive curriculum from ASA. Remote Pilot Ground School includes online textbook lessons, engaging videos, practice tests, course tracking, test-taking tips, and full-length sample exams.

asa2fly.com/UAS

— Since 1940 —

FAA-CT-8080-2H

Airman Knowledge Testing Supplement for Sport Pilot, Recreational Pilot, Remote Pilot, and Private Pilot

2018

U.S. Department of Transportation
FEDERAL AVIATION ADMINISTRATION
Flight Standards Service

Preface

This testing supplement supersedes FAA-CT-8080-2G, Airman Knowledge Testing Supplement for Sport Pilot, Recreational Pilot, and Private Pilot, dated 2016.

This Airman Knowledge Testing Supplement is designed by the Federal Aviation Administration (FAA) Flight Standards Service. It is intended for use by Airman Knowledge Testing (AKT) Organization Designation Authorization (ODA) Holders and other entities approved and/or authorized to administer airman knowledge tests on behalf of the FAA in the following knowledge areas:

Sport Pilot–Airplane (ASEL and ASES)
Sport Pilot–Gyroplane
Sport Pilot–Glider
Sport Pilot–Airship (LTA)
Sport Pilot–Balloon (LTA)
Sport Pilot–Weight-Shift Control (WSCS and WSCL)
Sport Pilot–Powered Parachute (PPL and PPS)

Recreational Pilot–Airplane (RPA)
Recreational Pilot–Rotorcraft/Helicopter (RPH)

Recreational Pilot–Rotorcraft/Gyroplane (RPG)
Private Pilot–Airplane/Recreational Pilot–Transition (PAT)
Private Pilot–Helicopter/Recreational Pilot–Transition (PHT)
Private Pilot–Gyroplane/Recreational Pilot–Transition (POT)
Private Pilot–Airplane (PAR)
Private Pilot–Rotorcraft/Helicopter (PRH)
Private Pilot–Rotorcraft/Gyroplane (PRO)
Private Pilot–Glider (POL)
Private Pilot–Free Balloon–Hot Air (PBH)
Private Pilot–Free Balloon–Gas (PBG)
Private Pilot–Lighter-Than-Air–Airship (PLA)
Private Pilot–Powered-Parachute (PPP)
Private Pilot–Weight-shift Control (PWS)

Unmanned Aircraft General–Small (UAG)

Comments regarding this supplement, or any Airman Testing publication, should be emailed to AFS630comments@faa.gov.

Contents

Preface iii
Contents v

Appendix 1

Legend 1. Sectional Aeronautical Chart. 1-1
Legend 2. Chart Supplement. 1-2
Legend 3. Chart Supplement. 1-3
Legend 4. Chart Supplement. 1-4
Legend 5. Chart Supplement. 1-5
Legend 6. Chart Supplement. 1-6
Legend 7. Chart Supplement. 1-7
Legend 8. Chart Supplement. 1-8
Legend 9. Chart Supplement. 1-9
Legend 10. Chart Supplement. 1-10
Legend 11. Chart Supplement. 1-11
Legend 12. Chart Supplement. 1-12
Legend 13. Chart Supplement. 1-13
Legend 14. Chart Supplement. 1-14
Legend 15. Chart Supplement. 1-15
Legend 16. Chart Supplement. 1-16
Legend 17. Chart Supplement. 1-17
Legend 18. Chart Supplement. 1-18
Legend 19. Chart Supplement. 1-19

Appendix 2

Figure 1. Lift Vector. 2-1
Figure 2. Load Factor Chart. 2-2
Figure 3. Altimeter. 2-3
Figure 4. Airspeed Indicator. 2-4
Figure 5. Turn Coordinator. 2-5
Figure 6. Heading Indicator. 2-6
Figure 7. Attitude Indicator. 2-7
Figure 8. Density Altitude Chart. 2-8
Figure 9. Control Position for Taxi. 2-9
Figure 10. Gyroplane Rotor Blade Position. 2-10
Figure 11. Glider Yaw String. 2-11
Figure 12. Aviation Routine Weather Reports (METAR). 2-12
Figure 13. Telephone Weather Briefing. 2-13
Figure 14. Pilot Weather Report. 2-14
Figure 15. Terminal Aerodrome Forecasts (TAF). 2-15
Figure 17. Winds and Temperatures Aloft Forecast. 2-16
Figure 18. Weather Depiction Chart. 2-17
Figure 19. Low-Level Significant Weather (SIGWX) Prognostic Charts. 2-18
Figure 20. Sectional Chart Excerpt. 2-19
Figure 21. Sectional Chart Excerpt. 2-20
Figure 22. Sectional Chart Excerpt. 2-21

Figure	Description	Page
Figure 23.	Sectional Chart Excerpt.	2-22
Figure 24.	Sectional Chart Excerpt.	2-23
Figure 25.	Sectional Chart Excerpt.	2-24
Figure 26.	Sectional Chart Excerpt.	2-25
Figure 27.	Time Conversion Table.	2-26
Figure 28.	VOR.	2-27
Figure 31.	Chart Supplement.	2-28
Figure 32.	Airplane Weight and Balance Tables.	2-29
Figure 33.	Airplane Weight and Balance Tables.	2-30
Figure 34.	Airplane Weight and Balance Graphs.	2-31
Figure 35.	Airplane Power Setting Table.	2-32
Figure 36.	Crosswind Component Graph.	2-33
Figure 37.	Airplane Landing Distance Graph.	2-34
Figure 38.	Airplane Landing Distance Table.	2-35
Figure 39.	Gyroplane Takeoff and Landing Graphs.	2-36
Figure 40.	Airplane Takeoff Distance Graph.	2-37
Figure 41.	Helicopter Weight and Balance Graph.	2-38
Figure 42.	Helicopter Weight and Balance Graphs.	2-39
Figure 43.	Helicopter CG Envelopes.	2-40
Figure 44.	Gyroplane Weight and Balance Graph.	2-41
Figure 45.	Gyroplane Weight and Balance Graph.	2-42
Figure 46.	Helicopter Height Velocity Diagram.	2-43
Figure 47.	VASI Illustrations.	2-44
Figure 48.	Airport Diagram.	2-45
Figure 49.	Airport Diagram.	2-46
Figure 50.	Wind Sock Airport Landing Indicator.	2-47
Figure 51.	Flight Plan Form.	2-48
Figure 52.	Chart Supplement.	2-49
Figure 53.	Glider Weight and Balance Diagram.	2-50
Figure 54.	Glider Performance Graph.	2-51
Figure 56.	Hot Air Balloon Performance Graph.	2-53
Figure 57.	Hot Air Balloon Performance Graph.	2-54
Figure 58.	Compass Card.	2-55
Figure 59.	Sectional Chart Excerpt.	2-56
Figure 60.	Weight and Balance Diagram.	2-57
Figure 61.	Weight and Balance Diagram.	2-58
Figure 62.	Rectangular Course.	2-59
Figure 63.	Chart Supplement.	2-60
Figure 64.	Airport Markings.	2-61
Figure 65.	U.S. Airport Signs.	2-62
Figure 66.	S-Turn Diagram.	2-63
Figure 67.	Weight and Balance Chart.	2-64
Figure 68.	Wind Triangle.	2-65
Figure 69.	Sectional Chart Excerpt.	2-66
Figure 70.	Sectional Chart Excerpt.	2-67
Figure 71.	Sectional Chart Excerpt.	2-68
Figure 72.	Velocity vs. G-Loads.	2-69
Figure 73.	Glider Hand Signals.	2-70
Figure 74.	Sectional Chart Excerpt.	2-71
Figure 75.	Sectional Chart Excerpt.	2-72
Figure 76.	Sectional Chart Excerpt.	2-73

Figure 77. Chart Supplement. 2-74
Figure 78. Sectional Chart Excerpt 2-75
Figure 79. Chart Supplement. 2-76
Figure 80. Sectional Chart Excerpt 2-77
Figure 81. Chart Supplement. 2-78
Figure 82. Altimeter 2-79

Appendix 1

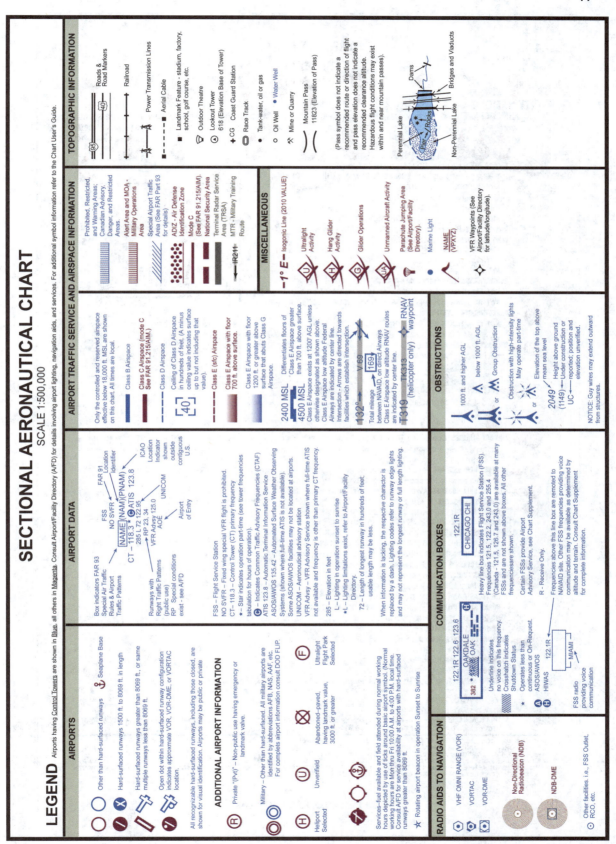

Legend 1. Sectional Aeronautical Chart.

Appendix 1

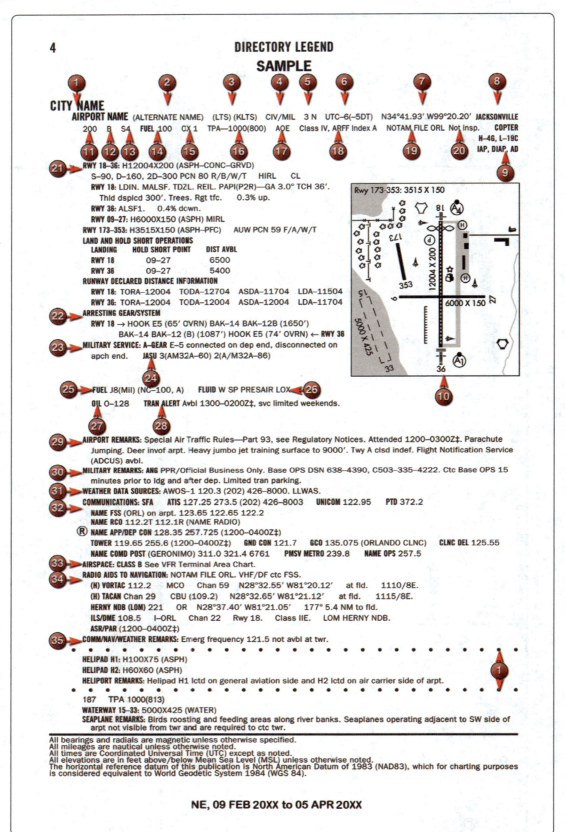

Legend 2. Chart Supplement.

Appendix 1

DIRECTORY LEGEND 5

SKETCH LEGEND

RUNWAYS/LANDING AREAS

- Hard Surfaced
- Metal Surface
- Sod, Gravel, etc.
- Light Plane, Ski Landing Area or Water
- Under Construction
- Closed
- Helicopter Landings Area
- Displaced Threshold
- Taxiway, Apron and Stopways

MISCELLANEOUS BASE AND CULTURAL FEATURES

- Buildings
- Power Lines
- Fence
- Towers
- Tanks
- Oil Well
- Smoke Stack
- Obstruction 5812
- Controlling Obstruction .... +5812
- Trees
- Populated Places
- Cuts and Fills ...... Cut   Fill
- Cliffs and Depressions
- Ditch
- Hill

RADIO AIDS TO NAVIGATION

- VORTAC
- VOR
- VOR/DME
- NDB
- TACAN
- NDB/DME

MISCELLANEOUS AERONAUTICAL FEATURES

- Airport Beacon
- Wind Cone
- Landing Tee
- Tetrahedron
- Control Tower .... or TWR

When control tower and rotating beacon are co-located beacon symbol will be used and further identified as TWR.

APPROACH LIGHTING SYSTEMS

A dot "•" portrayed with approach lighting letter identifier indicates sequenced flashing lights (F) installed with the approach lighting system e.g. (A1) Negative symbology, e.g. (A1). (V) indicates Pilot Controlled Lighting (PCL).

- Runway Centerline Lighting
- (A) Approach Lighting System ALSF-2
- (A1) Approach Lighting System ALSF-1
- (A2) Short Approach Lighting System SALS/SALSF
- (A3) Simplified Short Approach Lighting System (SSALR) with RAIL
- (A4) Medium Intensity Approach Lighting System (MALS and MALSF)/(SSALS and SSALF)
- (A5) Medium Intensity Approach Lighting System (MALSR) and RAIL
- Omnidirectional Approach Lighting System (ODALS)
- (D) Navy Parallel Row and Cross Bar
- Air Force Overrun
- (V) Visual Approach Slope Indicator with Standard Threshold Clearance provided
- (V2) Pulsating Visual Approach Slope Indicator (PVASI)
- (V3) Visual Approach Slope Indicator with a threshold crossing height to accomodate long bodied or jumbo aircraft
- (V4) Tri-color Visual Approach Slope Indicator (TRCV)
- (V5) Approach Path Alignment Panel (APAP)
- (P) Precision Approach Path Indicator (PAPI)

NE, 09 FEB 20XX to 05 APR 20XX

Legend 3. Chart Supplement.

Appendix 1

6   **DIRECTORY LEGEND**

LEGEND

This directory is a listing of data on record with the FAA on all open to the public airports, military facilities and selected private use facilities specifically requested by the Department of Defense (DoD) for which a DoD Instrument Approach Procedure has been published in the U.S. Terminal Procedures Publication. Additionally this listing contains data for associated terminal control facilities, air route traffic control centers, and radio aids to navigation within the conterminous United States, Puerto Rico and the Virgin Islands. Joint civil/military and civil airports are listed alphabetically by state, associated city and airport name and cross-referenced by airport name. Military facilities are listed alphabetically by state and official airport name and cross-referenced by associated city name. Navaids, flight service stations and remote communication outlets that are associated with an airport, but with a different name, are listed alphabetically under their own name, as well as under the airport with which they are associated.

The listing of an open to the public airport in this directory merely indicates the airport operator's willingness to accommodate transient aircraft, and does not represent that the facility conforms with any Federal or local standards, or that it has been approved for use on the part of the general public. Military and private use facilities published in this directory are open to civil pilots only in an emergency or with prior permission. See Special Notice Section, Civil Use of Military Fields.

The information on obstructions is taken from reports submitted to the FAA. Obstruction data has not been verified in all cases. Pilots are cautioned that objects not indicated in this tabulation (or on the airports sketches and/or charts) may exist which can create a hazard to flight operation. Detailed specifics concerning services and facilities tabulated within this directory are contained in the Aeronautical Information Manual, Basic Flight Information and ATC Procedures.

The legend items that follow explain in detail the contents of this Directory and are keyed to the circled numbers on the sample on the preceding pages.

 CITY/AIRPORT NAME

Civil and joint civil/military airports and facilities in this directory are listed alphabetically by state and associated city. Where the city name is different from the airport name the city name will appear on the line above the airport name. Airports with the same associated city name will be listed alphabetically by airport name and will be separated by a dashed rule line. A solid rule line will separate all others. FAA approved helipads and seaplane landing areas associated with a land airport will be separated by a dotted line. Military airports are listed alphabetically by state and official airport name.

 ALTERNATE NAME

Alternate names, if any, will be shown in parentheses.

 LOCATION IDENTIFIER

The location identifier is a three or four character FAA code followed by a four-character ICAO code assigned to airports. ICAO codes will only be published at joint civil/military, and military facilities. If two different military codes are assigned, both codes will be shown with the primary operating agency's code listed first. These identifiers are used by ATC in lieu of the airport name in flight plans, flight strips and other written records and computer operations. Zeros will appear with a slash to differentiate them from the letter "O".

 OPERATING AGENCY

Airports within this directory are classified into two categories, Military/Federal Government and Civil airports open to the general public, plus selected private use airports. The operating agency is shown for military, private use and joint civil/military airports. The operating agency is shown by an abbreviation as listed below. When an organization is a tenant, the abbreviation is enclosed in parenthesis. No classification indicates the airport is open to the general public with no military tenant.

A	US Army	MC	Marine Corps
AFRC	Air Force Reserve Command	N	Navy
AF	US Air Force	NAF	Naval Air Facility
ANG	Air National Guard	NAS	Naval Air Station
AR	US Army Reserve	NASA	National Air and Space Administration
ARNG	US Army National Guard	P	US Civil Airport Wherein Permit Covers
CG	US Coast Guard		Use by Transient Military Aircraft
CIV/MIL	Joint Use Civil/Military	PVT	Private Use Only (Closed to the Public)
DND	Department of National Defense Canada		

 AIRPORT LOCATION

Airport location is expressed as distance and direction from the center of the associated city in nautical miles and cardinal points, e.g., 4 NE.

 TIME CONVERSION

Hours of operation of all facilities are expressed in Coordinated Universal Time (UTC) and shown as "Z" time. The directory indicates the number of hours to be subtracted from UTC to obtain local standard time and local daylight saving time UTC–5(–4DT). The symbol ‡ indicates that during periods of Daylight Saving Time effective hours will be one hour earlier than shown. In those areas where daylight saving time is not observed the (–4DT) and ‡ will not be shown. Daylight saving time is in effect from 0200 local time the second Sunday in March to 0200 local time the first Sunday in November. Canada and all U.S. Conterminous States observe daylight saving time except Arizona and Puerto Rico, and the Virgin Islands. If the state observes daylight saving time and the operating times are other than daylight saving times, the operating hours will include the dates, times and no ‡ symbol will be shown, i.e., April 15–Aug 31 0630–1700Z, Sep 1–Apr 14 0600–1700Z.

NE, 09 FEB 20XX to 05 APR 20XX

Legend 4. Chart Supplement.

Appendix 1

DIRECTORY LEGEND 7

 GEOGRAPHIC POSITION OF AIRPORT—AIRPORT REFERENCE POINT (ARP)
Positions are shown as hemisphere, degrees, minutes and hundredths of a minute and represent the approximate geometric center of all usable runway surfaces.

 CHARTS
Charts refer to the Sectional Chart and Low and High Altitude Enroute Chart and panel on which the airport or facility is located. Helicopter Chart locations will be indicated as COPTER. IFR Gulf of Mexico West and IFR Gulf of Mexico Central will be depicted as GOMW and GOMC.

 INSTRUMENT APPROACH PROCEDURES, AIRPORT DIAGRAMS
IAP indicates an airport for which a prescribed (Public Use) FAA Instrument Approach Procedure has been published. DIAP indicates an airport for which a prescribed DoD Instrument Approach Procedure has been published in the U.S. Terminal Procedures. See the Special Notice Section of this directory, Civil Use of Military Fields and the Aeronautical Information Manual 5–4–5 Instrument Approach Procedure Charts for additional information. AD indicates an airport for which an airport diagram has been published. Airport diagrams are located in the back of each A/FD volume alphabetically by associated city and airport name.

 AIRPORT SKETCH
The airport sketch, when provided, depicts the airport and related topographical information as seen from the air and should be used in conjunction with the text. It is intended as a guide for pilots in VFR conditions. Symbology that is not self-explanatory will be reflected in the sketch legend. The airport sketch will be oriented with True North at the top. Airport sketches will be added incrementally.

 ELEVATION
The highest point of an airport's usable runways measured in feet from mean sea level. When elevation is sea level it will be indicated as "00". When elevation is below sea level a minus "−" sign will precede the figure.

 ROTATING LIGHT BEACON
B indicates rotating beacon is available. Rotating beacons operate sunset to sunrise unless otherwise indicated in the AIRPORT REMARKS or MILITARY REMARKS segment of the airport entry.

 SERVICING—CIVIL

S1:	Minor airframe repairs.	S5:	Major airframe repairs.
S2:	Minor airframe and minor powerplant repairs.	S6:	Minor airframe and major powerplant repairs.
S3:	Major airframe and minor powerplant repairs.	S7:	Major powerplant repairs.
S4:	Major airframe and major powerplant repairs.	S8:	Minor powerplant repairs.

 FUEL

CODE	FUEL	CODE	FUEL
80	Grade 80 gasoline (Red)	B+	Jet B, Wide-cut, turbine fuel with FS–II*, FP** minus 50° C.
100	Grade 100 gasoline (Green)		
100LL	100LL gasoline (low lead) (Blue)	J4 (JP4)	(JP–4 military specification) FP** minus 58° C.
115	Grade 115 gasoline (115/145 military specification) (Purple)		
A	Jet A, Kerosene, without FS–II*, FP** minus 40°C.	J5 (JP5)	(JP–5 military specification) Kerosene with FS–11, FP** minus 46°C.
A+	Jet A, Kerosene, with FS–II*, FP** minus 40°C.	J8 (JP8)	(JP–8 military specification) Jet A–1, Kerosene with FS–II*, FP** minus 47°C.
A1	Jet A–1, Kerosene, without FS–II*, FP** minus 47°C.	J8+100	(JP–8 military specification) Jet A–1, Kerosene with FS–II*, FP** minus 47°C, with-fuel additive package that improves thermo stability characteristics of JP-8.
A1+	Jet A–1, Kerosene with FS–II*, FP** minus 47° C.		
B	Jet B, Wide-cut, turbine fuel without FS–II*, FP** minus 50° C.	J	(Jet Fuel Type Unknown)
		MOGAS	Automobile gasoline which is to be used as aircraft fuel.

*(Fuel System Icing Inhibitor)
**(Freeze Point)

NOTE: Certain automobile gasoline may be used in specific aircraft engines if a FAA supplemental type certificate has been obtained. Automobile gasoline, which is to be used in aircraft engines, will be identified as "MOGAS", however, the grade/type and other octane rating will not be published.

Data shown on fuel availability represents the most recent information the publisher has been able to acquire. Because of a variety of factors, the fuel listed may not always be obtainable by transient civil pilots. Confirmation of availability of fuel should be made directly with fuel suppliers at locations where refueling is planned.

OXYGEN—CIVIL

OX 1	High Pressure	OX 3	High Pressure—Replacement Bottles
OX 2	Low Pressure	OX 4	Low Pressure—Replacement Bottles

TRAFFIC PATTERN ALTITUDE
Traffic Pattern Altitude (TPA)—The first figure shown is TPA above mean sea level. The second figure in parentheses is TPA above airport elevation. Multiple TPA shall be shown as "TPA—See Remarks" and detailed information shall be shown in the Airport or Military Remarks Section. Traffic pattern data for USAF bases, USN facilities, and U.S. Army airports (including those on which ACC or U.S. Army is a tenant) that deviate from standard pattern altitudes shall be shown in Military Remarks.

NE, 09 FEB 20XX to 05 APR 20XX

Legend 5. Chart Supplement.

Appendix 1

8 **DIRECTORY LEGEND**

17 AIRPORT OF ENTRY, LANDING RIGHTS, AND CUSTOMS USER FEE AIRPORTS

U.S. CUSTOMS USER FEE AIRPORT—Private Aircraft operators are frequently required to pay the costs associated with customs processing.

AOE—Airport of Entry. A customs Airport of Entry where permission from U.S. Customs is not required to land. However, at least one hour advance notice of arrival is required.

LRA—Landing Rights Airport. Application for permission to land must be submitted in advance to U.S. Customs. At least one hour advance notice of arrival is required.

NOTE: Advance notice of arrival at both an AOE and LRA airport may be included in the flight plan when filed in Canada or Mexico. Where Flight Notification Service (ADCUS) is available the airport remark will indicate this service. This notice will also be treated as an application for permission to land in the case of an LRA. Although advance notice of arrival may be relayed to Customs through Mexico, Canada, and U.S. Communications facilities by flight plan, the aircraft operator is solely responsible for ensuring that Customs receives the notification. (See Customs, Immigration and Naturalization, Public Health and Agriculture Department requirements in the International Flight Information Manual for further details.)

US Customs Air and Sea Ports, Inspectors and Agents
Northeast Sector (New England and Atlantic States—ME to MD)   407–975–1740
Southeast Sector (Atlantic States—DC, WV, VA to FL)   407–975–1780
Central Sector (Interior of the US, including Gulf states—MS, AL, LA) 407–975–1760
Southwest East Sector (OK and eastern TX)   407–975–1840
Southwest West Sector (Western TX, NM and AZ)   407–975–1820
Pacific Sector (WA, OR, CA, HI and AK)   407–975–1800

18 CERTIFICATED AIRPORT (14 CFR PART 139)

Airports serving Department of Transportation certified carriers and certified under 14 CFR part 139 are indicated by the Class and the ARFF Index; e.g. Class I, ARFF Index A, which relates to the availability of crash, fire, rescue equipment. Class I airports can have an ARFF Index A through E, depending on the aircraft length and scheduled departures. Class II, III, and IV will always carry an Index A.

14 CFR PART 139 CERTIFICATED AIRPORTS
AIRPORT CLASSIFICATIONS

Type of Air Carrier Operation	Class I	Class II	Class III	Class IV
Scheduled Air Carrier Aircraft with 31 or more passenger seats	X			
Unscheduled Air Carrier Aircraft with 31 or more passengers seats	X	X		X
Scheduled Air Carrier Aircraft with 10 to 30 passenger seats	X	X	X	

14 CFR–PART 139 CERTIFICATED AIRPORTS
INDICES AND AIRCRAFT RESCUE AND FIRE FIGHTING EQUIPMENT REQUIREMENTS

Airport Index	Required No. Vehicles	Aircraft Length	Scheduled Departures	Agent + Water for Foam
A	1	<90′	≥1	500#DC or HALON 1211 or 450#DC + 100 gal H_2O
B	1 or 2	≥90′, <126′	≥5	Index A + 1500 gal H_2O
		≥126′, <159′	<5	
C	2 or 3	≥126′, <159′	≥5	Index A + 3000 gal H_2O
		≥159′, <200′	<5	
D	3	≥159′, <200′		Index A + 4000 gal H_2O
		>200′	<5	
E	3	≥200′	≥5	Index A + 6000 gal H_2O

> Greater Than; < Less Than; ≥ Equal or Greater Than; ≤ Equal or Less Than; H_2O–Water; DC–Dry Chemical.

NOTE: The listing of ARFF index does not necessarily assure coverage for non-air carrier operations or at other than prescribed times for air carrier. ARFF Index Ltd.—indicates ARFF coverage may or may not be available, for information contact airport manager prior to flight.

 NOTAM SERVICE

All public use landing areas are provided NOTAM service. A NOTAM FILE identifier is shown for individual langing areas, e.g., "NOTAM FILE BNA". See the AIM, Basic Flight Information and ATC Procedures for a detailed description of NOTAMs.

NE, 09 FEB 20XX to 05 APR 20XX

Legend 6. Chart Supplement.

DIRECTORY LEGEND 9

Current NOTAMs are available from flight service stations at 1–800–WX–BRIEF (992–7433) or online through the FAA PilotWeb at https://pilotweb.nas.faa.gov. Military NOTAMs are available using the Defense Internet NOTAM Service (DINS) at https://www.notams.jcs.mil.

Pilots flying to or from airports not available through the FAA PilotWeb or DINS can obtain assistance from Flight Service.

All airports not inspected by FAA will be identified by the note: Not insp. This indicates that the airport information has been provided by the owner or operator of the field.

Runway information is shown on two lines. That information common to the entire runway is shown on the first line while information concerning the runway ends is shown on the second or following line. Runway direction, surface, length, width, weight bearing capacity, lighting, and slope, when available are shown for each runway. Multiple runways are shown with the longest runway first. Direction, length, width, and lighting are shown for sea-lanes. The full dimensions of helipads are shown, e.g., 50X150. Runway data that requires clarification will be placed in the remarks section.

RUNWAY DESIGNATION

Runways are normally numbered in relation to their magnetic orientation rounded off to the nearest 10 degrees. Parallel runways can be designated L (left)/R (right)/C (center). Runways may be designated as Ultralight or assault strips. Assault strips are shown by magnetic bearing.

RUNWAY DIMENSIONS

Runway length and width are shown in feet. Length shown is runway end to end including displaced thresholds, but excluding those areas designed as overruns.

RUNWAY SURFACE AND LENGTH

Runway lengths prefixed by the letter "H" indicate that the runways are hard surfaced (concrete, asphalt, or part asphalt–concrete). If the runway length is not prefixed, the surface is sod, clay, etc. The runway surface composition is indicated in parentheses after runway length as follows:

(AFSC)—Aggregate friction seal coat
(AMS)—Temporary metal planks coated with nonskid material
(ASPH)—Asphalt
(CONC)—Concrete
(DIRT)—Dirt
(GRVD)—Grooved
(GRVL)—Gravel, or cinders
(MATS)—Pierced steel planking, landing mats, membranes
(PEM)—Part concrete, part asphalt
(PFC)—Porous friction courses
(PSP)—Pierced steel plank
(RFSC)—Rubberized friction seal coat
(TURF)—Turf
(TRTD)—Treated
(WC)—Wire combed

RUNWAY WEIGHT BEARING CAPACITY

Runway strength data shown in this publication is derived from available information and is a realistic estimate of capability at an average level of activity. It is not intended as a maximum allowable weight or as an operating limitation. Many airport pavements are capable of supporting limited operations with gross weights in excess of the published figures. Permissible operating weights, insofar as runway strengths are concerned, are a matter of agreement between the owner and user. When desiring to operate into any airport at weights in excess of those published in the publication, users should contact the airport management for permission. Runway strength figures are shown in thousand of pounds, with the last three figures being omitted. Add 000 to figure following S, D, 2S, 2T, AUW, SWL, etc., for gross weight capacity. A blank space following the letter designator is used to indicate the runway can sustain aircraft with this type landing gear, although definite runway weight bearing capacity figures are not available, e.g., S, D. Applicable codes for typical gear configurations with S=Single, D=Dual, T=Triple and Q=Quadruple:

CURRENT	NEW	NEW DESCRIPTION
S	S	Single wheel type landing gear (DC3), (C47), (F15), etc.
D	D	Dual wheel type landing gear (BE1900), (B737), (A319), etc.
T	D	Dual wheel type landing gear (P3, C9).
ST	2S	Two single wheels in tandem type landing gear (C130).
TRT	2T	Two triple wheels in tandem type landing gear (C17), etc.
DT	2D	Two dual wheels in tandem type landing gear (B707), etc.
TT	2D	Two dual wheels in tandem type landing gear (B757, KC135).
SBTT	2D/D1	Two dual wheels in tandem/dual wheel body gear type landing gear (KC10).
None	2D/2D1	Two dual wheels in tandem/two dual wheels in tandem body gear type landing gear (A340–600).
DDT	2D/2D2	Two dual wheels in tandem/two dual wheels in double tandem body gear type landing gear (B747, E4).
TTT	3D	Three dual wheels in tandem type landing gear (B777), etc.
TT	D2	Dual wheel gear two struts per side main gear type landing gear (B52).
TDT	C5	Complex dual wheel and quadruple wheel combination landing gear (C5).

NE, 09 FEB 20XX to 05 APR 20XX

Legend 7. Chart Supplement.

Appendix 1

10   **DIRECTORY LEGEND**

    AUW—All up weight. Maximum weight bearing capacity for any aircraft irrespective of landing gear configuration.
    SWL—Single Wheel Loading. (This includes information submitted in terms of Equivalent Single Wheel Loading (ESWL) and Single Isolated Wheel Loading).
    PSI—Pounds per square inch. PSI is the actual figure expressing maximum pounds per square inch runway will support, e.g., (SWL 000/PSI 535).

Omission of weight bearing capacity indicates information unknown.

The ACN/PCN System is the ICAO standard method of reporting pavement strength for pavements with bearing strengths greater than 12,500 pounds. The Pavement Classification Number (PCN) is established by an engineering assessment of the runway. The PCN is for use in conjunction with an Aircraft Classification Number (ACN). Consult the Aircraft Flight Manual, Flight Information Handbook, or other appropriate source for ACN tables or charts. Currently, ACN data may not be available for all aircraft. If an ACN table or chart is available, the ACN can be calculated by taking into account the aircraft weight, the pavement type, and the subgrade category. For runways that have been evaluated under the ACN/PCN system, the PCN will be shown as a five-part code (e.g. PCN 80 R/B/W/T). Details of the coded format are as follows:

(1) The PCN NUMBER—The reported PCN indicates that an aircraft with an ACN equal or less than the reported PCN can operate on the pavement subject to any limitation on the tire pressure.

(2) The type of pavement:
    R — Rigid
    F — Flexible

(3) The pavement subgrade category:
    A — High
    B — Medium
    C — Low
    D — Ultra-low

(4) The maximum tire pressure authorized for the pavement:
    W — High, no limit
    X — Medium, limited to 217 psi
    Y — Low, limited to 145 psi
    Z — Very low, limited to 73 psi

(5) Pavement evaluation method:
    T — Technical evaluation
    U — By experience of aircraft using the pavement

NOTE: Prior permission from the airport controlling authority is required when the ACN of the aircraft exceeds the published PCN or aircraft tire pressure exceeds the published limits.

RUNWAY LIGHTING

Lights are in operation sunset to sunrise. Lighting available by prior arrangement only or operating part of the night and/or pilot controlled lighting with specific operating hours are indicated under airport or military remarks. At USN/USMC facilities lights are available only during airport hours of operation. Since obstructions are usually lighted, obstruction lighting is not included in this code. Unlighted obstructions on or surrounding an airport will be noted in airport or military remarks. Runway lights nonstandard (NSTD) are systems for which the light fixtures are not FAA approved L-800 series: color, intensity, or spacing does not meet FAA standards. Nonstandard runway lights, VASI, or any other system not listed below will be shown in airport remarks or military service. Temporary, emergency or limited runway edge lighting such as flares, smudge pots, lanterns or portable runway lights will also be shown in airport remarks or military service. Types of lighting are shown with the runway or runway end they serve.

NSTD—Light system fails to meet FAA standards.
LIRL—Low Intensity Runway Lights.
MIRL—Medium Intensity Runway Lights.
HIRL—High Intensity Runway Lights.
RAIL—Runway Alignment Indicator Lights.
REIL—Runway End Identifier Lights.
CL—Centerline Lights.
TDZL—Touchdown Zone Lights.
ODALS—Omni Directional Approach Lighting System.
AF OVRN—Air Force Overrun 1000′ Standard Approach Lighting System.
LDIN—Lead-In Lighting System.
MALS—Medium Intensity Approach Lighting System.
MALSF—Medium Intensity Approach Lighting System with Sequenced Flashing Lights.
MALSR—Medium Intensity Approach Lighting System with Runway Alignment Indicator Lights.
SALS—Short Approach Lighting System.
SALSF—Short Approach Lighting System with Sequenced Flashing Lights.
SSALS—Simplified Short Approach Lighting System.
SSALF—Simplified Short Approach Lighting System with Sequenced Flashing Lights.
SSALR—Simplified Short Approach Lighting System with Runway Alignment Indicator Lights.
ALSAF—High Intensity Approach Lighting System with Sequenced Flashing Lights.
ALSF1—High Intensity Approach Lighting System with Sequenced Flashing Lights, Category I, Configuration.
ALSF2—High Intensity Approach Lighting System with Sequenced Flashing Lights, Category II, Configuration.
SF—Sequenced Flashing Lights.
OLS—Optical Landing System.
WAVE–OFF.

NOTE: Civil ALSF2 may be operated as SSALR during favorable weather conditions. When runway edge lights are positioned more than 10 feet from the edge of the usable runway surface a remark will be added in the "Remarks" portion of the airport entry. This is applicable to Air Force, Air National Guard and Air Force Reserve Bases, and those joint civil/military airfields on which they are tenants.

NE, 09 FEB 20XX to 05 APR 20XX

Legend 8. Chart Supplement.

Appendix 1

DIRECTORY LEGEND 11

VISUAL GLIDESLOPE INDICATORS

APAP—A system of panels, which may or may not be lighted, used for alignment of approach path.
    PNIL   APAP on left side of runway   PNIR   APAP on right side of runway
PAPI—Precision Approach Path Indicator
    P2L   2-identical light units placed on left side of runway   P4L   4-identical light units placed on left side of runway
    P2R   2-identical light units placed on right side of runway   P4R   4-identical light units placed on right side of runway
PVASI—Pulsating/steady burning visual approach slope indicator, normally a single light unit projecting two colors.
    PSIL   PVASI on left side of runway   PSIR   PVASI on right side of runway
SAVASI—Simplified Abbreviated Visual Approach Slope Indicator
    S2L   2-box SAVASI on left side of runway   S2R   2-box SAVASI on right side of runway

TRCV—Tri-color visual approach slope indicator, normally a single light unit projecting three colors.
    TRIL   TRCV on left side of runway   TRIR   TRCV on right side of runway
VASI—Visual Approach Slope Indicator
    V2L   2-box VASI on left side of runway   V6L   6-box VASI on left side of runway
    V2R   2-box VASI on right side of runway   V6R   6-box VASI on right side of runway
    V4L   4-box VASI on left side of runway   V12   12-box VASI on both sides of runway
    V4R   4-box VASI on right side of runway   V16   16-box VASI on both sides of runway

NOTE: Approach slope angle and threshold crossing height will be shown when available; i.e., –GA 3.5° TCH 37'.

PILOT CONTROL OF AIRPORT LIGHTING

Key Mike	Function
7 times within 5 seconds	Highest intensity available
5 times within 5 seconds	Medium or lower intensity (Lower REIL or REIL-Off)
3 times within 5 seconds	Lowest intensity available (Lower REIL or REIL-Off)

Available systems will be indicated in the airport or military remarks, e.g., ACTIVATE HIRL Rwy 07–25, MALSR Rwy 07, and VASI Rwy 07—122.8.

Where the airport is not served by an instrument approach procedure and/or has an independent type system of different specification installed by the airport sponsor, descriptions of the type lights, method of control, and operating frequency will be explained in clear text. See AIM, "Basic Flight Information and ATC Procedures," for detailed description of pilot control of airport lighting.

RUNWAY SLOPE

When available, runway slope data will only be provided for those airports with an approved FAA instrument approach procedure. Runway slope will be shown only when it is 0.3 percent or greater. On runways less than 8000 feet, the direction of the slope up will be indicated, e.g., 0.3% up NW. On runways 8000 feet or greater, the slope will be shown (up or down) on the runway end line, e.g., RWY 13: 0.3% up., RWY 21: Pole. Rgt tfc. 0.4% down.

RUNWAY END DATA

Information pertaining to the runway approach end such as approach lights, touchdown zone lights, runway end identification lights, visual glideslope indicators, displaced thresholds, controlling obstruction, and right hand traffic pattern, will be shown on the specific runway end. "Rgt tfc"—Right traffic indicates right turns should be made on landing and takeoff for specified runway end.

LAND AND HOLD SHORT OPERATIONS (LAHSO)

LAHSO is an acronym for "Land and Hold Short Operations." These operations include landing and holding short of an intersection runway, an intersecting taxiway, or other predetermined points on the runway other than a runway or taxiway. Measured distance represents the available landing distance on the landing runway, in feet.

Specific questions regarding these distances should be referred to the air traffic manager of the facility concerned. The Aeronautical Information Manual contains specific details on hold–short operations and markings.

RUNWAY DECLARED DISTANCE INFORMATION

TORA—Take-off Run Available. The length of runway declared available and suitable for the ground run of an aeroplane take-off.
TODA—Take-off Distance Available. The length of the take–off run available plus the length of the clearway, if provided.
ASDA—Accelerate-Stop Distance Available. The length of the take–off run available plus the length of the stopway, if provided.
LDA—Landing Distance Available. The length of runway which is declared available and suitable for the ground run of an aeroplane landing.

(22) ARRESTING GEAR/SYSTEMS

Arresting gear is shown as it is located on the runway. The a–gear distance from the end of the appropriate runway (or into the overrun) is indicated in parentheses. A–Gear which has a bi–direction capability and can be utilized for emergency approach end engagement is indicated by a (B). The direction of engaging device is indicated by an arrow. Up to 15 minutes advance notice may be required for rigging A–Gear for approach and engagement. Airport listing may show availability of other than US Systems. This information is provided for emergency requirements only. Refer to current aircraft operating manuals for specific engagement weight and speed criteria based on aircraft structural restrictions and arresting system limitations.

Following is a list of current systems referenced in this publication identified by both Air Force and Navy terminology:

NE, 09 FEB 20XX to 05 APR 20XX

Legend 9. Chart Supplement.

Appendix 1

12   **DIRECTORY LEGEND**

BI-DIRECTIONAL CABLE (B)

TYPE	DESCRIPTION
BAK-9	Rotary friction brake.
BAK-12A	Standard BAK-12 with 950 foot run out, 1-inch cable and 40,000 pound weight setting. Rotary friction brake.
BAK-12B	Extended BAK-12 with 1200 foot run, 1¼ inch Cable and 50,000 pounds weight setting. Rotary friction brake.
E28	Rotary Hydraulic (Water Brake).
M21	Rotary Hydraulic (Water Brake) Mobile.

The following device is used in conjunction with some aircraft arresting systems:

| BAK-14 | A device that raises a hook cable out of a slot in the runway surface and is remotely positioned for engagement by the tower on request. (In addition to personnel reaction time, the system requires up to five seconds to fully raise the cable.) |
| H | A device that raises a hook cable out of a slot in the runway surface and is remotely positioned for engagement by the tower on request. (In addition to personnel reaction time, the system requires up to one and one-half seconds to fully raise the cable.) |

UNI-DIRECTIONAL CABLE

TYPE	DESCRIPTION
MB60	Textile brake—an emergency one-time use, modular braking system employing the tearing of specially woven textile straps to absorb the kinetic energy.
E5/E5-1/E5-3	Chain Type. At USN/USMC stations E-5 A-GEAR systems are rated, e.g., E-5 RATING-13R-1100 HW (DRY), 31L/R-1200 STD (WET). This rating is a function of the A-GEAR chain weight and length and is used to determine the maximum aircraft engaging speed. A dry rating applies to a stabilized surface (dry or wet) while a wet rating takes into account the amount (if any) of wet overrun that is not capable of withstanding the aircraft weight. These ratings are published under Military Service.

FOREIGN CABLE

TYPE	DESCRIPTION	US EQUIVALENT
44B-3H	Rotary Hydraulic) (Water Brake)	
CHAG	Chain	E-5

UNI-DIRECTIONAL BARRIER

TYPE	DESCRIPTION
MA-1A	Web barrier between stanchions attached to a chain energy absorber.
BAK-15	Web barrier between stanchions attached to an energy absorber (water squeezer, rotary friction, chain). Designed for wing engagement.

NOTE: Landing short of the runway threshold on a runway with a BAK-15 in the underrun is a significant hazard. The barrier in the down position still protrudes several inches above the underrun. Aircraft contact with the barrier short of the runway threshold can cause damage to the barrier and substantial damage to the aircraft.

OTHER

TYPE	DESCRIPTION
EMAS	Engineered Material Arresting System, located beyond the departure end of the runway, consisting of high energy absorbing materials which will crush under the weight of an aircraft.

㉓ MILITARY SERVICE

Specific military services available at the airport are listed under this general heading. Remarks applicable to any military service are shown in the individual service listing.

㉔ JET AIRCRAFT STARTING UNITS (JASU)

The numeral preceding the type of unit indicates the number of units available. The absence of the numeral indicates ten or more units available. If the number of units is unknown, the number one will be shown. Absence of JASU designation indicates non-availability.

The following is a list of current JASU systems referenced in this publication:

USAF JASU (For variations in technical data, refer to T.O. 35-1-7.)

ELECTRICAL STARTING UNITS:

A/M32A-86	AC: 115/200v, 3 phase, 90 kva, 0.8 pf, 4 wire
	DC: 28v, 1500 amp, 72 kw (with TR pack)
MC-1A	AC: 115/208v, 400 cycle, 3 phase, 37.5 kva, 0.8 pf, 108 amp, 4 wire
	DC: 28v, 500 amp, 14 kw
MD-3	AC: 115/208v, 400 cycle, 3 phase, 60 kva, 0.75 pf, 4 wire
	DC: 28v, 1500 amp, 45 kw, split bus
MD-3A	AC: 115/208v, 400 cycle, 3 phase, 60 kva, 0.75 pf, 4 wire
	DC: 28v, 1500 amp, 45 kw, split bus
MD-3M	AC: 115/208v, 400 cycle, 3 phase, 60 kva, 0.75 pf, 4 wire
	DC: 28v, 500 amp, 15 kw

NE, 09 FEB 20XX to 05 APR 20XX

Legend 10. Chart Supplement.

1-10

Appendix 1

DIRECTORY LEGEND 13

MD–4	AC: 120/208v, 400 cycle, 3 phase, 62.5 kva, 0.8 pf, 175 amp, "WYE" neutral ground, 4 wire, 120v, 400 cycle, 3 phase, 62.5 kva, 0.8 pf, 303 amp, "DELTA" 3 wire, 120v, 400 cycle, 1 phase, 62.5 kva, 0.8 pf, 520 amp, 2 wire

AIR STARTING UNITS

AM32–95	150 +/– 5 lb/min (2055 +/– 68 cfm) at 51 +/– 2 psia
AM32A–95	150 +/– 5 lb/min @ 49 +/– 2 psia (35 +/– 2 psig)
LASS	150 +/– 5 lb/min @ 49 +/– 2 psia
MA–1A	82 lb/min (1123 cfm) at 130° air inlet temp, 45 psia (min) air outlet press
MC–1	15 cfm, 3500 psia
MC–1A	15 cfm, 3500 psia
MC–2A	15 cfm, 200 psia
MC–11	8,000 cu in cap, 4000 psig, 15 cfm

COMBINED AIR AND ELECTRICAL STARTING UNITS:

AGPU	AC: 115/200v, 400 cycle, 3 phase, 30 kw gen
	DC: 28v, 700 amp
	AIR: 60 lb/min @ 40 psig @ sea level
AM32A–60*	AIR: 120 +/– 4 lb/min (1644 +/– 55 cfm) at 49 +/– 2 psia
	AC: 120/208v, 400 cycle, 3 phase, 75 kva, 0.75 pf, 4 wire, 120v, 1 phase, 25 kva
	DC: 28v, 500 amp, 15 kw
AM32A–60A	AIR: 150 +/– 5 lb/min (2055 +/– 68 cfm) at 51 +/– psia
	AC: 120/208v, 400 cycle, 3 phase, 75 kva, 0.75 pf, 4 wire
	DC: 28v, 200 amp, 5.6 kw
AM32A–60B*	AIR: 130 lb/min, 50 psia
	AC: 120/208v, 400 cycle, 3 phase, 75 kva, 0.75 pf, 4 wire
	DC: 28v, 200 amp, 5.6 kw

*NOTE: During combined air and electrical loads, the pneumatic circuitry takes preference and will limit the amount of electrical power available.

USN JASU
ELECTRICAL STARTING UNITS:

NC–8A/A1	DC: 500 amp constant, 750 amp intermittent, 28v;
	AC: 60 kva @ .8 pf, 115/200v, 3 phase, 400 Hz.
NC–10A/A1/B/C	DC: 750 amp constant, 1000 amp intermittent, 28v;
	AC: 90 kva, 115/200v, 3 phase, 400 Hz.

AIR STARTING UNITS:

GTC–85/GTE–85	120 lbs/min @ 45 psi.
MSU–200NAV/A/U47A–5	204 lbs/min @ 56 psia.
WELLS AIR START SYSTEM	180 lbs/min @ 75 psi or 120 lbs/min @ 45 psi. Simultaneous multiple start capability.

COMBINED AIR AND ELECTRICAL STARTING UNITS:

NCPP–105/RCPT	180 lbs/min @ 75 psi or 120 lbs/min @ 45 psi. 700 amp, 28v DC. 120/208v, 400 Hz AC, 30 kva.

JASU (ARMY)

59B2–1B	28v, 7.5 kw, 280 amp.

OTHER JASU
ELECTRICAL STARTING UNITS (DND):

CE12	AC 115/200v, 140 kva, 400 Hz, 3 phase
CE13	AC 115/200v, 60 kva, 400 Hz, 3 phase
CE14	AC/DC 115/200v, 140 kva, 400 Hz, 3 phase, 28vDC, 1500 amp
CE15	DC 22–35v, 500 amp continuous 1100 amp intermittent
CE16	DC 22–35v, 500 amp continuous 1100 amp intermittent soft start

AIR STARTING UNITS (DND):

CA2	ASA 45.5 psig, 116.4 lb/min

COMBINED AIR AND ELECTRICAL STARTING UNITS (DND)

CEA1	AC 120/208v, 60 kva, 400 Hz, 3 phase DC 28v, 75 amp
	AIR 112.5 lb/min, 47 psig

ELECTRICAL STARTING UNITS (OTHER)

C–26	28v 45kw 115–200v 15kw 380–800 Hz 1 phase 2 wire
C–26–B, C–26–C	28v 45kw: Split Bus: 115–200v 15kw 380–800 Hz 1 phase 2 wire
E3	DC 28v/10kw

AIR STARTING UNITS (OTHER):

A4	40 psi/2 lb/sec (LPAS Mk12, Mk12L, Mk12A, Mk1, Mk2B)
MA–1	150 Air HP, 115 lb/min 50 psia
MA–2	250 Air HP, 150 lb/min 75 psia

CARTRIDGE:

MXU–4A	USAF

NE, 09 FEB 20XX to 05 APR 20XX

Legend 11. Chart Supplement.

Appendix 1

14   **DIRECTORY LEGEND**

 FUEL—MILITARY

Fuel available through US Military Base supply, DESC Into–Plane Contracts and/or reciprocal agreement is listed first and is followed by (Mil). At commercial airports where Into–Plane contracts are in place, the name of the refueling agent is shown. Military fuel should be used first if it is available. When military fuel cannot be obtained but Into–Plane contract fuel is available, Government aircraft must refuel with the contract fuel and applicable refueling agent to avoid any breach in contract terms and conditions. Fuel not available through the above is shown preceded by NC (no contract). When fuel is obtained from NC sources, local purchase procedures must be followed. The US Military Aircraft Identaplates DD Form 1896 (Jet Fuel), DD Form 1897 (Avgas) and AF Form 1245 (Avgas) are used at military installations only. The US Government Aviation Into–Plane Reimbursement (AIR) Card (currently issued by AVCARD) is the instrument to be used to obtain fuel under a DESC Into–Plane Contract and for NC purchases if the refueling agent at the commercial airport accepts the AVCARD. A current list of contract fuel locations is available online at www.desc.dla.mil/Static/ProductsAndServices.asp; click on the Commercial Airports button.

See legend item 14 for fuel code and description.

 SUPPORTING FLUIDS AND SYSTEMS—MILITARY

CODE
ADI   Anti–Detonation Injection Fluid—Reciprocating Engine Aircraft.
W   Water Thrust Augmentation—Jet Aircraft.
WAI   Water–Alcohol Injection Type, Thrust Augmentation—Jet Aircraft.
SP   Single Point Refueling.
PRESAIR   Air Compressors rated 3,000 PSI or more.
De–Ice   Anti–icing/De–icing/Defrosting Fluid (MIL-A-8243).

OXYGEN:
LPOX   Low pressure oxygen servicing.
HPOX   High pressure oxygen servicing.
LHOX   Low and high pressure oxygen servicing.
LOX   Liquid oxygen servicing.
OXRB   Oxygen replacement bottles. (Maintained primarily at Naval stations for use in acft where oxygen can be replenished only by replacement of cylinders.)
OX   Indicates oxygen servicing when type of servicing is unknown.

NOTE: Combinations of above items is used to indicate complete oxygen servicing available;

LHOXRB   Low and high pressure oxygen servicing and replacement bottles;
LPOXRB   Low pressure oxygen replacement bottles only, etc.

NOTE: Aircraft will be serviced with oxygen procured under military specifications only. Aircraft will not be serviced with medical oxygen.

NITROGEN:
LPNIT — Low pressure nitrogen servicing.
HPNIT — High pressure nitrogen servicing.
LHNIT — Low and high pressure nitrogen servicing.

 OIL—MILITARY

US AVIATION OILS (MIL SPECS):

CODE	GRADE, TYPE
O–113	1065, Reciprocating Engine Oil (MIL-L-6082)
O–117	1100, Reciprocating Engine Oil (MIL-L-6082)
O–117+	1100, O–117 plus cyclohexanone (MIL-L-6082)
O–123	1065, (Dispersant), Reciprocating Engine Oil (MIL-L-22851 Type III)
O–128	1100, (Dispersant), Reciprocating Engine Oil (MIL-L-22851 Type II)
O–132	1005, Jet Engine Oil (MIL-L-6081)
O–133	1010, Jet Engine Oil (MIL-L-6081)
O–147	None, MIL-L-6085A Lubricating Oil, Instrument, Synthetic
O–148	None, MIL-L-7808 (Synthetic Base) Turbine Engine Oil
O–149	None, Aircraft Turbine Engine Synthetic, 7.5c St
O–155	None, MIL-L-6086C, Aircraft, Medium Grade
O–156	None, MIL-L-23699 (Synthetic Base), Turboprop and Turboshaft Engines
JOAP/SOAP	Joint Oil Analysis Program. JOAP support is furnished during normal duty hours, other times on request. (JOAP and SOAP programs provide essentially the same service, JOAP is now the standard joint service supported program.)

28 TRANSIENT ALERT (TRAN ALERT)—MILITARY

Tran Alert service is considered to include all services required for normal aircraft turn-around, e.g., servicing (fuel, oil, oxygen, etc.), debriefing to determine requirements for maintenance, minor maintenance, inspection and parking assistance of transient aircraft. Drag chute repack, specialized maintenance, or extensive repairs will be provided within the capabilities and priorities of the base. Delays can be anticipated after normal duty hours/holidays/weekends regardless of the hours of transient maintenance operation. Pilots should not expect aircraft to be serviced for TURN-AROUNDS during time periods when servicing or maintenance manpower is not available. In the case of airports not operated exclusively by US military, the servicing indicated by the remarks will not always be available for US military

NE, 09 FEB 20XX to 05 APR 20XX

Legend 12. Chart Supplement.

Appendix 1

DIRECTORY LEGEND 15

aircraft. When transient alert services are not shown, facilities are unknown. NO PRIORITY BASIS—means that transient alert services will be provided only after all the requirements for mission/tactical assigned aircraft have been accomplished.

 AIRPORT REMARKS

The Attendance Schedule is the months, days and hours the airport is actually attended. Airport attendance does not mean watchman duties or telephone accessibility, but rather an attendant or operator on duty to provide at least minimum services (e.g., repairs, fuel, transportation).

Airport Remarks have been grouped in order of applicability. Airport remarks are limited to those items of information that are determined essential for operational use, i.e., conditions of a permanent or indefinite nature and conditions that will remain in effect for more than 30 days concerning aeronautical facilities, services, maintenance available, procedures or hazards, knowledge of which is essential for safe and efficient operation of aircraft. Information concerning permanent closing of a runway or taxiway will not be shown. A note "See Special Notices" shall be applied within this remarks section when a special notice applicable to the entry is contained in the Special Notices section of this publication.

Parachute Jumping indicates parachute jumping areas associated with the airport. See Parachute Jumping Area section of this publication for additional Information.

Landing Fee indicates landing charges for private or non-revenue producing aircraft. In addition, fees may be charged for planes that remain over a couple of hours and buy no services, or at major airline terminals for all aircraft.

Note: Unless otherwise stated, remarks including runway ends refer to the runway's approach end.

 MILITARY REMARKS

Military Remarks published at a joint Civil/Military facility are remarks that are applicable to the Military. At Military Facilities all remarks will be published under the heading Military Remarks. Remarks contained in this section may not be applicable to civil users. The first group of remarks is applicable to the primary operator of the airport. Remarks applicable to a tenant on the airport are shown preceded by the tenant organization, i.e., (A) (AF) (N) (ANG), etc. Military airports operate 24 hours unless otherwise specified. Airport operating hours are listed first (airport operating hours will only be listed if they are different than the airport attended hours or if the attended hours are unavailable) followed by pertinent remarks in order of applicability. Remarks will include information on restrictions, hazards, traffic pattern, noise abatement, customs/agriculture/immigration, and miscellaneous information applicable to the Military.

Type of restrictions:

CLOSED: When designated closed, the airport is restricted from use by all aircraft unless stated otherwise. Any closure applying to specific type of aircraft or operation will be so stated. USN/USMC/USAF airports are considered closed during non–operating hours. Closed airports may be utilized during an emergency provided there is a safe landing area.

OFFICIAL BUSINESS ONLY: The airfield is closed to all transient military aircraft for obtaining routine services such as fueling, passenger drop off or pickup, practice approaches, parking, etc. The airfield may be used by aircrews and aircraft if official government business (including civilian) must be conducted on or near the airfield and prior permission is received from the airfield manager.

AF OFFICIAL BUSINESS ONLY OR NAVY OFFICIAL BUSINESS ONLY: Indicates that the restriction applies only to service indicated.

PRIOR PERMISSION REQUIRED (PPR): Airport is closed to transient aircraft unless approval for operation is obtained from the appropriate commander through Chief, Airfield Management or Airfield Operations Officer. Official Business or PPR does not preclude the use of US Military airports as an alternate for IFR flights. If a non–US military airport is used as a weather alternate and requires a PPR, the PPR must be requested and confirmed before the flight departs. The purpose of PPR is to control volume and flow of traffic rather than to prohibit it. Prior permission is required for all aircraft requiring transient alert service outside the published transient alert duty hours. All aircraft carrying hazardous materials must obtain prior permission as outlined in AFJI 11–204, AR 95–27, OPNAVINST 3710.7.

Note: OFFICIAL BUSINESS ONLY AND PPR restrictions are not applicable to Special Air Mission (SAM) or Special Air Resource (SPAR) aircraft providing person or persons on aboard are designated Code 6 or higher as explained in AFJMAN 11–213, AR 95–11, OPNAVINST 3722–8J. Official Business Only or PPR do not preclude the use of the airport as an alternate for IFR flights.

 WEATHER DATA SOURCES

Weather data sources will be listed alphabetically followed by their assigned frequencies and/or telephone number and hours of operation.

ASOS—Automated Surface Observing System. Reports the same as an AWOS–3 plus precipitation identification and intensity, and freezing rain occurrence;

AWOS—Automated Weather Observing System
 AWOS–A—reports altimeter setting (all other information is advisory only).
 AWOS–AV—reports altimeter and visibility.
 AWOS–1—reports altimeter setting, wind data and usually temperature, dew point and density altitude.
 AWOS–2—reports the same as AWOS–1 plus visibility.
 AWOS–3—reports the same as AWOS–1 plus visibility and cloud/ceiling data.
 AWOS–3P reports the same as the AWOS–3 system, plus a precipitation identification sensor.
 AWOS–3PT reports the same as the AWOS–3 system, plus precipitation identification sensor and a thunderstorm/lightning reporting capability.
 AWOS–3T reports the same as AWOS–3 system and includes a thunderstorm/lightning reporting capability.

NE, 09 FEB 20XX to 05 APR 20XX

Legend 13. Chart Supplement.

16 **DIRECTORY LEGEND**

See AIM, Basic Flight Information and ATC Procedures for detailed description of Weather Data Sources.

AWOS–4—reports same as AWOS–3 system, plus precipitation occurence, type and accumulation, freezing rain, thunderstorm, and runway surface sensors.
HIWAS—See RADIO AIDS TO NAVIGATION
LAWRS—Limited Aviation Weather Reporting Station where observers report cloud height, weather, obstructions to vision, temperature and dewpoint (in most cases), surface wind, altimeter and pertinent remarks.
LLWAS—indicates a Low Level Wind Shear Alert System consisting of a center field and several field perimeter anemometers.
SAWRS—identifies airports that have a Supplemental Aviation Weather Reporting Station available to pilots for current weather information.
SWSL—Supplemental Weather Service Location providing current local weather information via radio and telephone.
TDWR—indicates airports that have Terminal Doppler Weather Radar.
WSP—indicates airports that have Weather System Processor.

When the automated weather source is broadcast over an associated airport NAVAID frequency (see NAVAID line), it shall be indicated by a bold ASOS, AWOS, or HIWAS followed by the frequency, identifier and phone number, if available.

 COMMUNICATIONS

Airport terminal control facilities and radio communications associated with the airport shall be shown. When the call sign is not the same as the airport name the call sign will be shown. Frequencies shall normally be shown in descending order with the primary frequency listed first. Frequencies will be listed, together with sectorization indicated by outbound radials, and hours of operation. Communications will be listed in sequence as follows:

Single Frequency Approach (SFA), Common Traffic Advisory Frequency (CTAF), Automatic Terminal Information Service (ATIS) and Aeronautical Advisory Stations (UNICOM) or (AUNICOM) along with their frequency is shown, where available, on the line following the heading "COMMUNICATIONS." When the CTAF and UNICOM frequencies are the same, the frequency will be shown as CTAF/UNICOM 122.8.

The FSS telephone nationwide is toll free 1–800–WX–BRIEF (1–800–992–7433). When the FSS is located on the field it will be indicated as "on arpt". Frequencies available at the FSS will follow in descending order. Remote Communications Outlet (RCO) providing service to the airport followed by the frequency and FSS RADIO name will be shown when available.

FSS's provide information on airport conditions, radio aids and other facilities, and process flight plans. Airport Advisory Service (AAS) is provided on the CTAF by FSS's for select non-tower airports or airports where the tower is not in operation. (See AIM, Para 4–1–9 Traffic Advisory Practices at Airports Without Operating Control Towers or AC 90–42C.)

Aviation weather briefing service is provided by FSS specialists. Flight and weather briefing services are also available by calling the telephone numbers listed.

Remote Communications Outlet (RCO)—An unmanned air/ground communications facility that is remotely controlled and provides UHF or VHF communications capability to extend the service range of an FSS.

Civil Communications Frequencies-Civil communications frequencies used in the FSS air/ground system are operated on 122.0, 122.2, 123.6; emergency 121.5; plus receive-only on 122.1.
  a. 122.0 is assigned as the Enroute Flight Advisory Service frequency at selected FSS RADIO outlets.
  b. 122.2 is assigned as a common enroute frequency.
  c. 123.6 is assigned as the airport advisory frequency at select non-tower locations. At airports with a tower, FSS may provide airport advisories on the tower frequency when tower is closed.
  d. 122.1 is the primary receive-only frequency at VOR's.
  e. Some FSS's are assigned 50 kHz frequencies in the 122–126 MHz band (eg. 122.45). Pilots using the FSS A/G system should refer to this directory or appropriate charts to determine frequencies available at the FSS or remoted facility through which they wish to communicate.

Emergency frequency 121.5 and 243.0 are available at all Flight Service Stations, most Towers, Approach Control and RADAR facilities.

Frequencies published followed by the letter "T" or "R", indicate that the facility will only transmit or receive respectively on that frequency. All radio aids to navigation (NAVAID) frequencies are transmit only.

TERMINAL SERVICES

SFA—Single Frequency Approach.
CTAF—A program designed to get all vehicles and aircraft at airports without an operating control tower on a common frequency.
ATIS—A continuous broadcast of recorded non-control information in selected terminal areas.
D–ATIS—Digital ATIS provides ATIS information in text form outside the standard reception range of conventional ATIS via landline & data link communications and voice message within range of existing transmitters.
AUNICOM—Automated UNICOM is a computerized, command response system that provides automated weather, radio check capability and airport advisory information selected from an automated menu by microphone clicks.
UNICOM—A non-government air/ground radio communications facility which may provide airport information.
PTD—Pilot to Dispatcher.
APP CON—Approach Control. The symbol Ⓡ indicates radar approach control.
TOWER—Control tower.
GCA—Ground Control Approach System.
GND CON—Ground Control.
GCO—Ground Communication Outlet—An unstaffed, remotely controlled, ground/ground communications facility. Pilots at

NE, 09 FEB 20XX to 05 APR 20XX

Legend 14. Chart Supplement.

DIRECTORY LEGEND   17

uncontrolled airports may contact ATC and FSS via VHF to a telephone connection to obtain an instrument clearance or close a VFR or IFR flight plan. They may also get an updated weather briefing prior to takeoff. Pilots will use four "key clicks" on the VHF radio to contact the appropriate ATC facility or six "key clicks" to contact the FSS. The GCO system is intended to be used only on the ground.

DEP CON—Departure Control. The symbol Ⓡ indicates radar departure control.
CLNC DEL—Clearance Delivery.
PRE TAXI CLNC—Pre taxi clearance.

VFR ADVSY SVC—VFR Advisory Service. Service provided by Non-Radar Approach Control.
  Advisory Service for VFR aircraft (upon a workload basis) ctc APP CON.
COMD POST—Command Post followed by the operator call sign in parenthesis.
PMSV—Pilot-to-Metro Service call sign, frequency and hours of operation, when full service is other than continuous. PMSV installations at which weather observation service is available shall be indicated, following the frequency and/or hours of operation as "Wx obsn svc 1900–0000Z‡" or "other times" may be used when no specific time is given. PMSV facilities manned by forecasters are considered "Full Service". PMSV facilities manned by weather observers are listed as "Limited Service".
OPS—Operations followed by the operator call sign in parenthesis.
CON
RANGE
FLT FLW—Flight Following
MEDIVAC
NOTE: Communication frequencies followed by the letter "X" indicate frequency available on request.

 AIRSPACE

Information concerning Class B, C, and part-time D and E surface area airspace shall be published with effective times. Class D and E surface area airspace that is continuous as established by Rulemaking Docket will not be shown.
CLASS B—Radar Sequencing and Separation Service for all aircraft in CLASS B airspace.
CLASS C—Separation between IFR and VFR aircraft and sequencing of VFR arrivals to the primary airport.
TRSA—Radar Sequencing and Separation Service for participating VFR Aircraft within a Terminal Radar Service Area.
Class C, D, and E airspace described in this publication is that airspace usually consisting of a 5 NM radius core surface area that begins at the surface and extends upward to an altitude above the airport elevation (charted in MSL for Class C and Class D). Class E surface airspace normally extends from the surface up to but not including the overlying controlled airspace.
When part-time Class C or Class D airspace defaults to Class E, the core surface area becomes Class E. This will be formatted as:
AIRSPACE: CLASS C svc "times" ctc **APP CON** other times CLASS E:
or
AIRSPACE: CLASS D svc "times" other times CLASS E.
When a part-time Class C, Class D or Class E surface area defaults to Class G, the core surface area becomes Class G up to, but not including, the overlying controlled airspace. Normally, the overlying controlled airspace is Class E airspace beginning at either 700' or 1200' AGL and may be determined by consulting the relevant VFR Sectional or Terminal Area Charts. This will be formatted as:
AIRSPACE: CLASS C svc "times" ctc **APP CON** other times CLASS G, with CLASS E 700' (or 1200') AGL & abv:
or
AIRSPACE: CLASS D svc "times" other times CLASS G with CLASS E 700' (or 1200') AGL & abv:
or
AIRSPACE: CLASS E svc "times" other times CLASS G with CLASS E 700' (or 1200') AGL & abv.
NOTE: AIRSPACE SVC "TIMES" INCLUDE ALL ASSOCIATED ARRIVAL EXTENSIONS. Surface area arrival extensions for instrument approach procedures become part of the primary core surface area. These extensions may be either Class D or Class E airspace and are effective concurrent with the times of the primary core surface area. For example, when a part-time Class C, Class D or Class E surface area defaults to Class G, the associated arrival extensions will default to Class G at the same time. When a part-time Class C or Class D surface area defaults to Class E, the arrival extensions will remain in effect as Class E airspace.
NOTE: CLASS E AIRSPACE EXTENDING UPWARD FROM 700 FEET OR MORE ABOVE THE SURFACE, DESIGNATED IN CONJUNCTION WITH AN AIRPORT WITH AN APPROVED INSTRUMENT PROCEDURE.
Class E 700' AGL (shown as magenta vignette on sectional charts) and 1200' AGL (blue vignette) areas are designated when necessary to provide controlled airspace for transitioning to/from the terminal and enroute environments. Unless otherwise specified, these 700'/1200' AGL Class E airspace areas remain in effect continuously, regardless of airport operating hours or surface area status. These transition areas should not be confused with surface areas or arrival extensions.
(See Chapter 3, AIRSPACE, in the Aeronautical Information Manual for further details)

NE, 09 FEB 20XX to 05 APR 20XX

Legend 15. Chart Supplement.

Appendix 1

18   DIRECTORY LEGEND

㉞ RADIO AIDS TO NAVIGATION

The Airport/Facility Directory lists, by facility name, all Radio Aids to Navigation that appear on FAA, AeroNav Products Visual or IFR Aeronautical Charts and those upon which the FAA has approved an Instrument Approach Procedure, with exception of selected TACANs. Military TACAN information will be published for Military facilities contained in this publication. All VOR, VORTAC, TACAN, ILS and MLS equipment in the National Airspace System has an automatic monitoring and shutdown feature in the event of malfunction. Unmonitored, as used in this publication, for any navigational aid, means that monitoring personnel cannot observe the malfunction or shutdown signal. The NAVAID NOTAM file identifier will be shown as "NOTAM FILE IAD" and will be listed on the Radio Aids to Navigation line. When two or more NAVAIDS are listed and the NOTAM file identifier is different from that shown on the Radio Aids to Navigation line, it will be shown with the NAVAID listing. NOTAM file identifiers for ILSs and its components (e.g., NDB (LOM) are the same as the associated airports and are not repeated. Automated Surface Observing System (ASOS), Automated Weather Observing System (AWOS), and Hazardous Inflight Weather Advisory Service (HIWAS) will be shown when this service is broadcast over selected NAVAIDs.

NAVAID information is tabulated as indicated in the following sample:

Note: Those DME channel numbers with a (Y) suffix require TACAN to be placed in the "Y" mode to receive distance information.

HIWAS—Hazardous Inflight Weather Advisory Service is a continuous broadcast of inflight weather advisories including summarized SIGMETs, convective SIGMETs, AIRMETs and urgent PIREPs. HIWAS is presently broadcast over selected VOR's throughout the U.S.

ASR/PAR—Indicates that Surveillance (ASR) or Precision (PAR) radar instrument approach minimums are published in the U.S. Terminal Procedures. Only part-time hours of operation will be shown.

RADIO CLASS DESIGNATIONS
VOR/DME/TACAN Standard Service Volume (SSV) Classifications

SSV Class	Altitudes	Distance (NM)
(T) Terminal	1000' to 12,000'	25
(L) Low Altitude	1000' to 18,000'	40
(H) High Altitude	1000' to 14,500'	40
	14,500' to 18,000'	100
	18,000' to 45,000'	130
	45,000' to 60,000'	100

NOTE: Additionally, (H) facilities provide (L) and (T) service volume and (L) facilities provide (T) service. Altitudes are with respect to the station's site elevation. Coverage is not available in a cone of airspace directly above the facility.

CONTINUED ON NEXT PAGE

NE, 09 FEB 20XX to 05 APR 20XX

Legend 16. Chart Supplement.

DIRECTORY LEGEND
CONTINUED FROM PRECEDING PAGE

19

The term VOR is, operationally, a general term covering the VHF omnidirectional bearing type of facility without regard to the fact that the power, the frequency protected service volume, the equipment configuration, and operational requirements may vary between facilities at different locations.

AB	Automatic Weather Broadcast.
DF	Direction Finding Service.
DME	UHF standard (TACAN compatible) distance measuring equipment.
DME(Y)	UHF standard (TACAN compatible) distance measuring equipment that require TACAN to be placed in the "Y" mode to receive DME.
GS	Glide slope.
H	Non-directional radio beacon (homing), power 50 watts to less than 2,000 watts (50 NM at all altitudes).
HH	Non-directional radio beacon (homing), power 2,000 watts or more (75 NM at all altitudes).
H-SAB	Non-directional radio beacons providing automatic transcribed weather service.
ILS	Instrument Landing System (voice, where available, on localizer channel).
IM	Inner marker.
ISMLS	Interim Standard Microwave Landing System.
LDA	Localizer Directional Aid.
LMM	Compass locator station when installed at middle marker site (15 NM at all altitudes).
LOM	Compass locator station when installed at outer marker site (15 NM at all altitudes).
MH	Non-directional radio beacon (homing) power less than 50 watts (25 NM at all altitudes).
MLS	Microwave Landing System.
MM	Middle marker.
OM	Outer marker.
S	Simultaneous range homing signal and/or voice.
SABH	Non-directional radio beacon not authorized for IFR or ATC. Provides automatic weather broadcasts.
SDF	Simplified Direction Facility.
TACAN	UHF navigational facility-omnidirectional course and distance information.
VOR	VHF navigational facility-omnidirectional course only.
VOR/DME	Collocated VOR navigational facility and UHF standard distance measuring equipment.
VORTAC	Collocated VOR and TACAN navigational facilities.
W	Without voice on radio facility frequency.
Z	VHF station location marker at a LF radio facility.

NE, 09 FEB 20XX to 05 APR 20XX

Legend 17. Chart Supplement.

20 DIRECTORY LEGEND
ILS FACILITY PEFORMANCE CLASSIFICATION CODES

Codes define the ability of an ILS to support autoland operations. The two portions of the code represent Official Category and farthest point along a Category I, II, or III approach that the Localizer meets Category III structure tolerances.

Official Category: I, II, or III; the lowest minima on published or unpublished procedures supported by the ILS.

Farthest point of satisfactory Category III Localizer performance for Category I, II, or III approaches: A – 4 NM prior to runway threshold, B – 3500 ft prior to runway threshold, C – glide angle dependent but generally 750–1000 ft prior to threshold, T – runway threshold, D – 3000 ft after runway threshold, and E – 2000 ft prior to stop end of runway.

ILS information is tabulated as indicated in the following sample:

ILS/DME   108.5   I–ORL   Chan 22   Rwy 18.   Class IIE.   LOM HERNY NDB.

ILS Facility Performance Classification Code

FREQUENCY PAIRING PLAN AND MLS CHANNELING

MLS CHANNEL	VHF FREQUENCY	TACAN CHANNEL	MLS CHANNEL	VHF FREQUENCY	TACAN CHANNEL	MLS CHANNEL	VHF FREQUENCY	TACAN CHANNEL
500	108.10	18X	568	109.45	31Y	636	114.15	88Y
502	108.30	20X	570	109.55	32Y	638	114.25	89Y
504	108.50	22X	572	109.65	33Y	640	114.35	90Y
506	108.70	24X	574	109.75	34Y	642	114.45	91Y
508	108.90	26X	576	109.85	35Y	644	114.55	92Y
510	109.10	28X	578	109.95	36Y	646	114.65	93Y
512	109.30	30X	580	110.05	37Y	648	114.75	94Y
514	109.50	32X	582	110.15	38Y	650	114.85	95Y
516	109.70	34X	584	110.25	39Y	652	114.95	96Y
518	109.90	36X	586	110.35	40Y	654	115.05	97Y
520	110.10	38X	588	110.45	41Y	656	115.15	98Y
522	110.30	40X	590	110.55	42Y	658	115.25	99Y
524	110.50	42X	592	110.65	43Y	660	115.35	100Y
526	110.70	44X	594	110.75	44Y	662	115.45	101Y
528	110.90	46X	596	110.85	45Y	664	115.55	102Y
530	111.10	48X	598	110.95	46Y	666	115.65	103Y
532	111.30	50X	600	111.05	47Y	668	115.75	104Y
534	111.50	52X	602	111.15	48Y	670	115.85	105Y
536	111.70	54X	604	111.25	49Y	672	115.95	106Y
538	111.90	56X	606	111.35	50Y	674	116.05	107Y
540	108.05	17Y	608	111.45	51Y	676	116.15	108Y
542	108.15	18Y	610	111.55	52Y	678	116.25	109Y
544	108.25	19Y	612	111.65	53Y	680	116.35	110Y
546	108.35	20Y	614	111.75	54Y	682	116.45	111Y
548	108.45	21Y	616	111.85	55Y	684	116.55	112Y
550	108.55	22Y	618	111.95	56Y	686	116.65	113Y
552	108.65	23Y	620	113.35	80Y	688	116.75	114Y
554	108.75	24Y	622	113.45	81Y	690	116.85	115Y
556	108.85	25Y	624	113.55	82Y	692	116.95	116Y
558	108.95	26Y	626	113.65	83Y	694	117.05	117Y
560	109.05	27Y	628	113.75	84Y	696	117.15	118Y
562	109.15	28Y	630	113.85	85Y	698	117.25	119Y
564	109.25	29Y	632	113.95	86Y			
566	109.35	30Y	634	114.05	87Y			

FREQUENCY PAIRING PLAN AND MLS CHANNELING

The following is a list of paired VOR/ILS VHF frequencies with TACAN channels and MLS channels.

TACAN CHANNEL	VHF FREQUENCY	MLS CHANNEL	TACAN CHANNEL	VHF FREQUENCY	MLS CHANNEL	TACAN CHANNEL	VHF FREQUENCY	MLS CHANNEL
2X	134.5	-	19Y	108.25	544	25X	108.80	-
2Y	134.55	-	20X	108.30	502	25Y	108.85	556
11X	135.4	-	20Y	108.35	546	26X	108.90	508
11Y	135.45	-	21X	108.40	-	26Y	108.95	558
12X	135.5	-	21Y	108.45	548	27X	109.00	-
12Y	135.55	-	22X	108.50	504	27Y	109.05	560
17X	108.00	-	22Y	108.55	550	28X	109.10	510
17Y	108.05	540	23X	108.60	-	28Y	109.15	562
18X	108.10	500	23Y	108.65	552	29X	109.20	-
18Y	108.15	542	24X	108.70	506	29Y	109.25	564
19X	108.20	-	24Y	108.75	554	30X	109.30	512

NE, 09 FEB 20XX to 05 APR 20XX

Legend 18. Chart Supplement.

Appendix 1

DIRECTORY LEGEND 21

TACAN CHANNEL	VHF FREQUENCY	MLS CHANNEL	TACAN CHANNEL	VHF FREQUENCY	MLS CHANNEL	TACAN CHANNEL	VHF FREQUENCY	MLS CHANNEL
30Y	109.35	566	63X	133.60	-	95Y	114.85	650
31X	109.40	-	63Y	133.65	-	96X	114.90	-
31Y	109.45	568	64X	133.70	-	96Y	114.95	652
32X	109.50	514	64Y	133.75	-	97X	115.00	-
32Y	109.55	570	65X	133.80	-	97Y	115.05	654
33X	109.60	-	65Y	133.85	-	98X	115.10	-
33Y	109.65	572	66X	133.90	-	98Y	115.15	656
34X	109.70	516	66Y	133.95	-	99X	115.20	-
34Y	109.75	574	67X	134.00	-	99Y	115.25	658
35X	109.80	-	67Y	134.05	-	100X	115.30	-
35Y	109.85	576	68X	134.10	-	100Y	115.35	660
36X	109.90	518	68Y	134.15	-	101X	115.40	-
36Y	109.95	578	69X	134.20	-	101Y	115.45	662
37X	110.00	-	69Y	134.25	-	102X	115.50	-
37Y	110.05	580	70X	112.30	-	102Y	115.55	664
38X	110.10	520	70Y	112.35	-	103X	115.60	-
38Y	110.15	582	71X	112.40	-	103Y	115.65	666
39X	110.20	-	71Y	112.45	-	104X	115.70	-
39Y	110.25	584	72X	112.50	-	104Y	115.75	668
40X	110.30	522	72Y	112.55	-	105X	115.80	-
40Y	110.35	586	73X	112.60	-	105Y	115.85	670
41X	110.40	-	73Y	112.65	-	106X	115.90	-
41Y	110.45	588	74X	112.70	-	106Y	115.95	672
42X	110.50	524	74Y	112.75	-	107X	116.00	-
42Y	110.55	590	75X	112.80	-	107Y	116.05	674
43X	110.60	-	75Y	112.85	-	108X	116.10	-
43Y	110.65	592	76X	112.90	-	108Y	116.15	676
44X	110.70	526	76Y	112.95	-	109X	116.20	-
44Y	110.75	594	77X	113.00	-	109Y	116.25	678
45X	110.80	-	77Y	113.05	-	110X	116.30	-
45Y	110.85	596	78X	113.10	-	110Y	116.35	680
46X	110.90	528	78Y	113.15	-	111X	116.40	-
46Y	110.95	598	79X	113.20	-	111Y	116.45	682
47X	111.00	-	79Y	113.25	-	112X	116.50	-
47Y	111.05	600	80X	113.30	-	112Y	116.55	684
48X	111.10	530	80Y	113.35	620	113X	116.60	-
48Y	111.15	602	81X	113.40	-	113Y	116.65	686
49X	111.20	-	81Y	113.45	622	114X	116.70	-
49Y	111.25	604	82X	113.50	-	114Y	116.75	688
50X	111.30	532	82Y	113.55	624	115X	116.80	-
50Y	111.35	606	83X	113.60	-	115Y	116.85	690
51X	111.40	-	83Y	113.65	626	116X	116.90	-
51Y	111.45	608	84X	113.70	-	116Y	116.95	692
52X	111.50	534	84Y	113.75	628	117X	117.00	-
52Y	111.55	610	85X	113.80	-	117Y	117.05	694
53X	111.60	-	85Y	113.85	630	118X	117.10	-
53Y	111.65	612	86X	113.90	-	118Y	117.15	696
54X	111.70	536	86Y	113.95	632	119X	117.20	-
54Y	111.75	614	87X	114.00	-	119Y	117.25	698
55X	111.80	-	87Y	114.05	634	120X	117.30	-
55Y	111.85	616	88X	114.10	-	120Y	117.35	-
56X	111.90	538	88Y	114.15	636	121X	117.40	-
56Y	111.95	618	89X	114.20	-	121Y	117.45	-
57X	112.00	-	89Y	114.25	638	122X	117.50	-
57Y	112.05	-	90X	114.30	-	122Y	117.55	-
58X	112.10	-	90Y	114.35	640	123X	117.60	-
58Y	112.15	-	91X	114.40	-	123Y	117.65	-
59X	112.20	-	91Y	114.45	642	124X	117.70	-
59Y	112.25	-	92X	114.50	-	124Y	117.75	-
60X	133.30	-	92Y	114.55	644	125X	117.80	-
60Y	133.35	-	93X	114.60	-	125Y	117.85	-
61X	133.40	-	93Y	114.65	646	126X	117.90	-
61Y	133.45	-	94X	114.70	-	126Y	117.95	-
62X	133.50	-	94Y	114.75	648			
62Y	133.55	-	95X	114.80	-			

(35) COMM/NAV/WEATHER REMARKS:
These remarks consist of pertinent information affecting the current status of communications, NAVAIDs and weather.

NE, 09 FEB 20XX to 05 APR 20XX

Legend 19. Chart Supplement.

Appendix 1

Appendix 2

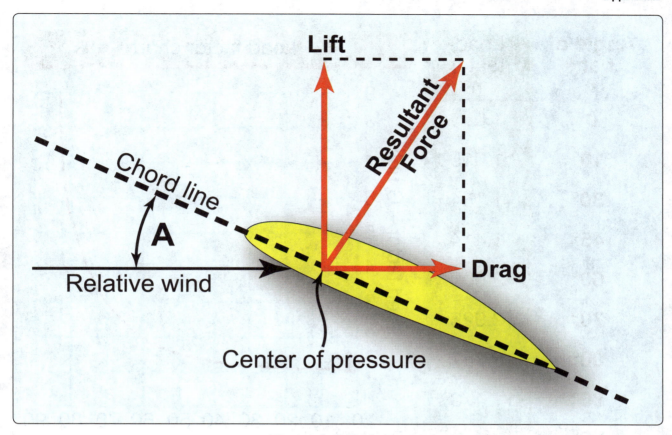

Figure 1. Lift Vector.

Appendix 2

Figure 2. Load Factor Chart.

Appendix 2

Figure 3. Altimeter.

Appendix 2

Figure 4. Airspeed Indicator.

Appendix 2

Figure 5. Turn Coordinator.

2-5

Appendix 2

Figure 6. Heading Indicator.

Appendix 2

Figure 7. Attitude Indicator.

2-7

Appendix 2

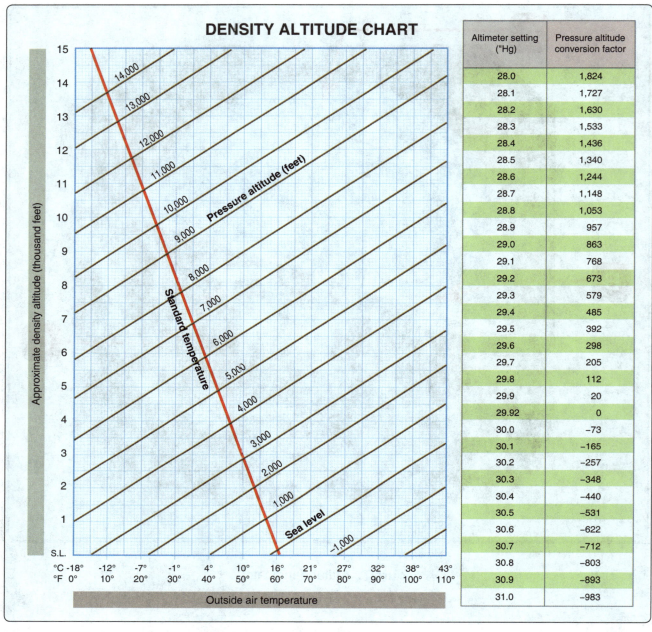

Figure 8. Density Altitude Chart.

Appendix 2

Figure 9. Control Position for Taxi.

2-9

Appendix 2

Figure 10. Gyroplane Rotor Blade Position.

Figure 11. Glider Yaw String.

Appendix 2

```
METAR KINK 121845Z 11012G18KT 15SM SKC 25/17 A3000

METAR KBOI 121854Z 13004KT 30SM SCT150 17/6 A3015

METAR KLAX 121852Z 25004KT 6SM BR SCT007 SCT250 16/15 A2991

SPECI KMDW 121856Z 32005KT 1 1/2SM RA OVC007 17/16 A2980 RMK RAB35

SPECI KJFK 121853Z 18004KT 1/2SM FG R04/2200 OVC005 20/18 A3006
```

Figure 12. Aviation Routine Weather Reports (METAR).

Appendix 2

This is a telephone weather briefing from the Dallas FSS for local operation of gliders and lighter-than-air at Caddo Mills, Texas (about 30 miles east of Dallas). The briefing is at 13Z.

"There are no adverse conditions reported or forecast for today."

"A weak low pressure over the Texas Panhandle and eastern New Mexico is causing a weak southerly flow over the area."

"Current weather here at Dallas is wind south 5 knots, visibility 12 miles, clear, temperature 21, dewpoint 9, altimeter 29 point 78."

"By 15Z, we should have a few scattered cumuliform clouds at 5 thousand AGL, with higher scattered cirrus at 25 thousand MSL. After 20Z, the wind should pick up to about 15 knots from the south."

"The winds aloft are: 3 thousand 170 at 7, temperature 20; 6 thousand 200 at 18, temperature 14; 9 thousand 210 at 22, temperature 8; 12 thousand 225 at 27, temperature 0; 18 thousand 240 at 30, temperature −7."

Figure 13. Telephone Weather Briefing.

Appendix 2

UA/OV KOKC-KTUL/TM 1800/FL120/TP BE90/SK BKN018-TOP055/OVC072-TOP089/CLR ABV/TA M7/WV 08021/TB LGT 055-072/IC LGT-MOD RIME 072-089

Figure 14. Pilot Weather Report.

Appendix 2

```
TAF

KMEM  121720Z 1218/1324 20012KT 5SM HZ BKN030 PROB40 1220/1222 1SM TSRA OVC008CB
      FM122200 33015G20KT P6SM BKN015 OVC025 PROB40 1220/1222 3SM SHRA
      FM120200 35012KT OVC008 PROB40 1202/1205 2SM-RASN BECMG 1306/1308 02008KT BKN012
      BECMG 1310/1312 00000KT 3SM BR SKC TEMPO 1212/1214 1/2SM FG
      FM131600 VRB06KT P6SM SKC=

KOKC  051130Z 0512/0618 14008KT 5SM BR BKN030 TEMPO 0513/0516 1 1/2SM BR
      FM051600 18010KT P6SM SKC BECMG 0522/0524 20013G20KT 4SM SHRA OVC020
      PROB40 0600/0606 2SM TSRA OVC008CB BECMG 0606/0608 21015KT P6SM SCT040=
```

Figure 15. Terminal Aerodrome Forecasts (TAF).

Appendix 2

```
FB WBC 151745
DATA BASED ON 151200Z
VALID 1600Z FOR USE 1800-0300Z. TEMPS NEG ABV 24000
```

FT	3000	6000	9000	12000	18000	24000	30000	34000	39000
ALS			2420	2635-08	2535-18	2444-30	245945	246755	246862
AMA		2714	2725+00	2625-04	2531-15	2542-27	265842	256352	256762
DEN			2321-04	2532-08	2434-19	2441-31	235347	236056	236262
HLC		1707-01	2113-03	2219-07	2330-17	2435-30	244145	244854	245561
MKC	0507	2006+03	2215-01	2322-06	2338-17	2348-29	236143	237252	238160
STL	2113	2325+07	2332+02	2339-04	2356-16	2373-27	239440	730649	731960

Figure 17. Winds and Temperatures Aloft Forecast.

Appendix 2

Figure 18. Weather Depiction Chart.

Appendix 2

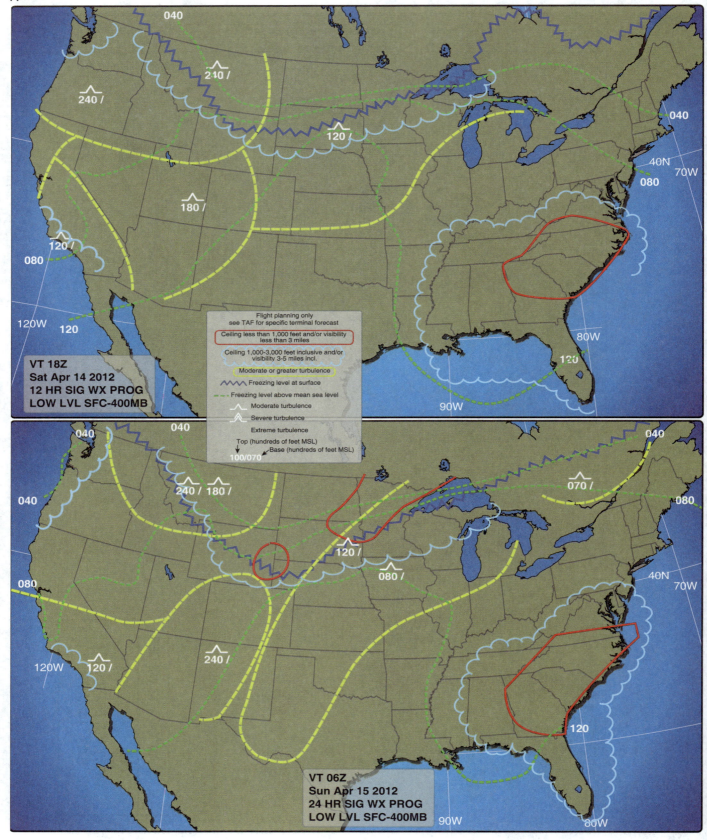

Figure 19. Low-Level Significant Weather (SIGWX) Prognostic Charts.

2-18

Appendix 2

Figure 20. Sectional Chart Excerpt.
NOTE: Chart is not to scale and should not be used for navigation. Use associated scale.

Appendix 2

Figure 21. Sectional Chart Excerpt.
NOTE: Chart is not to scale and should not be used for navigation. Use associated scale.

Appendix 2

Figure 22. Sectional Chart Excerpt.
NOTE: Chart is not to scale and should not be used for navigation. Use associated scale.

Appendix 2

Figure 23. Sectional Chart Excerpt.
NOTE: Chart is not to scale and should not be used for navigation. Use associated scale.

Appendix 2

Figure 24. Sectional Chart Excerpt.
NOTE: Chart is not to scale and should not be used for navigation. Use associated scale.

Appendix 2

Figure 25. Sectional Chart Excerpt.
NOTE: Chart is not to scale and should not be used for navigation. Use associated scale.

Appendix 2

Figure 26. Sectional Chart Excerpt.
NOTE: Chart is not to scale and should not be used for navigation. Use associated scale.

Appendix 2

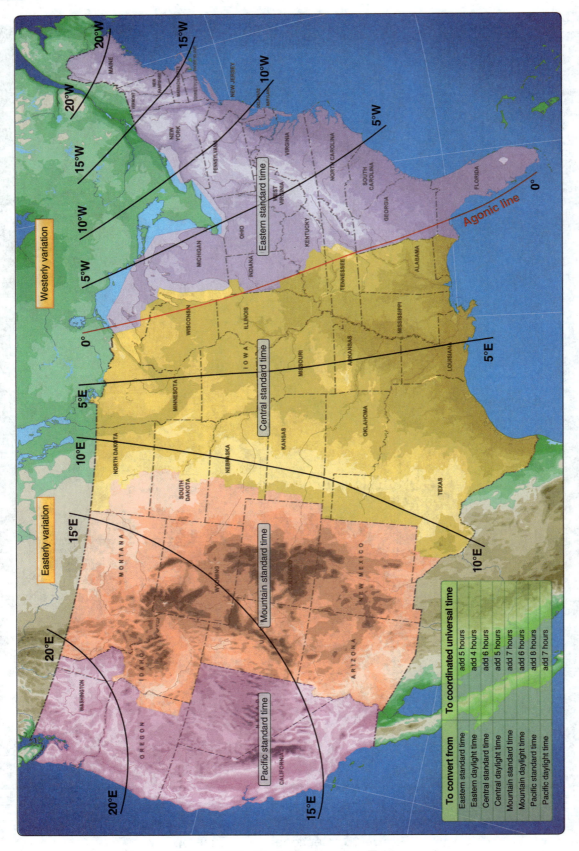

Figure 27. Time Conversion Table.

2-26

Appendix 2

Figure 28. VOR.

Appendix 2

IDAHO

COEUR D'ALENE–PAPPY BOYINGTON FLD (COE) 9 NW UTC−8(−7DT) GREAT FALLS
N47°46.46′ W116°49.18′ H−1C, L−13B
2320 B S4 **FUEL** 100, JET A OX 1, 2, 3, 4 Class IV, ARFF Index A NOTAM FILE COE IAP
RWY 05−23: H7400X100 (ASPH−GRVD) S−57, D−95, 2S−121, 2D−165 HIRL 0.6% up NE
  RWY 05: MALSR (NSTD). PAPI(P4R)—GA 3.0° TCH 56′.
  RWY 23: REIL. PAPI(P4R)—GA 3.0° TCH 50′.
RWY 01−19: H5400X75 (ASPH) S−50, D−83, 2S−105, 2D−150
  MIRL 0.3% up N
  RWY 01: REIL. PAPI(P2L)—GA 3.0° TCH 39′. Rgt tfc.
  RWY 19: PAPI(P2L)—GA 3.0° TCH 41′.
RUNWAY DECLARED DISTANCE INFORMATION
  RWY 01: TORA−5400 TODA−5400 ASDA−5400 LDA−5400
  RWY 05: TORA−7400 TODA−7400 ASDA−7400 LDA−7400
  RWY 19: TORA−5400 TODA−5400 ASDA−5400 LDA−5400
  RWY 23: TORA−7400 TODA−7400 ASDA−7400 LDA−7400
AIRPORT REMARKS: Attended Mon−Fri 1500−0100Z‡. For after hrs fuel-self svc avbl or call 208−772−6404, 208−661−4174, 208−661−7449, 208−699−5433. Self svc fuel avbl with credit card. 48 hr PPR for unscheduled ops with more than 30 passenger seats call arpt manager 208−446−1860. Migratory birds on and invof arpt Oct−Nov. Remote cntl airstrip is 2.3 miles west AER 05. Arpt conditions avbl on AWOS. Rwy 05 NSTD MALSR, thld bar extends 5′ byd rwy edge lgts each side. ACTIVATE MIRL Rwy 01−19, HIRL Rwy 05−23, REIL Rwy 01 and Rwy 23, MALSR Rwy 05—CTAF. PAPI Rwy 01, Rwy 19, Rwy 05, and Rwy 23 opr continuously.
WEATHER DATA SOURCES: AWOS−3 135.075 (208) 772−8215.
  HIWAS 108.8 COE.
COMMUNICATIONS: CTAF/UNICOM 122.8
  RCO 122.05 (BOISE RADIO)
  ® **SPOKANE APP/DEP CON** 132.1
AIRSPACE: CLASS E svc continuous.
RADIO AIDS TO NAVIGATION: NOTAM FILE COE.
  (T) VORW/DME 108.8 COE Chan 25 N47°46.42′ W116°49.24′ at fld. 2320/19E. **HIWAS.**
    DME portion unusable:
    220°−240° byd 15 NM   280°−315° byd 15 NM blo 11,000′.
  POST FALLS NDB (MHW) 347 LEN N47°44.57′ W116°57.66′ 053° 6.0 NM to fld.
  ILS 110.7 I−COE Rwy 05 Class ID. Localizer unusable 25° left and right of course.

Figure 31. Chart Supplement.

Useful load weights and moments

Baggage or 5th seat occupant
ARM 140

Weight	Moment/100
10	14
20	28
30	42
40	56
50	70
60	84
70	98
80	112
90	126
100	140
110	154
120	168
130	182
140	196
150	210
160	224
170	238
180	252
190	266
200	280
210	294
220	308
230	322
240	336
250	350
260	364
270	378

Occupants

Front seats ARM 85		Rear seats ARM 121	
Weight	Moment/100	Weight	Moment/100
120	102	120	145
130	110	130	157
140	119	140	169
150	128	150	182
160	136	160	194
170	144	170	206
180	153	180	218
190	162	190	230
200	170	200	242

Usable fuel
Main wing tanks ARM 75

Gallons	Weight	Moment/100
5	30	22
10	60	45
15	90	68
20	120	90
25	150	112
30	180	135
35	210	158
40	240	180
44	264	198

Auxiliary wing tanks ARM 94

Gallons	Weight	Moment/100
5	30	28
10	60	56
15	90	85
19	114	107

*Oil

Quarts	Weight	Moment/100
10	19	5

*Included in basic empty weight.

Empty weight~2,015
MOM/100~1,554

Moment limits vs weight
Moment limits are based on the following weight and center of gravity limit data (landing gear down).

Weight condition	Forward CG limit	AFT CG limit
2,950 lb (takeoff or landing)	82.1	84.7
2,525 lb	77.5	85.7
2,475 lb or less	77.0	85.7

Figure 32. Airplane Weight and Balance Tables.

Appendix 2

Moment limits vs weight (continued)

Weight	Minimum Moment 100	Maximum Moment 100	Weight	Minimum Moment 100	Maximum Moment 100
2,100	1,617	1,800	2,500	1,932	2,143
2,110	1,625	1,808	2,510	1,942	2,151
2,120	1,632	1,817	2,520	1,953	2,160
2,130	1,640	1,825	2,530	1,963	2,168
2,140	1,648	1,834	2,540	1,974	2,176
2,150	1,656	1,843	2,550	1,984	2,184
2,160	1,663	1,851	2,560	1,995	2,192
2,170	1,671	1,860	2,570	2,005	2,200
2,180	1,679	1,868	2,580	2,016	2,208
2,190	1,686	1,877	2,590	2,026	2,216
2,200	1,694	1,885	2,600	2,037	2,224
2,210	1,702	1,894	2,610	2,048	2,232
2,220	1,709	1,903	2,620	2,058	2,239
2,230	1,717	1,911	2,630	2,069	2,247
2,240	1,725	1,920	2,640	2,080	2,255
2,250	1,733	1,928	2,650	2,090	2,263
2,260	1,740	1,937	2,660	2,101	2,271
2,270	1,748	1,945	2,670	2,112	2,279
2,280	1,756	1,954	2,680	2,123	2,287
2,290	1,763	1,963	2,690	2,133	2,295
2,300	1,771	1,971	2,700	2,144	2,303
2,310	1,779	1,980	2,710	2,155	2,311
2,320	1,786	1,988	2,720	2,166	2,319
2,330	1,794	1,997	2,730	2,177	2,326
2,340	1,802	2,005	2,740	2,188	2,334
2,350	1,810	2,014	2,750	2,199	2,342
2,360	1,817	2,023	2,760	2,210	2,350
2,370	1,825	2,031	2,770	2,221	2,358
2,380	1,833	2,040	2,780	2,232	2,366
2,390	1,840	2,048	2,790	2,243	2,374
2,400	1,848	2,057	2,800	2,254	2,381
2,410	1,856	2,065	2,810	2,265	2,389
2,420	1,863	2,074	2,820	2,276	2,397
2,430	1,871	2,083	2,830	2,287	2,405
2,440	1,879	2,091	2,840	2,298	2,413
2,450	1,887	2,100	2,850	2,309	2,421
2,460	1,894	2,108	2,860	2,320	2,428
2,470	1,902	2,117	2,870	2,332	2,436
2,480	1,911	2,125	2,880	2,343	2,444
2,490	1,921	2,134	2,890	2,354	2,452
			2,900	2,365	2,460
			2,910	2,377	2,468
			2,920	2,388	2,475
			2,930	2,399	2,483
			2,940	2,411	2,491
			2,950	2,422	2,499

Figure 33. Airplane Weight and Balance Tables.

Appendix 2

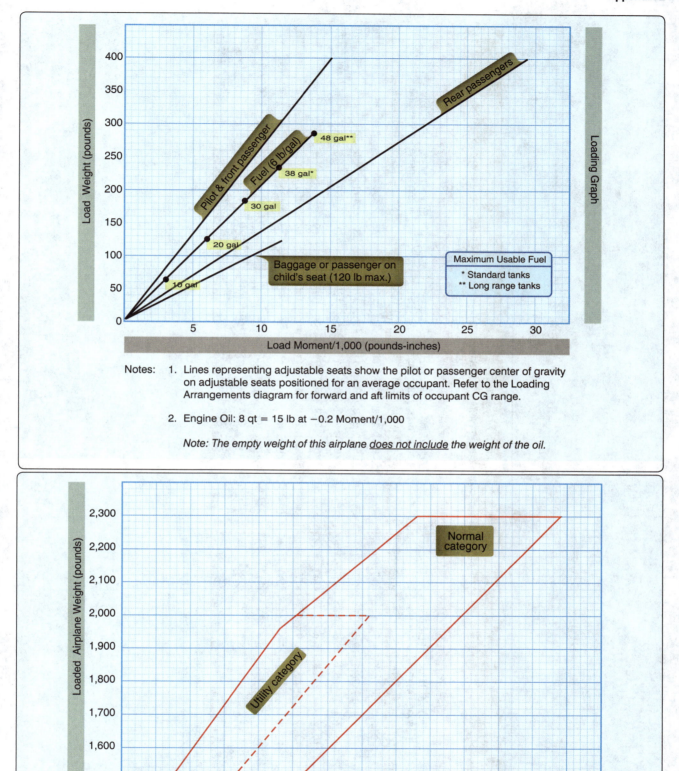

Figure 34. Airplane Weight and Balance Graphs.

2-31

Appendix 2

Cruise power settings
65% Maximum continuous power (or full throttle 2,800 pounds)

Press ALT.	ISA −20 °C (−36 °F)									Standard day (ISA)									ISA +20 °C (+36 °F)								
	IOAT		Engine speed	MAN. press	Fuel flow per engine		TAS		IOAT		Engine speed	MAN. press	Fuel flow per engine		TAS		IOAT		Engine speed	MAN. press	Fuel flow per engine		TAS	
Feet	°F	°C	RPM	IN HG	PSI	GPH	KTS	MPH	°F	°C	RPM	IN HG	PSI	GPH	KTS	MPH	°F	°C	RPM	IN HG	PSI	GPH	KTS	MPH
SL	27	−3	2,450	20.7	6.6	11.5	147	169	63	17	2,450	21.2	6.6	11.5	150	173	99	37	2,450	21.8	6.6	11.5	153	176
2,000	19	−7	2,450	20.4	6.6	11.5	149	171	55	13	2,450	21.0	6.6	11.5	153	176	91	33	2,450	21.5	6.6	11.5	156	180
4,000	12	−11	2,450	20.1	6.6	11.5	152	175	48	9	2,450	20.7	6.6	11.5	156	180	84	29	2,450	21.3	6.6	11.5	159	183
6,000	5	−15	2,450	19.8	6.6	11.5	155	178	41	5	2,450	20.4	6.6	11.5	158	182	79	26	2,450	21.0	6.6	11.5	161	185
8,000	−2	−19	2,450	19.5	6.6	11.5	157	181	36	2	2,450	20.2	6.6	11.5	161	185	72	22	2,450	20.8	6.6	11.5	164	189
10,000	−8	−22	2,450	19.2	6.6	11.5	160	184	28	−2	2,450	19.9	6.6	11.5	163	188	64	18	2,450	20.3	6.5	11.4	166	191
12,000	−15	−26	2,450	18.8	6.4	11.5	162	186	21	−6	2,450	18.8	6.1	10.9	163	188	57	14	2,450	18.8	5.9	10.6	163	188
14,000	−22	−30	2,450	17.4	5.8	10.5	159	183	14	−10	2,450	17.4	5.6	10.1	160	184	50	10	2,450	17.4	5.4	9.8	160	184
16,000	−29	−34	2,450	16.1	5.3	9.7	156	180	7	−14	2,450	16.1	5.1	9.4	156	180	43	6	2,450	16.1	4.9	9.1	155	178

Note: 1. Full throttle manifold pressure settings are approximate.
2. Shaded area represents operation with full throttle.

Figure 35. Airplane Power Setting Table.

Appendix 2

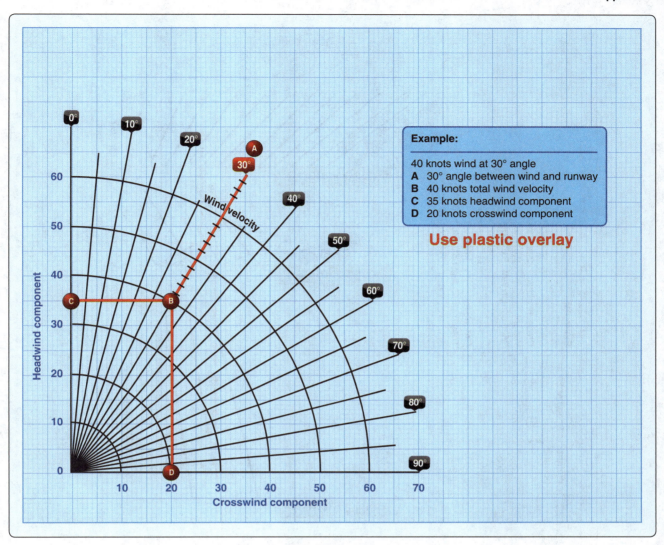

Figure 36. Crosswind Component Graph.

2-33

Appendix 2

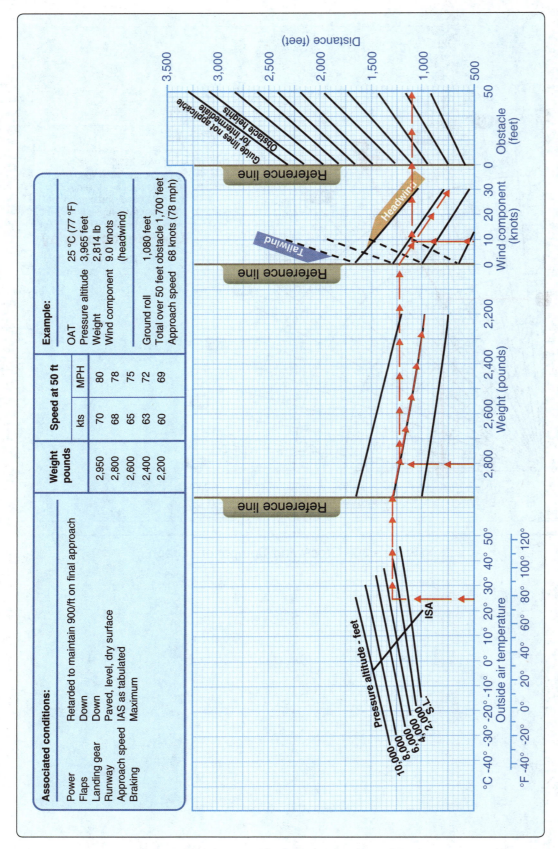

Figure 37. Airplane Landing Distance Graph.

2-34

Appendix 2

Landing distance

Flaps lowered to 40° – Power off
Hard surface runway – Zero wind

Gross weight lb	Approach speed, IAS, MPH	At sea level & 59 °F Ground roll	At sea level & 59 °F Total to clear 50 feet OBS	At 2,500 feet & 50 °F Ground roll	At 2,500 feet & 50 °F Total to clear 50 feet OBS	At 5,000 feet & 41 °F Ground roll	At 5,000 feet & 41 °F Total to clear 50 feet OBS	At 7,500 feet & 32 °F Ground roll	At 7,500 feet & 32 °F Total to clear 50 feet OBS
1,600	60	445	1,075	470	1,135	495	1,195	520	1,255

NOTE:
1. Decrease the distances shown by 10% for each 4 knots of headwind.
2. Increase the distance by 10% for each 60 °F temperature increase above standard.
3. For operation on a dry, grass runway, increase distance (both "ground roll" and "total to clear 50 feet obstacle") by 20% of the "total to clear 50 feet obstacle" figure.

Figure 38. Airplane Landing Distance Table.

2-35

Appendix 2

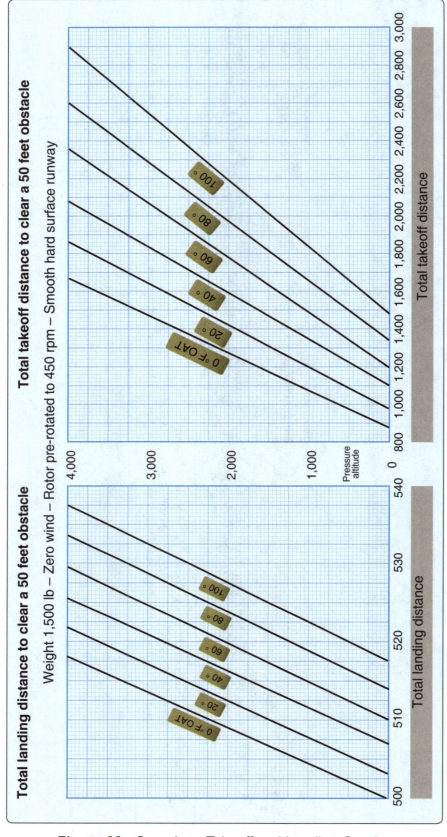

Figure 39. Gyroplane Takeoff and Landing Graphs.

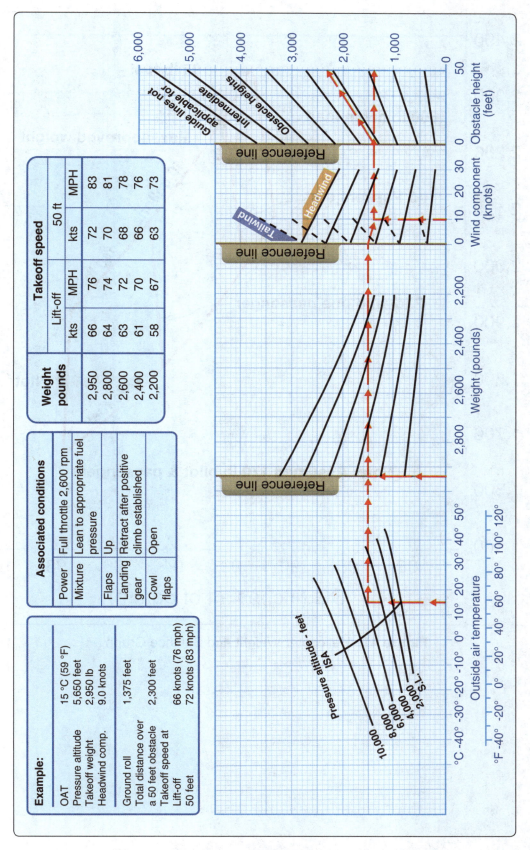

Figure 40. Airplane Takeoff Distance Graph.

Appendix 2

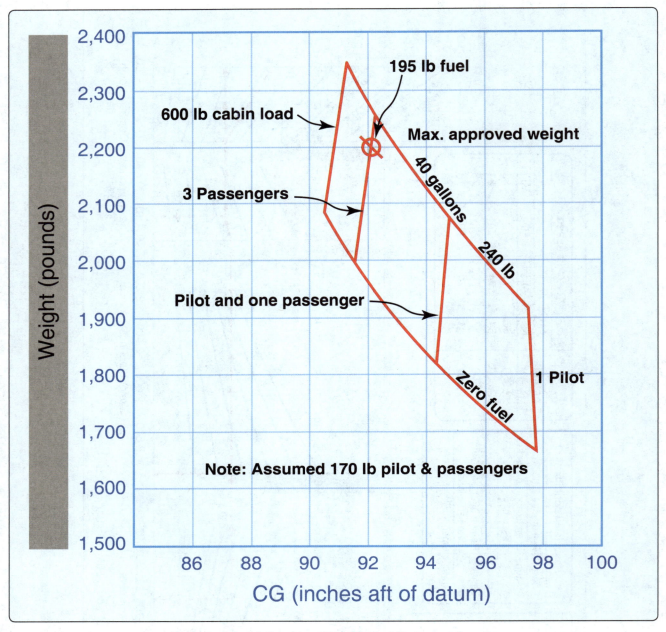

Figure 41. Helicopter Weight and Balance Graph.

Appendix 2

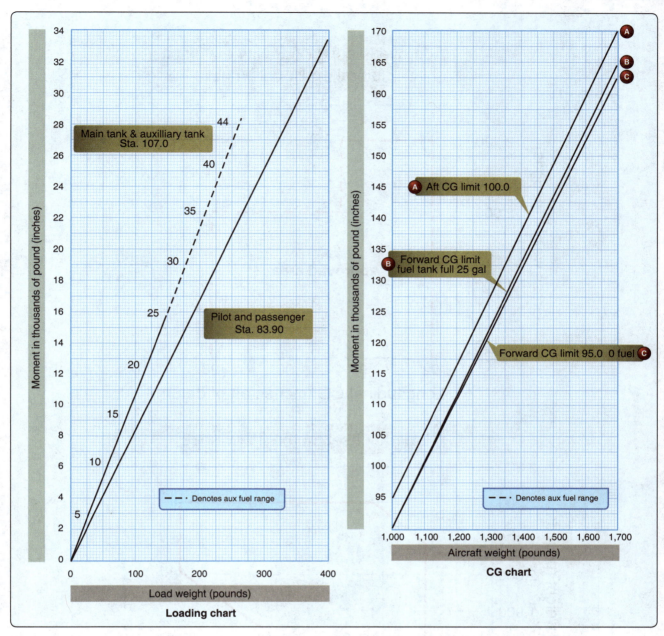

Figure 42. Helicopter Weight and Balance Graphs.

Appendix 2

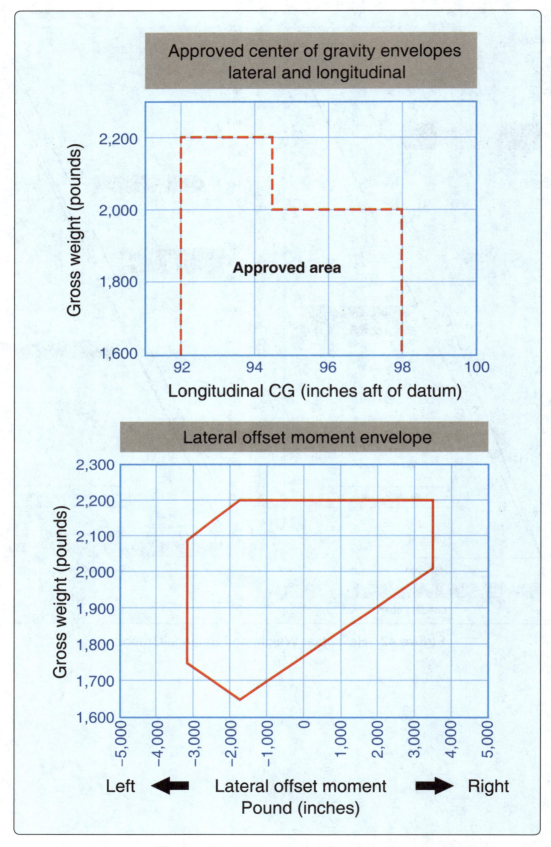

Figure 43. Helicopter CG Envelopes.

2-40

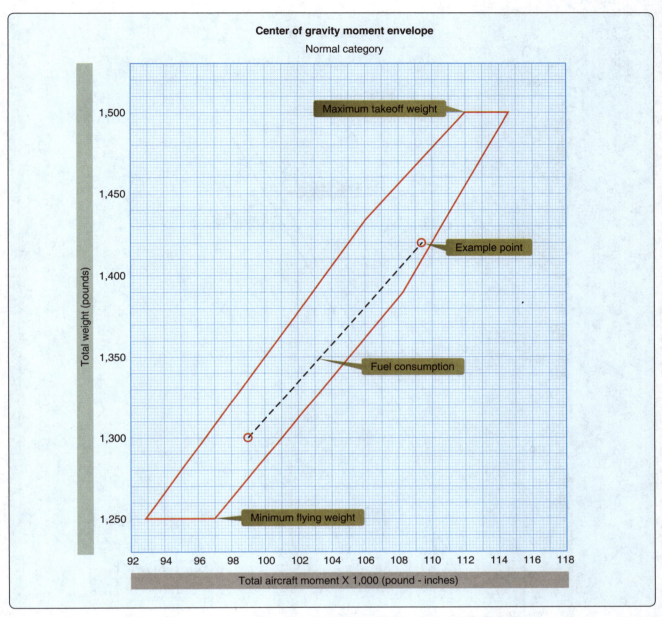

Figure 44. Gyroplane Weight and Balance Graph.

Appendix 2

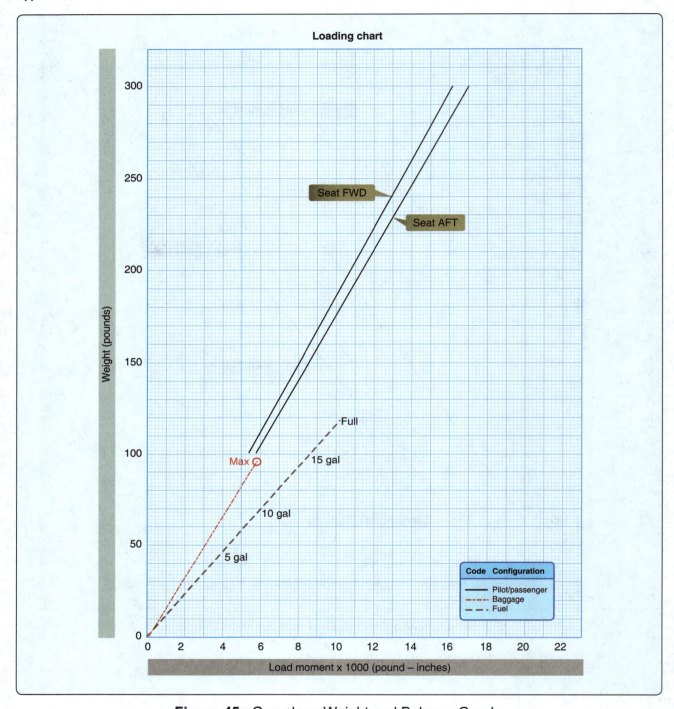

Figure 45. Gyroplane Weight and Balance Graph.

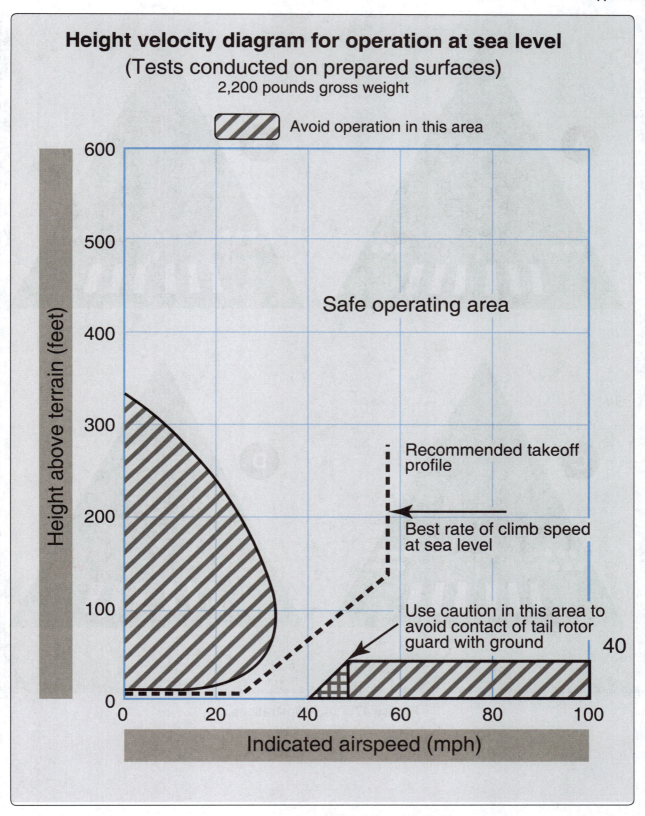

Figure 46. Helicopter Height Velocity Diagram.

Appendix 2

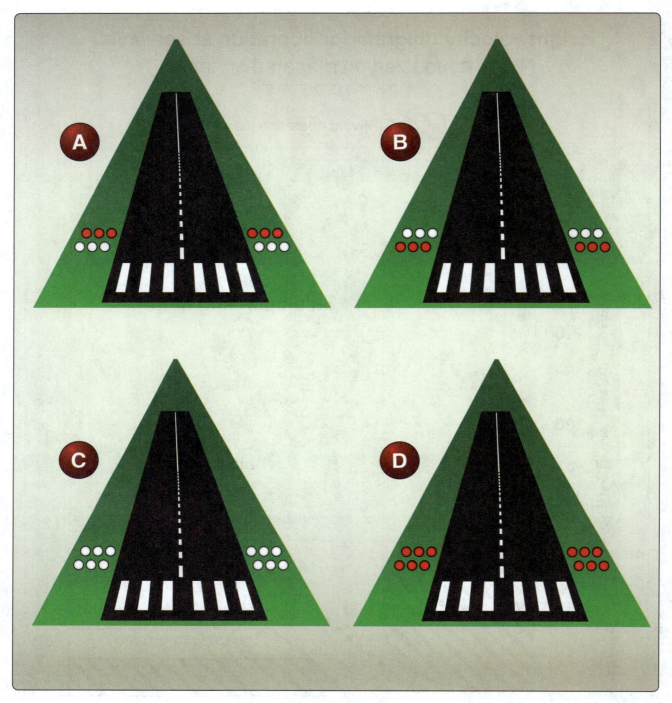

Figure 47. VASI Illustrations.

Appendix 2

Figure 48. Airport Diagram.

2-45

Appendix 2

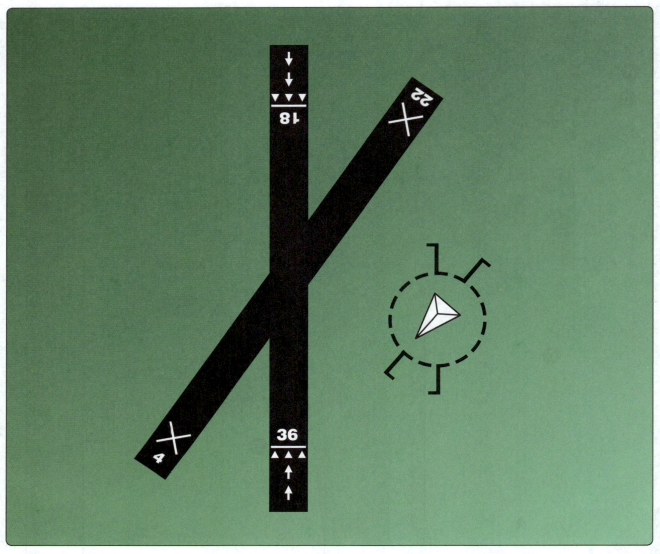

Figure 49. Airport Diagram.

2-46

Appendix 2

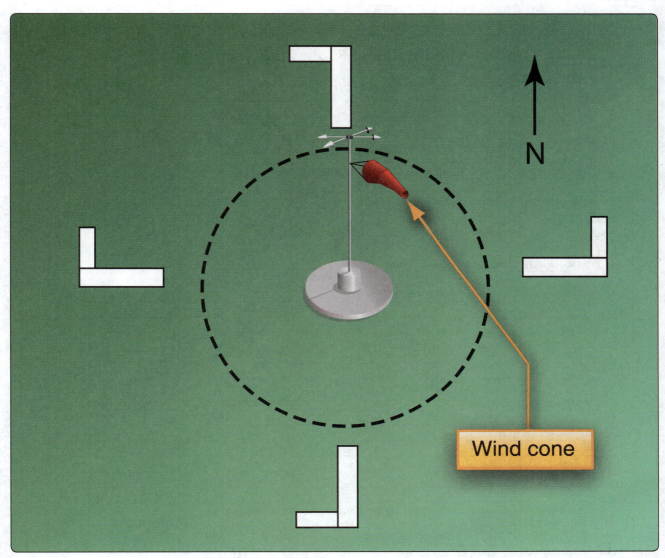

Figure 50. Wind Sock Airport Landing Indicator.

Appendix 2

Figure 51. Flight Plan Form.

NEBRASKA

LINCOLN (LNK) 4 NW UTC–6(–5DT) N40°51.05' W96°45.55' OMAHA
  1219 B S4 **FUEL** 100LL, JET A TPA—See Remarks ARFF Index—See Remarks H–5C, L–10I
  NOTAM FILE LNK IAP, AD
  RWY 18–36: H12901X200 (ASPH–CONC–GRVD) S–100, D–200,
    2S–175, 2D–400 HIRL
    RWY 18: MALSR. PAPI(P4L)—GA 3.0° TCH 55'. Rgt tfc. 0.4%
      down.
    RWY 36: MALSR. PAPI(P4L)—GA 3.0° TCH 57'.
  RWY 14–32: H8649X150 (ASPH–CONC–GRVD) S–80, D–170,
    2S–175, 2D–280 MIRL
    RWY 14: REIL. VASI(V4L)—GA 3.0° TCH 48'. Thld dsplcd 363'.
    RWY 32: VASI(V4L)—GA 3.0° TCH 50'. Thld dsplcd 470'.
      Pole. 0.3% up.
  RWY 17–35: H5800X100 (ASPH–CONC–AFSC) S–49, D–60
      HIRL 0.8% up S
    RWY 17: REIL. PAPI(P4L)—GA 3.0° TCH 44'.
    RWY 35: ODALS. PAPI(P4L)—GA 3.0° TCH 30'. Rgt tfc.
  RUNWAY DECLARED DISTANCE INFORMATION
    RWY 14: TORA–8649 TODA–8649 ASDA–8649 LDA–8286
    RWY 17: TORA–5800 TODA–5800 ASDA–5400 LDA–5400
    RWY 18: TORA–12901 TODA–12901 ASDA–12901 LDA–12901
    RWY 32: TORA–8649 TODA–8649 ASDA–8286 LDA–7816
    RWY 35: TORA–5800 TODA–5800 ASDA–5800 LDA–5800
    RWY 36: TORA–12901 TODA–12901 ASDA–12901 LDA–12901
  AIRPORT REMARKS: Attended continuously. Birds invof arpt. Rwy 18 designated calm wind rwy. Rwy 32 apch holdline
    on South A twy. TPA–2219 (1000), heavy military jet 3000 (1781). Class I, ARFF Index B. ARFF Index C level
    equipment provided. Rwy 18–36 touchdown and rollout rwy visual range avbl. When twr clsd MIRL Rwy 14–32
    preset on low ints, HIRL Rwy 18–36 and Rwy 17–35 preset on med ints, ODALS Rwy 35 operate continuously on
    med ints, MALSR Rwy 18 and Rwy 36 operate continuously and REIL Rwy 14 and Rwy 17 operate continuously
    on low ints. VASI Rwy 14 and Rwy 32, PAPI Rwy 17, Rwy 35, Rwy 18 and Rwy 36 on continuously.
  WEATHER DATA SOURCES: ASOS (402) 474–9214. LLWAS
  COMMUNICATIONS: CTAF 118.5 **ATIS** 118.05 **UNICOM** 122.95
    RCO 122.65 (COLUMBUS RADIO)
  ® **APP/DEP CON** 124.0 (180°–359°) 124.8 (360°–179°)
    TOWER 118.5 125.7 (1130–0600Z‡) **GND CON** 121.9 **CLNC DEL** 120.7
  AIRSPACE: CLASS C svc 1130–0600Z‡ ctc **APP CON** other times CLASS E.
  RADIO AIDS TO NAVIGATION: NOTAM FILE LNK.
    (H) VORTACW 116.1 LNK Chan 108 N40°55.43' W96°44.52' 181° 4.4 NM to fld. 1370/9E
    POTTS NDB (MHW/LOM) 385 LN N40°44.83' W96°45.75' 355° 6.2 NM to fld. Unmonitored when twr clsd.
    ILS 111.1 I–OCZ Rwy 18. Class IB OM unmonitored.
    ILS 109.9 I–LNK Rwy 36 Class IA LOM POTTS NDB. MM unmonitored. LOM unmonitored when twr
      clsd.
  COMM/NAV/WEATHER REMARKS: Emerg frequency 121.5 not available at twr.

LOUP CITY MUNI (Ø F4) 1 NW UTC–6(–5DT) N41°17.20' W98°59.41' OMAHA
  2071 B **FUEL** 100LL NOTAM FILE OLU L–10H, 12H
  RWY 16–34: H3200X60 (CONC) S–12.5 MIRL
    RWY 34: Trees.
  RWY 04–22: 2040X100 (TURF)
    RWY 04: Tree. **RWY 22:** Road.
  AIRPORT REMARKS: Unattended. For svc call 308–745–1344/1244/0664.
  COMMUNICATIONS: CTAF 122.9
  RADIO AIDS TO NAVIGATION: NOTAM FILE OLU.
    WOLBACH (H) VORTAC 114.8 OBH Chan 95 N41°22.54' W98°21.22' 253° 29.3 NM to fld. 2010/7E.

MARTIN FLD (See SO SIOUX CITY)

Figure 52. Chart Supplement.

Appendix 2

Figure 53. Glider Weight and Balance Diagram.

Figure 54. Glider Performance Graph.

Appendix 2

Figure 55. Standard Soaring Signals.

2-52

Appendix 2

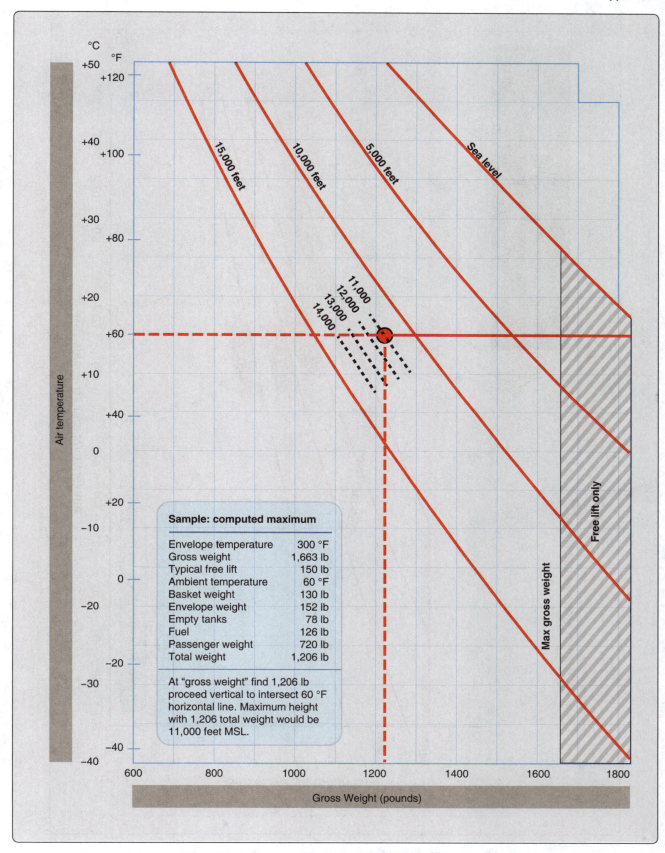

Figure 56. Hot Air Balloon Performance Graph.

2-53

Appendix 2

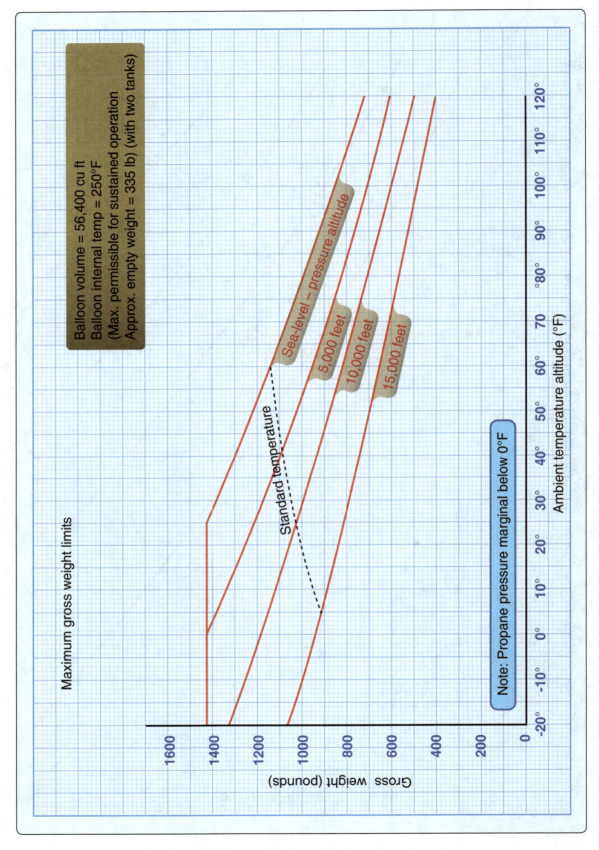

Figure 57. Hot Air Balloon Performance Graph.

2-54

For	N	30	60	E	120	150
Steer	0	27	56	85	116	148
For	S	210	240	W	300	330
Steer	181	214	244	274	303	332

Figure 58. Compass Card.

Appendix 2

Figure 59. Sectional Chart Excerpt.
Note: Chart is not to scale and should not be used for navigation. Use associated scale.

Figure 60. Weight and Balance Diagram.

Appendix 2

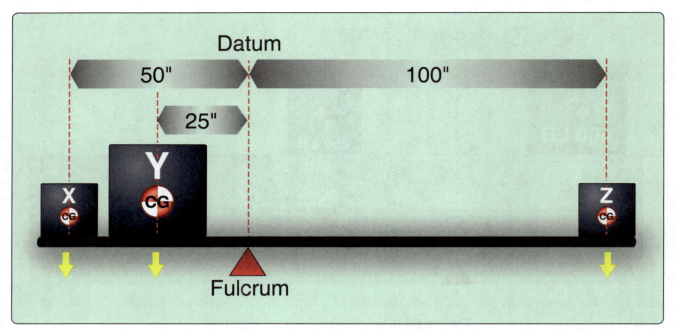

Figure 61. Weight and Balance Diagram.

Figure 62. Rectangular Course.

OHIO

TOLEDO

TOLEDO EXECUTIVE (TDZ) 6 SE UTC–5(–4DT) N41°33.90' W83°28.93'   DETROIT
  623   B   S4   **FUEL** 100LL, JET A   OX 1, 3   NOTAM FILE TDZ   H–10G, L–28J
  RWY 14–32: H5829X100 (ASPH–GRVD)   S–63, D–85, 2S–107   MIRL   IAP
    RWY 14: REIL. PAPI(P4L)—GA 3.0° TCH 34'. Thld dsplcd 225'.
    Tower.
    RWY 32: VASI(V4L)—GA 3.0° TCH 43'. Thld dsplcd 351'. Road.
  RWY 04–22: H3799X75 (ASPH)   S–63, D–85, 2S–107   MIRL
    RWY 04: REIL. PAPI(P4L)—GA 3.5° TCH 35'. Thld dsplcd 100'.
    Road.
    RWY 22: REIL. PAPI(P4L)—GA 3.0° TCH 25'. Thld dsplcd 380'.
    Railroad.
  AIRPORT REMARKS: Attended Mon–Fri continuously, Sat–Sun
    1300–0100Z‡. Parallel twy Rwy 04–22 and Rwy 14–32 35' wide.
    Seagulls on and invof arpt. Ldg fee. ACTIVATE MIRL Rwy 04–22
    and Rwy 14–32, REIL and PAPI Rwy 04, Rwy 22, Rwy 14 and VASI
    Rwy 32—CTAF.
  WEATHER DATA SOURCES: ASOS 121.575 (419) 838–5034.
  COMMUNICATIONS: CTAF/UNICOM 123.05
  ® APP/DEP CON 126.1   CLNC DEL 125.6
  RADIO AIDS TO NAVIGATION: NOTAM FILE CLE.
    WATERVILLE (L) VOR/DME 113.1   VWV   Chan 78   N41°27.09'
    W83°38.32'   048° 9.8 NM to fld. 664/2W.

TOLEDO EXPRESS (TOL) 10 W UTC–5(–4DT) N41°35.21' W83°48.47'   DETROIT
  683   B   S4   **FUEL** 100LL, JET A   OX 3   LRA   Class I, ARFF Index B   NOTAM FILE TOL   H–10G, L–28J
  RWY 07–25: H10599X150 (ASPH–GRVD)   S–100, D–174, 2S–175, 2D–300, 2D/2D2–550   IAP, AD
    HIRL   CL
    RWY 07: ALSF2. TDZL. Trees.
    RWY 25: MALSR. VASI(V4L)—GA 3.0° TCH 51'. Trees.   0.3% up.
  RWY 16–34: H5599X150 (ASPH–GRVD)   S–100, D–174, 2S–175,
    2D–300   MIRL
    RWY 16: REIL. PAPI(P4L)—GA 3.0° TCH 48'. Trees.
    RWY 34: REIL.
  RUNWAY DECLARED DISTANCE INFORMATION
    RWY 07:   TORA 10599   TODA 10599   ASDA 10599   LDA 10599
    RWY 16:   TORA 5599   TODA 5599   ASDA 5599   LDA 5599
    RWY 25:   TORA 10599   TODA 10599   ASDA 10599   LDA 10599
    RWY 34:   TORA 5599   TODA 5599   ASDA 5599   LDA 5599
  ARRESTING GEAR/SYSTEM
    RWY 07 ←BAK–12   BAK–12 →RWY 25
  AIRPORT REMARKS: Attended continuously. Fuel and svc avbl
    1300–0500Z‡. Birds on and invof arpt. Twy A west of Rwy 16 and
    the ramp between Twy B9 and B13 not visible from twr. Twy D
    intersection of Twy D1, heavy acft use minimal power to reduce
    foreign object damage on Air National Guard ramp. Customs:
    Sat–Sun req must be made prior to 2200Z‡ on Fri, phone 419–259–6424.
  WEATHER DATA SOURCES: ASOS (419) 865–8351.
  COMMUNICATIONS: ATIS 118.75   UNICOM 122.95
  ® APP/DEP CON 126.1 (360°–179°) 134.35 (180°–359°) 123.975
    TOWER 118.1   GND CON 121.9   CLNC DEL 121.75
  AIRSPACE: CLASS C svc continuous ctc APP CON
  RADIO AIDS TO NAVIGATION: NOTAM FILE CLE.
    WATERVILLE (L) VOR/DME 113.1   VWV   Chan 78   N41°27.09' W83°38.32'   319° 11.1 NM to fld. 664/2W.
    TOPHR NDB (LOM) 219   TO   N41°33.21' W83°55.27'   074° 5.5 NM to fld. Unmonitored. NOTAM FILE TOL.
    ILS 109.7.   I–TOL   Rwy 07.   Class IE.   LOM TOPHR NDB.
    ILS 108.7.   I–BQE   Rwy 25.   Class IA.   LOC unusable 0.4 NM inbound. ILS unmonitored when twr clsd.
    ASR

SEAGATE HELISTOP (6T2) 00 N UTC–5(–4DT) N41°39.25' W83°31.88'   DETROIT
  650   NOTAM FILE CLE
  HELIPAD H1: H50X50 (CONC)
  HELIPORT REMARKS: Unattended. ACTIVATE orange perimeter lgts—CTAF. Helipad H1 NSTD 1–box (2 VASIS). Helipad
    H1 not marked with "H." Helipad H1 perimeter lgts.
  COMMUNICATIONS: CTAF/UNICOM 123.05

Figure 63. Chart Supplement.

Appendix 2

Figure 64. Airport Markings.

2-61

Appendix 2

Figure 65. U.S. Airport Signs.

2-62

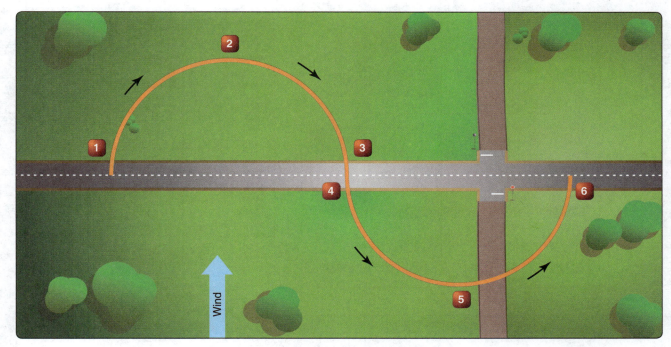

Figure 66. S-Turn Diagram.

Appendix 2

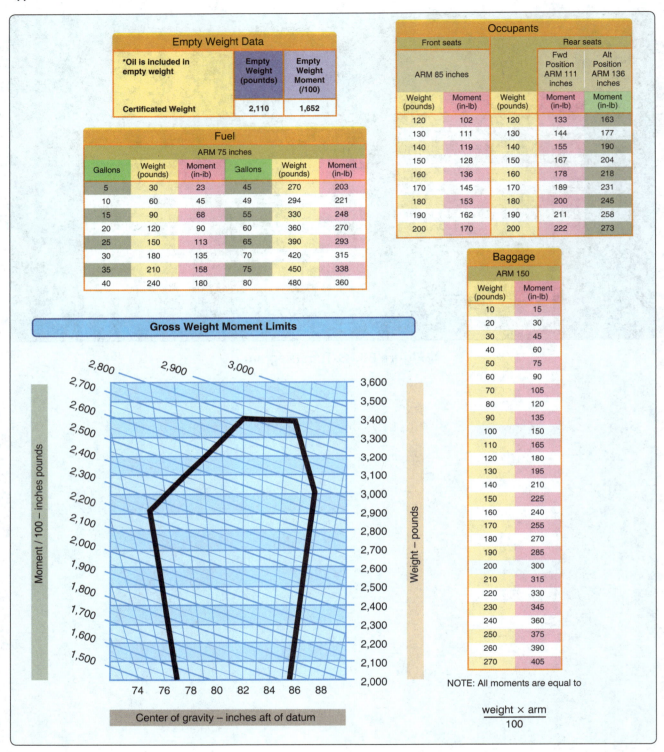

Figure 67. Weight and Balance Chart.

Figure 68. Wind Triangle.

2-65

Appendix 2

Figure 69. Sectional Chart Excerpt.
NOTE: Chart is not to scale and should not be used for navigation. Use associated scale.

Appendix 2

Figure 70. Sectional Chart Excerpt.
NOTE: Chart is not to scale and should not be used for navigation. Use associated scale.

Appendix 2

Figure 71. Sectional Chart Excerpt.
NOTE: Chart is not to scale and should not be used for navigation. Use associated scale.

2-68

Appendix 2

Figure 72. Velocity vs. G-Loads.

2-69

Appendix 2

Figure 73. Glider Hand Signals.

Appendix 2

Figure 74. Sectional Chart Excerpt.
NOTE: Chart is not to scale and should not be used for navigation. Use associated scale.

Appendix 2

Figure 75. Sectional Chart Excerpt.
NOTE: Chart is not to scale and should not be used for navigation. Use associated scale.

Appendix 2

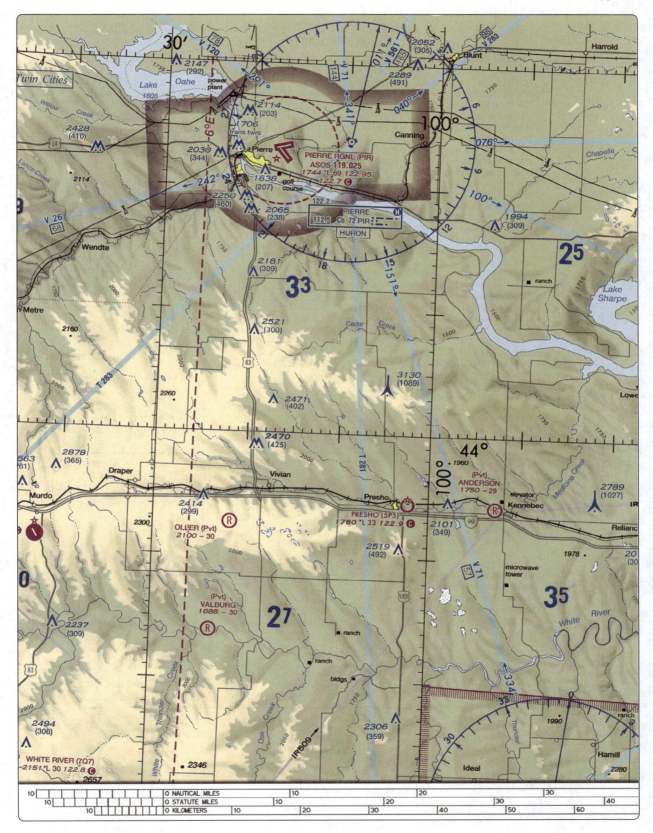

Figure 76. Sectional Chart Excerpt.
NOTE: Chart is not to scale and should not be used for navigation. Use associated scale.

2-73

Appendix 2

340   SOUTH DAKOTA

PIERRE RGNL (PIR) 3 E UTC −6(−5DT) N44°22.96′ W100°17.16′   **OMAHA**
1744   B   S4   **FUEL** 100LL, JET A   OX 1, 2, 3, 4   Class I, ARFF Index A   NOTAM FILE PIR   H−2I, L−12H
RWY 13−31: H6900X100 (ASPH−GRVD)   S−91, D−108, 2S−137, 2D−168   HIRL   IAP
   RWY 13: REIL. PAPI(P4L)—GA 3.0 ° TCH 52′.
   RWY 31: MALSR. PAPI(P4L)—GA 3.0 ° TCH 52′.
RWY 07−25: H6881X150 (ASPH−GRVD)   S−91, D−114, 2S−145, 2D−180   HIRL   0.6% up W
   RWY 07: REIL. PAPI(P4L)—GA 3.0 ° TCH 47′. Tank.
   RWY 25: REIL. PAPI(P4L)—GA 3.0 ° TCH 54′.
RUNWAY DECLARED DISTANCE INFORMATION
   RWY 07:   TORA−6881   TODA−6881   ASDA−6830   LDA−6830
   RWY 13:   TORA−6900   TODA−6900   ASDA−6900   LDA−6900
   RWY 25:   TORA−6881   TODA−6881   ASDA−6881   LDA−6881
   RWY 31:   TORA−6900   TODA−6900   ASDA−6900   LDA−6900
AIRPORT REMARKS: Attended Mon−Fri 1100−0600Z‡, Sat−Sun 1100−0400Z‡. For attendant other times call 605−224−9000/8621. Arpt conditions unmonitored during 0530−1000Z‡. Numerous non−radio acft operating in area. Birds on and invof arpt and within a 25 NM radius. No line of sight between rwy ends of Rwy 07−25. ARFF provided for part 121 air carrier ops only. 48 hr PPR for unscheduled acr ops involving acft designed for 31 or more passenger seats call 605−773−7447 or 605−773−7405. Taxiway C is 50′ wide and restricted to acft 75,000 pounds or less. ACTIVATE HIRL Rwy 13−31 and Rwy 07−25, MALSR Rwy 31, REIL Rwy 07, Rwy 13 and Rwy 25, PAPI Rwy 07, Rwy 25, Rwy 13 and Rwy 31—CTAF 122.7. NOTE: See Special Notices Section—Aerobatic Practice Areas.
WEATHER DATA SOURCES: ASOS 119.025 (605) 224−6087.   **HIWAS** 112.5 PIR.
COMMUNICATIONS: CTAF 122.7   **UNICOM** 122.95
   RCO 122.2 (HURON RADIO)
® **MINNEAPOLIS CENTER APP/DEP CON** 125.1
RADIO AIDS TO NAVIGATION: NOTAM FILE PIR.
   (L) **VORTACW** 112.5   PIR   Chan 72   N44°23.67′ W100°09.77′   251° 5.3 NM to fld. 1789/11E.   **HIWAS.**
   ILS/DME 111.9   I−PIR   Chan 56   Rwy 31.   Class IA   ILS GS unusable for coupled apch blo 2,255′. GS unusable blo 2135′.

PINE RIDGE (IEN) 2 E UTC −7(−6DT) N43°01.35′ W102°30.66′   **CHEYENNE**
3333   B   NOTAM FILE IEN   H−5B, L−12G
RWY 12−30: H5000X60 (ASPH)   S−12   MIRL   0.7% up SE   IAP
   RWY 12: P−line.
   RWY 30: PAPI(P2L)—GA 3.0 ° TCH 26′. Fence.
RWY 06−24: H3003X50 (ASPH)   S−12   0.7% up NE
   RWY 24: Fence.
AIRPORT REMARKS: Unattended. Rwy 06−24 CLOSED indef. MIRL Rwy 12−30 and PAPI Rwy 30 opr dusk−0530Z‡, after 0530Z‡ ACTIVATE—CTAF.
WEATHER DATA SOURCES: ASOS 126.775 (605) 867−1584.
COMMUNICATIONS: CTAF 122.9
   DENVER CENTER APP/DEP CON 127.95
RADIO AIDS TO NAVIGATION: NOTAM FILE RAP.
   RAPID CITY (H) VORTAC 112.3   RAP   Chan 70   N43°58.56′ W103°00.74′   146° 61.3 NM to fld. 3160/13E.

Figure 77. Chart Supplement.

Appendix 2

Figure 78. Sectional Chart Excerpt.
NOTE: Chart is not to scale and should not be used for navigation. Use associated scale.

64 IOWA

SIOUX CITY N42°20.67' W96°19.42' NOTAM FILE SUX OMAHA
  (L) **VORTAC** 116.5 SUX Chan 112 313° 4.4 NM to Sioux Gateway/Col Bud Day Fld. 1087/9E. HIWAS. L-12I
  VOR unusable:
    280°-292° byd 25 NM   306°-350° byd 20 NM blo 3,000'
    293°-305° byd 20 NM blo 4,500'   350°-280° byd 30 NM blo 3,000'
    293°-305° byd 35 NM
  RCO 122.45 122.1R 116.5T (FORT DODGE RADIO)

SIOUX CITY
SIOUX GATEWAY/COL BUD DAY FLD (SUX) 6 S UTC -6(-5DT) N42°24.16' W96°23.06' OMAHA
  1098 B S4 **FUEL** 100LL, 115, JET A OX 1, 2, 3, 4 Class I, ARFF Index—See Remarks H-5C, L-12I
  NOTAM FILE SUX   IAP, AD
  RWY 13-31: H9002X150 (CONC-GRVD) S-100, D-120, 2S-152,
    2D-220 HIRL
    RWY 13: MALS. VASI(V4L)—GA 3.0° TCH 49'. Tree.
    RWY 31: MALSR. VASI(V4L)—GA 3.0° TCH 50'.
  RWY 17-35: H6600X150 (ASPH-PFC) S-65, D-80, 2S-102,
    2D-130 MIRL
    RWY 17: REIL. VASI(V4R)—GA 3.0° TCH 50'. Trees.
    RWY 35: PAPI(P4L)—GA 3.0° TCH 54'. Pole.
  LAND AND HOLD SHORT OPERATIONS
    LANDING   HOLD SHORT POINT   DIST AVBL
    RWY 13   17-35   5400
    RWY 17   13-31   5650
  ARRESTING GEAR/SYSTEM
    RWY 13 ←BAK-14 BAK-12B(B) (1392')
                BAK-14 BAK-12B(B) (1492') →RWY 31
  AIRPORT REMARKS: Attended continuously. PAEW 0330-1200Z ‡ during
    inclement weather Nov-Apr. AER 31-BAK-12/14 located (1492')
    from thld. Airfield surface conditions not monitored by arpt
    management between 0600-1000Z ‡ daily. Rwy 13-BAK-12/14
    located (1392') from thld. All A-gear avbl only during ANG flying ops. Twr has limited visibility southeast of
    ramp near ARFF bldg and northeast of Rwy 31 touchdown zone. Rwy 31 is calm wind rwy. Class I, ARFF Index
    B. ARFF Index E fire fighting equipment avbl on request. Twy F unlit, retro-reflective markers in place. Portions
    of Twy A SE of Twy B not visible by twr and is designated a non-movement area. Rwy 13-31 touchdown and
    rollout rwy visual range avbl. When twr clsd, ACTIVATE HIRL Rwy 13-31; MIRL Rwy 17-35; MALS Rwy 13;
    MALSR Rwy 31; and REIL Rwy 17-CTAF.
  WEATHER DATA SOURCES: ASOS (712) 255-6474. HIWAS 116.5 SUX. LAWRS.
  COMMUNICATIONS: CTAF 118.7 ATIS 119.45 UNICOM 122.95
    SIOUX CITY RCO 122.45 122.1R 116.5T (FORT DODGE RADIO)
  ® **SIOUX CITY APP/DEP CON** 124.6 (1200-0330Z ‡)
  ® **MINNEAPOLIS CENTER APP/DEP CON** 124.1 (0330-1200Z ‡)
    SIOUX CITY TOWER 118.7 (1200-0330Z ‡) **GND CON** 121.9
  AIRSPACE: CLASS D svc 1200-0330Z ‡ other times CLASS E.
  RADIO AIDS TO NAVIGATION: NOTAM FILE SUX.
    SIOUX CITY (L) **VORTAC** 116.5 SUX Chan 112 N42°20.67' W96°19.42' 313° 4.4 NM to fld. 1087/9E.
      HIWAS.
    NDB (MHW) 233 GAK N42°24.49' W96°23.16' at fld.
    SALIX NDB (MHW/LOM) 414 SU N42°19.65' W96°17.43' 311° 6.1 NM to fld. Unmonitored.
    TOMMI NDB (MHW/LOM) 305 OI N42°27.61' W96°27.73' 128° 4.9 NM to fld. Unmonitored.
    ILS 109.3 I-SUX Rwy 31 Class IT. LOM SALIX NBD. ILS Unmonitored when twr clsd. Glide path
      unusable coupled approach (CPD) blo 1805'.
    ILS 111.3 I-OIQ Rwy 13 LOM TOMMI NDB. Localizer shutdown when twr clsd.
    ASR (1200-0330Z ‡)

SNORE N43°13.96' W95°19.66' NOTAM FILE SPW. OMAHA
  NDB (LOM) 394 SP 121° 6.8 NM to Spencer Muni.

SOUTHEAST IOWA RGNL (See BURLINGTON)

Figure 79. Chart Supplement.

Appendix 2

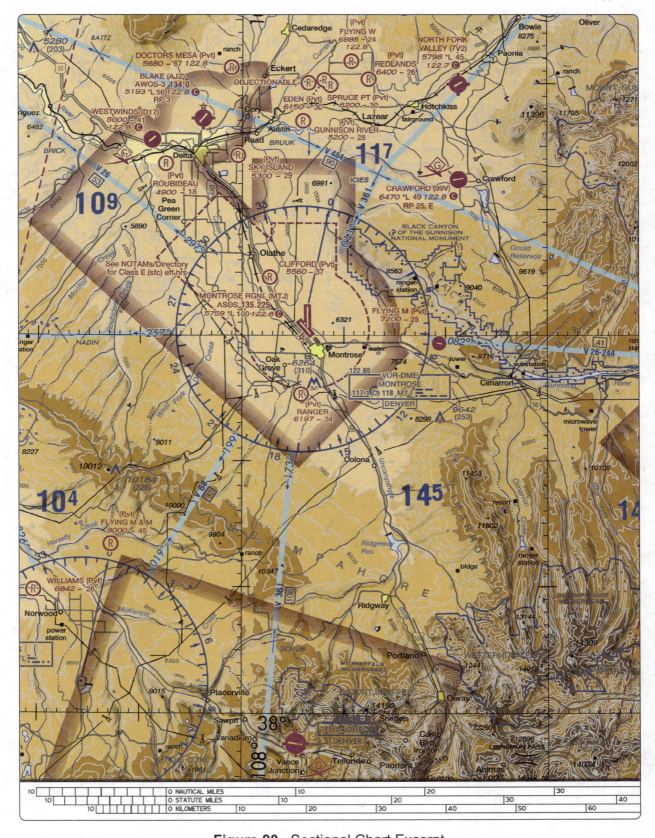

Figure 80. Sectional Chart Excerpt.
NOTE: Chart is not to scale and should not be used for navigation. Use associated scale.

216　　　　　　　　　　　　　　COLORADO

CRAWFORD　(99V)　2 W　UTC −7(−6DT)　N38°42.25′ W107°38.62′　　　　DENVER
6470　S2　OX 4　TPA—7470(1000)　NOTAM FILE DEN　　　　　　　　　　　　L−9E
RWY 07−25: H4900X20 (ASPH)　　LIRL (NSTD)
　RWY 07: VASI (NSTD). Trees.　　　**RWY 25:** VASI (NSTD) Tank. Rgt tfc.
RWY E−W: 2500X125 (TURF)
　RWY E: Rgt tfc.　　**RWY W:** Trees.
AIRPORT REMARKS: Attended continuously. Rwy 07−25 west 1300 ′ only 25′ wide. Heavy glider ops at arpt. Land to the
　east tkf to the west winds permitting. 100LL fuel avbl for emergency use only. Pedestrians, motor vehicles, deer
　and wildlife on and invof arpt. Unlimited vehicle use on arpt. Rwy West has +15 ′ building 170′ from thld 30′ left,
　+10′ road 100′ from thld centerline. +45′ tree 100′ L of Rwy 07 extended centerline 414 ′ from rwy end. −8′ to
　−20′ terrain off both sides of first 674 ′ of Rwy 25 end. E−W rwy occasionally has 6 inch diameter irrigation
　pipes crossing rwy width in various places. Rwy 07 has 20 ′ trees and −10′ to 20′ terrain 20′ right of rwy first
　150′. E−W rwy consists of +12 inch alfalfa vegetation during various times of the year. Arpt lgts opr
　dusk−0800Z‡. Rwy 07 1 box VASI left side for local operators only or PPR call 970−921−7700 or
　970−921−3018. Rwy 07−25 LIRL on N side from Rwy 25 end W 3800 ′. Rwy 07 1300′ from end E 300′. No thld
　lgts Rwy 07−25 3800′ usable for ngt ops.
COMMUNICATIONS: CTAF/UNICOM 122.8
RADIO AIDS TO NAVIGATION: NOTAM FILE MTJ.
　MONTROSE (H) VORW/DME 117.1　　MTJ　Chan 118　N38 °30.39′ W107°53.96′　　033° 16.9 NM to fld. 5713/12E.

CREEDE
MINERAL CO MEM　(C24)　2 E　UTC −7(−6DT)　N37°49.33′ W106°55.79′　　　　DENVER
8680　NOTAM FILE DEN　　　　　　　　　　　　　　　　　　　　　　　　　　　H−3E, L−9E
RWY 07−25: H6880X60 (ASPH)　S−12.5, D−70, 2D−110
　RWY 07: Thld dsplcd 188 ′.　　　**RWY 25:** Road.
AIRPORT REMARKS: Unattended. Elk and deer on and invof arpt. Glider and hang glider activity on and in vicinity of
　arpt. Mountains in all directions. Departure to NE avoid over flight of trailers and resident homes, climb to 200 ′
　above ground level on centerline extended prior to turn. Acft stay to right of valley on apch and/or departure
　route. 2′ cable fence around apron.
COMMUNICATIONS: CTAF 122.9
RADIO AIDS TO NAVIGATION: NOTAM FILE DEN.
　BLUE MESA (H) VORW/DME 114.9　　HBU　Chan 96　N38 °27.13′ W107°02.39′　　158° 38.1 NM to fld. 8730/14E.

CUCHARA VALLEY AT LA VETA　(See LA VETA)

DEL NORTE
ASTRONAUT KENT ROMINGER　(8V1)　3 N　UTC −7(−6DT)　N37°42.83′ W106°21.11′　　　DENVER
7949　NOTAM FILE DEN　　　　　　　　　　　　　　　　　　　　　　　　　　　H−3E, L−9E
RWY 06−24: 6050X75 (ASPH)　　1.1% up SW
RWY 03−21: 4670X60 (TURF−DIRT)
　RWY 21: Mountain.
AIRPORT REMARKS: Unattended. Wildlife on and invof arpt. Unlimited vehicle access on arpt. Mountainous terrain
　surrounds arpt in all directions.
COMMUNICATIONS: CTAF 122.9
RADIO AIDS TO NAVIGATION: NOTAM FILE ALS.
　ALAMOSA (H) VORTACW 113.9　　ALS　Chan 86　N37 °20.95′ W105°48.93′　　298° 33.7 NM to fld. 7535/13E.

Figure 81. Chart Supplement.

Appendix 2

Figure 82. Altimeter.

2-79